Courage & Compassion: A Civil War Soldier Speaks

To Calvin Cole
Enjoy!
Patda Jim

by Patda Jim

Warren Publishing Group

Cover Artwork Compliments of
Auggie Romero

www.battlegeartoys.com

BattleGear Toys is an American company which offers 1/6th scale military uniforms and accessories of museum quality with unparalleled detail and craftsmanship.

Layout by Joe Anziano (www.AdvantagePD.com)

For information regarding permissions, write to:
Warren Publishing Group: Publisher, 6725 Oak Manor Drive, Bradenton, FL 34202

ISBN:13: 978-1-4507-8943-1
Library of Congress Number: ☐1-645688031

Printed in the USA
Printed in October, 2011

Dedication & Special Thanks to:

Robert Peterson and all his Waterhouse relatives who gave me special insights to the family and allowed me to live within William Waterhouse through his original Letters and Journal.

The Maitland, Florida residents: Marjorie Tope, Irene Logan, Andrea Cox, Betty Sample, the Greenport Historical Society, other members of the Maitland Historical Society offering tidbits of information on W. Waterhouse's life and keeping his home as a memorial.

Authors Charles A. Mills of *The Hidden History of Northern Virginia,* Shelby Foote of *The Civil War, A Narrative* and the many other histories of the Civil War in Northern Virginia that I devoured.

And Especially to Alfred H. Guernsey and Henry M. Alden for compiling the vast information and innumerous letters and battle accounts written by the many generals and leaders of the Civil War era in *Harper's Pictorial History of the Civil War*. Also to my sister Bib for finding this book.

My heartfelt admiration and thanks go to all the soldiers and helpers of this ghastly war which took more lives than all the other battles combined since its birth until today. They were brave Americans each fighting for a cause they believed in under the worst conditions and type of warfare. Having ancestors who fought on both sides, leads me to bless all the souls lost during the Civil War and wonder at their awesome bravery.

Map of
VIRGINIA
AND NEIGHBORING STATES
showing
the location of Battles in the Civil War 1861-1865
Battles are shown in gothic type thus ; Bull Run
Battles in which New York Regiments were engaged thus ;
Railroads at time of War
Turnpikes and Plank Roads
Union States thus ; Confederate States thus ;
Modern names are in parenthesis.
SCALE OF MILES
PENNSYLVANIA
W. VIRGINIA
VIRGINIA
NORTH CAROLINA
Gettysburg
Hanover
Chambersburg
Hagerstown
Williamsport
South Mt
Antietam
Cramptons Pass
Harper's F.
Monocacy
Baltimore
Washington
Alexandria
Annapolis
Cedar Creek
Front Royal
Chantilly
Bull Run
Auburn
Beverly Ford
Brandy Sta.
Cross Keys
Cedar Mountain
Fredericksburg
Chancellorsville
Salem Church
Spotsylvania
Trevilian Sta.
North Anna
Hanover C.H.
Cold Harbor
Mechanicsville
Richmond
Fair Oaks
Glendale
Malvern Hill
Drewry's Bluff
Deep Bottom
Petersburg
Five Forks
Hatcher's Run
Dinwiddie C.H.
Ream's Sta.
Appomattox C.H.
Westpoint
Williamsburg
Yorktown
Big Bethel
Hampton Roads
Norfolk
Suffolk
Franklin
Potomac River
Longitude West from Greenwich
www.historymap.com

1

GREENPORT, LONG ISLAND – SEPTEMBER 1, 1861

"I am going to go fight the rebs!" I blurted out as soon as my father's 'Amen' finished his prayer. Every Sunday our Waterhouse routine started after breakfast with a gathering in the dining room for the reading of a chapter from the Bible by my mother, followed by Pa's prayer. Not a word of what Ma read went into my head. The excitement inside me since I had made my decision on Saturday had kept me awake all night. I could hold it no longer.

All held their breath. Wide eyes went from me to Pa, wondering which of us would speak first. Pa nodded, as I had spoken with him during the week to have his consent. After all I would not be there to help with his shoe business. I had explained that he had four other sons, John, George, Henry and Edward, to help him and none were old enough to go fight the cause of the Federal government.

Pa explained to the family, "William came to me early in the week about this. I asked him to think about it long and hard before making a final decision. I wanted him to know that war is not a game, played hiding in yards and using sticks for guns. The fighting we are hearing stories about from the survivors are horrible. He has made his own decision and I will stand by him."

These words and the reminder I might not be returning, he had said to me before, which had caused me the great struggle in my thoughts and dreams during the last few days. I had turned nineteen on February 11, finished school, worked with my father some and with my uncle at carpentry, enjoyed the company of my friends, and admittedly was looking for a future and a mate to go along the way with me.

My mother's tears started immediately. Putting my arms around her, I hugged her and said, "I will be fine. I am not leaving for good, just a little while until we teach those southerners how to be Americans." The weakness in my knees told me I might not return.

Brother Johnny, fired the questions fast, "Have you really signed up? What regiment will you go in? When are you leaving? Will they take me, too?"

"Last week, when I made a delivery in Greenport, someone said to me, 'You look able-bodied. We need people like you to show these rebels they can't treat slaves like animals. There is a man at the court house right now signing people up to go in the Federal army to show those southerners some manners.' So I started to go by the court house just to see. I have been thinking about it a lot. But, when I got to the Post Office, there was a guy there with a great horse. His name is Captain Pratt. Both he and the horse were in uniform. Looked real military. I went to pet the horse's nose and he whinnied and nuzzled my hand."

"The Captain said, 'You want a horse like this?' 'Of course,' I said, 'That would be nice.' He said, 'Join the 5th Calvary of New York and you can have a horse just like this as well as stand up for our cause against those rebs.' We talked for about a half hour more. That horse kept nuzzling me. He was nicer and bigger than any horse we have ever had for the carriage...so I told him, 'yes, I would think about it'. Then I talked it over with Pa. He had me think about it this week, but yesterday I went and signed up."

"Just like that?" Georgie blurted.

"Just like that. I have been so excited ever since."

"Did you ever get to the court house?" Johnny asked.

"No, so I am in the Calvary instead of the army."

My sister, Amelia, and her husband, Horace, as well as my little brothers all hugged me or gave me pats on the shoulders.

Pa quieted us all by giving another long prayer, asking God to watch over me; for our government to be strong; our army to be courageous and bring the war to a quick victory for us. He ended, "We pray, Heavenly Father, to protect young William, grant him the courage and good judgment he will need. Let him be prepared to die for one cannot win a battle unless one is prepared to fight to the finish."

We found our coats and went to church. I sang every song with a strong voice trying to build up my confidence that was dwindling. Once they made the announcement at the end of the service, everyone came to wish me 'God Speed.' All the young ladies came up also, each one looking at me with awe. This almost made me change my mind, but I knew that I had committed and had only one short week before deporting to Company E, 5th Regiment, New York Calvary on September 9 to be mustered in on September 10, 1861.

When we returned home, my brothers had more questions.

"When do you have to go and where?"

"A week from tomorrow. Through the west side of Long Island and into New York to Stapleton, Staten Island for a few weeks training, then they ship me and my horse on a boat to Baltimore or wherever I am sent to battle."

"Wow, that's fast. Do you have to ride your horse to New York?"

"No," I laughed until my side hurt. "It is much too far; I'll go by train." I remembered this laughter the first week after receiving my horse when I was never off of it and had so much muscle pain, I couldn't walk straight for days.

"What are you going to do until you leave?"

"There are many things I have to do to get ready and people I want to say good-bye to. It gives me enough time to get my list of supplies ready to take. Mother will help me, and hopefully Father will give me a pair of proper boots."

"He will if Mother asks him to. Will they pay you to do this?"

"Of course, do you expect me to do it just for the fun of it?"

"Will you have to kill anyone?"

"Of course, I will be learning how to run a saber straight through a man while I am galloping by. It is like when we used to play with our tin soldiers, but this time will be for real, which Pa has explained to me."

"Real blood...not sure I would like to do that."

"I guess when it is your blood or theirs, it does not bother you. Think I will take a walk to find Henry or Dan, Fred or John."

As I started down the front steps, my legs seemed a bit wobbly and my stomach queasy. As soon as I walked past the last house on the block, I ran to the trees in the park and wretched my insides out, and then had to sit on the ground for a good long time before I felt I could stand or walk.

2

SAYING GOODBYE

Walking toward the wharves, I took a good look at Greenport, street by street.

Being Sunday, it was quieter with only a few horses and carriages stirring up the dirt. It was just a village inside the town of Southold, but it was distinct for our population of over seven hundred people. I passed a few couples, every woman in a fashionable slim long skirt and beautifully lace decorated blouse, but bundled up with a shawl to keep out the September cool breezes. Greenport always had wind, being at the end of Long Island and surrounded by the Long Island Sound and the Peconic Bay, prime location with our sixty-seven slips inviting the international ships who wanted to save the ninety-five mile route into New York Harbor. The New York Railroad could take goods from Greenport into New York or the Cross Sound Ferry would carry them into Connecticut.

Each of the hundred two-story wooden houses sat high off the ground with eight to ten steps up to the front porch, which was covered by an extension of the roof. Not often did we need to be that far off the ground, but when the storms and high water came, it made those extra steps well worth having. The paned windows showed shades and sometimes curtains. The streets, side walks and paths to the houses were covered with crushed oyster shells mixed with a lot of loose dirt.

When would it rain to keep this dust down? I asked myself. Probably after I leave. The summer rains were long over. It was already September and the trees had lost most of their leaves and now showed only the lonely branches. Passing Webb's meat market, I wondered who was delivering the grocery orders now that his son had enlisted. Next I saw on the Petty Ice House in the back a sign that read, 'No More Until It Snows.' Wondering what David Petty did with his spare time in summer, I decided he probably still went to Silver Lake, but got fish instead of ice. It amazed me to think that ice could stay as many months as it did wrapped in hay and straw. That Ice House had to be well built.

The Ye Clarke House hotel, which was built by Captain John Clarke for the whalers over twenty years ago, looked closed up with whaling almost an item of the past. There had been rumors that some whalers were being used in the slave trade. The hotel had to rely on summer visitors and they were gone now until next summer. Note: in the November 21, 1861 edition of the *Suffolk Times* said the Whaler Augusta had been caught off coast of Greenport after being refitted for slave running. The 1861 *Suffolk Times* article concluded, "The mysterious maneuverings of this vessel have caused a great deal of excitement and speculation in this village, and yesterday a large concourse of people were assembled on the wharf to witness the departure of the doomed bark."

I slowly looked at Father's Store and thought of all the shoes he had made for the townspeople, plus the fancy shoes for women from ports like France and the sturdy choices for men that he bought from all over the world. Maybe all those shoes I have had to repair would help me fix my own when I need it. Now I had to learn about shoes for my horse. 'MY horse, MY horse,' I repeated loudly.

"What horse, you nut? You have no horse." Dan came up behind me.

"No, but I am going to."

"Where you going to steal it from?"

"I will tell you when we find the others."

"This should be really good."

As we reached our favorite meeting point between two large storehouses on the wharf, almost at the end of Shipping Row, Henry was chasing John's cap, which the wind was determined to toss over the edge into the murky waters fifteen feet below. How many caps and scarves among other things have we lost like that? It was Fred who grabbed it right on the edge.

"Good catch," yelled Dan. "Come over here. William has a big story to tell us."

We all huddled between two large storage bins where we had kept warm many times before, even putting some wood on top for a roof to keep us dry from rain or high surf.

"So, what is this big story you are going to tell us?" asked Fred.

"He is going to have his own horse," informed Dan, snapping his suspenders.

"Really?" chimed in John.

I told them exactly what I told my brothers. Word for word, but I could tell they thought it a great joke.

"No joke," I confirmed. "The announcement was made this morning in church. You should have been there; all the girls were awed over my decision. I leave you a week from yesterday. Someone has to represent Greenport in this fight against the greedy Southerners, so I will be the one to do this duty."

With that, they all jumped on me and started pounding on me – a gesture we had done all our lives when any of us stepped on any of the others.

"Is the guy still in town?" asked Henry. "I would go in a minute."

"No, he left last night. And you cannot go because you are the only son and your family needs you," I responded.

"But your family needs you, also. Who is going to help at the shoe store?" John always tried to keep the rest of us in line. I thought he would be a preacher in a few years.

"That is a good question that I have battled in my head for a long time. I think I really don't want to work in the shoe store and there are always my four brothers coming along to do that. This way I have time to see if there is something else I want to do. Maybe even stay in the Federal forces when the war is over."

"You really are going to do this?"

"I really am. Now I want each of you to make me a promise...don't marry all the best girls before I return. Leave one or two for me to choose from when I return." For two hours more, we stayed there and discussed the war, the battles I might have to fight, my possible demise, any killing I might do and then what they were going to do. Finally we ended the way we always did, by going over all the list of available girls in town and how to pursue them. For our finale, we moved to the end of the beach, racing down the three flights of stairs, pushing and tumbling our way down the sixty wooden steps to the rocks below, but the cold winds made us cut our beach visit short. We left with the promise to meet again once before I left. A promise we were not able to keep.

My mother took charge of the supplies I needed. She went to the military office in town and received a list of suggested items. Then she called on Mrs. Andrews whose husband had left to join the Burnside Expedition a few months before. The items suggested from Mrs. Andrews proved to be the most needed and wanted after reaching our encampment and lasted the longest in our many battle camps. Especially appreciated were the warm sox with two extra toes and heels in each, the wool vests to wear under the shirt or uniform and the wool leg warmers from knee to heel. Thank you, Mrs. Andrews! Ma and Aunt Fan washed, sewed and darned all week so that I would start with clean, strong clothes.

Pa handed me a new pair of heavy boots and issued his words, “God hold you in his hand, Son.”

Excitement ruled my thoughts and actions in that last week. All my life I had watched the eighty ships each month that sailed in and out of the Greenport Harbor and continued to wonder where they were going or what other places were like. Now, I would be going and find out for myself. I felt the adventure and thrill of what might be coming.

Only, as I waved good-bye to my family lined up on the porch did my heart sink a little, then a lot, as I turned and waved good-bye.

3

TRAINING CAMP –STAPLETON AND CAMP SCOTT –STATEN ISLAND SEPTEMBER 10- MID DECEMBER, 1861

Nothing turns out to be the same as one imagines and so it became with me as I traveled through Long Island. My name had been on the train transport, but no one acknowledged me. There were two other fellows whose names were on the list, but from the villages of Southhold and Orient, near Greenport. I did not say anything to them, because I did not want to seem as uninformed as I felt.

It surprised me to travel from town to town and none was as nice as Greenport. They seemed empty and shabby compared to our busy port city. We crossed to New York on a ferry, bigger than the one we have that crosses into Connecticut. Finally upon arrival to the other side, we saw a man in uniform with an open scroll. As I went toward him, I recognized him as Captain Pratt who signed me up at the Post Office.

He asked me my name. I said, "William H. Waterhouse, the same as I told you a week ago." The look he gave me warned that I better not appear sassy. I decided right then to think hard before I said or answered anything. I liked this man and did not want him annoyed with me.

One of the others noticed it also and

answered the question, "Byron G. Wilmot, sir." The man smiled at him.

The next did the same, "Eugene B. Barnes, sir." Too bad I was first. Another lesson I needed to learn fast. A few others joined us who were also on the ferry, but had not been on the train.

New York appeared very crowded and noisy. We were put in the back of a large wagon with our bags and had to wait for two other ferries from different directions to land before we could move. In the end we were about fifteen people of different ages and now very cold. I was glad to have my gloves, coat and hat. As we traveled to the Staten Island ferry, being pulled by six beautiful horses, bigger than we have in Long Island, the air was freezing and it was best to huddle next to one's neighbor. With the noise and the wind, talking became impossible; thus we all settled in silence to start thinking exactly to what and why we had signed our life away. I can truly say that nothing so far was anything like what I had imagined. And I had just begun.

~ ~ ~ ~

Camp Stapleton had buildings. I had imagined tents, so this mistake in my ideas of things to come turned out better. We were assigned the 'guard house.' It had cots lined up on each side all the way down. Each cot had a thin mattress and two blankets. These too were thin.

A tough looking man with a short beard announced, "In thirty minutes you will be taken to the mess hall to eat. Bring your tin plate and your tin cup if you want your eats."

Mother had questioned this on the list, but had given me a generous size of each, as she shook her head. I needed to thank her.

After we ate and washed our utensils, we were shown the toilets and sinks. "At 5:30 you will be awakened. At 6:00 you will be ready to move out," ordered the same man as we were taken back to our room. "All lamps out in thirty minutes." And he was gone. Each of us tried to put our things from the bag we brought into a wooden box at the end of each cot. What did not fit stayed in the bag under the cot. There was a lock with a key on top of each box. I was careful only to leave non necessary things in the bag under the cot.

Not being warm, not completely full of food, and not comfortable, I finally went to sleep, not full of excitement, but full of fear. This was going to be hard and I prayed I would have the courage to be brave to fight for my country and our beliefs as a private in Captain Pratt's Company called the Ira Harris Guard.

~ ~ ~ ~

The first day a bit of excitement erupted. That bugle sound at 5:30 made everyone jump up quickly. Then the fight for the toilet and face water recalled where we were. After breakfast, we were put in a line. I made sure I was not first or even near it. We marched to another building where we would be issued our 'kit,' not our uniforms as they would come later, but empty guns, knives, and items we would need for the early training. That afternoon, we started our regime of rigid drilling as a dismounted cavalry. We were told we had to be in perfect shape before we met out horses in about three weeks. If today's drills were an example, then we would be the toughest regiment around and soon.

A riot almost started when we were told that our monthly pay would be $13, not the $14 promised first. This bothered some to the point they were thinking of quitting, but I didn't come in to make money but to fight the vermin trying to split our country.

Speaking of vermin, we found a lot in our quarter's building, which had previously been occupied by Sickle's regiment; so were moved into tents immediately. Since we had to be moved, they decided to pitch the tents at Camp Scott, better ground for our drilling skills. Seven full companies had been mustered into service and three skeleton companies remained to be filled up. We would have our horses and full equipments before we started for the seat of war, scheduled in a month. There were then eight hundred able bodied men in the regiment, which was to be brought up to fourteen hundred.

October 7, 1861, we were officially mustered into the service of the United States as Company E, Fifth Regiment, in Captain Pratt's Company called the Ira Harris Guard of the New York Cavalry. On October 16, 1861, it was designated as the First Ira Harris Guard in honor of Senator Ira Harris. The bounty of $100 promised by the government would be given at the end of the three year contract.

I was a private. Company E had recruited principally from Allegany, Kennedy, Richburg, Belmont, East Rushford, Friendship, Ellicottville, Cuba, Black Creek, Little Valley, Scio, Genesee, Farmersville, Great Valley and Wellsville communities of New York. Just a few of us were from Suffolk County.

Within the week, we secured our tents at Camp Scott, near Old Town, a close distance to the water. We could see at least two hundred horses grazing around us. It was like a minnow on the end of a fishing line that we would finally be able to meet them soon. First we drilled; then started the gun practices. The shooting was easier. Although we did not use our gun in Greenport much, still my father had taken me out a few times to make sure I knew how to fill and shoot our house gun in case there was any need to protect our family. I can say I became a good marksman because the stories we heard, one had to be if he ever wanted to return. Evidently the rebels grew up hitting the eyes out of snakes and legs off frogs since they were two years old.

As our month in training came to an end, we were issued our uniforms, all but the overcoat, so I was happy to still have mine from home. I sent the rest of my outer clothes home in a box. Maybe someone could use them. After we were told the cost of all this, they gave us the option to pay right then or have it taken out of our pay. We figured it would take only a couple of months or more to finish the payments, so we all opted for a minimum each month to be taken. It was certain we were not going anywhere to buy anything and probably would have no need for full pay for many months.

November 2nd, we met our horses. Not many of us were expert riders. The ones from farms fared much better than we city fellows; so we were divided immediately.

The intense training was for those of us being taught how to ride a horse fast and slow, turn on a dime, care for the horse and its hardware in every way, and jump on and off, sometimes in full gallop. Many the nights, it hurt just to lie down. The most essential thing I learned was the importance of the cool-down of the horse, his bath and brushing. This procedure made you and the horse a pair. Its significance in your life weighed in with each stroke; its value to your life and success sealed.

We were told not to love our horse, because it might not be with us very long. It might be shot out from under us or we may even have to use one of our precious bullets to kill it if necessary, meaning its wounds would be too extensive. The word they used was to respect our animal, because it could mean if we lived or died. I already had a great feeling for my horse there, but he would not go with me when my orders came to go to battle as I had understood at first. His name, Star, because of the white star or spot on his forehead, taught me a lot and I had great confidence in him. Sometimes he made decisions for me, but that is not good in the war, so we came to terms that I would be the master and make the decisions. I would miss him, but where we were to be sent had just acquired new horses.

November 3rd, we received our overcoats, sabers, and saddle bags. A new bugle call woke us earlier every morning now that we had to water and feed the horses and ready the equipment. Once in awhile when it was our turn, we had to stay up all night watching the stables for theft or fire. We were all ready for our orders. Our regiment was ready. Everyday we waited to be told where we would be sent; could be west, south or southwest. News of the battles clearly lined up Virginia or Maryland to protect the Washington district or New Mexico for the fiery battles way out there. We did not care where, but we felt we were ready and wanted to find those rebels. The last month, when our destination did not become visible, rumors started they did not need us and we may be sent home. None wanted this to happen. At least once we all wanted to come face to face with the enemy.

So, we waited. We left New York on November 18, 1861, and served in the Department of Annapolis, Md., from November, 1861, through March, 1862.

4

CAMP HARRIS – ANNAPOLIS, MARYLAND - END OF 1861 THROUGH MARCH 1862

Christmas here was sad. The weight of being far from my family caught up with me. I think it started when we crossed the New York state line and moved south. Our trip on the boat to Baltimore proved very interesting, following the coast and seeing the lovely countryside. I think they took us this way to show us what we were fighting for and why we needed to make this commitment. It was a short way from Baltimore to Annapolis by train with beautiful old homes all along the way.

On the 28th of November, we pitched our tents about three miles from Annapolis, at Camp Harris, where we were instructed by Gen. John P. Hatch, a strict disciplinarian of the United States Army. I was made Corporal on January 1, 1862. Not sure it was any different than private.

Our encampment kept us well cared for, as were our horses. We drilled every day and waited, but got no orders to move to battle, although we knew we were not far from many conflicts. Remembering we were more or less passed over back in New York to receive marching orders, it seemed again we were left out of any movement toward the battles. They even decreased our regiment in number. Anxiously and innocently, we all wished to taste our first clash with the enemy.

My horse here, although named Tiny, sure was fast. I think they gave him to me, matching my 5 feet, 8 inch stature. He had brown eyes and a gray coat; I had gray eyes and brown hair. We made a great team and we were ready to go! It was apparent that all of us in the regiment had time on our hands, with all the antics we played on each other in our fifteen feet in diameter tents with fifteen of us living together. Waiting is always difficult. Each day with the news of different battles, some successes and some not, intensified our desire to be a part of it. Idle time opened too many thoughts of home and freedom.

More drilling, again and again, and no action unsettled us. Our daily schedule: 7:00 am breakfast; water, feed horses; clean horse equipment at 8:30 am; dress parade at 9:00 am; mounted drill from 10:00 am until 11:00 am followed by a half hour rest; saber drill until 12 noon; lunch at 2:00 pm; followed by a mounted drill; 4:30 pm supper; water and feed the horses; roll call at 8:30 pm; lights out at 9:00 pm. We were regularly inspected by the Medical Officer, due to the number living in a small area and the winter cold. He sent a number of persons home and out of the service.

The heavy winter rains and snow left the mud so thick, the horses had trouble walking. Then began the spring winds blowing our tents down; the likes I had never seen.

After the Federal disasters of the 1861 Bull Run and Ball's Bluff, and the bad first three months of 1862, there were many changes in the federal forces of the Potomac area.

McClellan was relieved of his duties as head of the many Federal armies throughout, and put in charge of only the Army of the Potomac. His brigadier generals were McDowell, Sumner, Heintzelman and Keyes. All four of these had suggested to have less regiments of cavalry; thus creating a period of inactivity for these units.

My thoughts were mainly of my family. I wrote to my Mother to share with Pa and the boys. My sister Cinty (Cynthia) lived in Chicago with her husband William Willis and daughter, Louie. They turned out to be stanch supporters of me during the war. My other sister, Mela (Amelia) lived in Greenport with her husband, Horace Penny, until they moved to New York City. Horace served in the navy on the Bark Clara Haxall.

They all kept many of my letters, which I will share with you as we proceed.

January 11, 1862 letter to Sister Cinty :

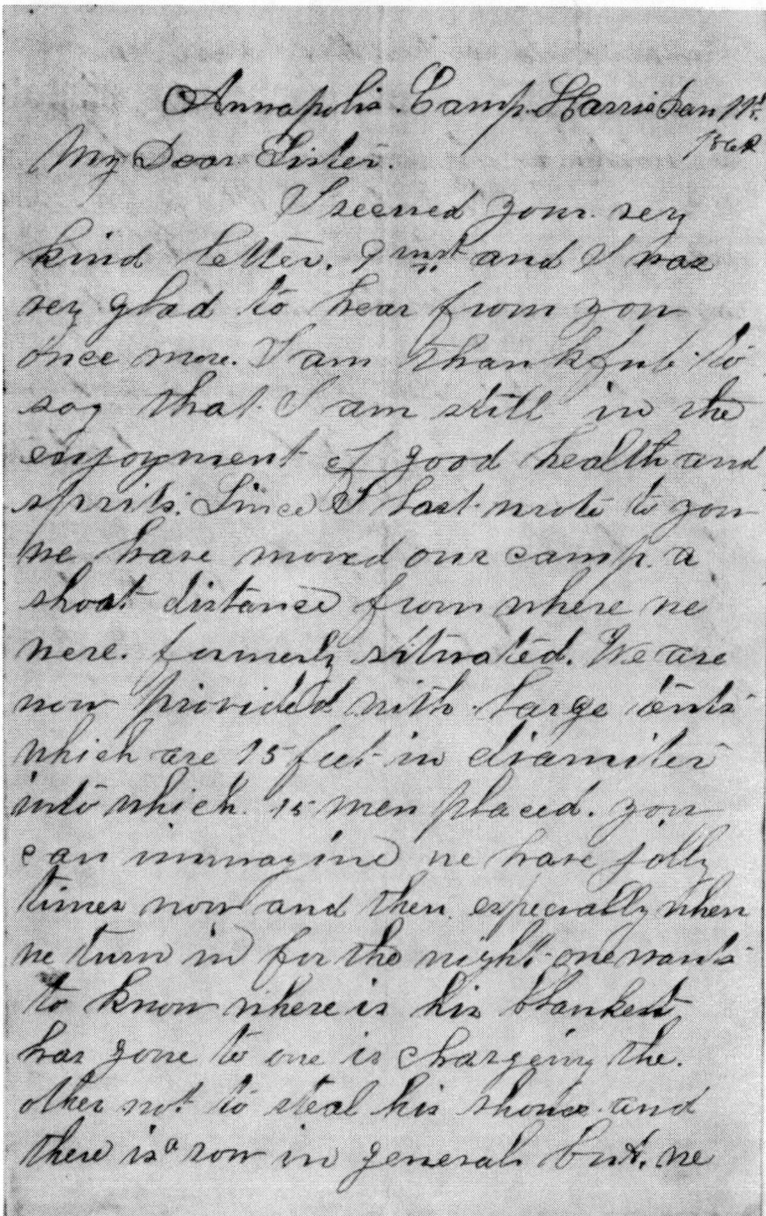
Annapolis Camp Harrison Jan 11th 1862

My Dear Sister:

I received your very kind letter 9 inst and I was very glad to hear from you once more. I am thankful to say that I am still in the enjoyment of good health and spirits. Since I last wrote to you we have moved our camp a short distance from where we were formerly situated. We are now provided with large tents which are 15 feet in diameter into which 15 men placed. you can immagine we have jolly times now and then especially when we turn in for the night one wants to know where is his blanket has gone to one is charging the other not to steal his shoes and there is a row in general but we

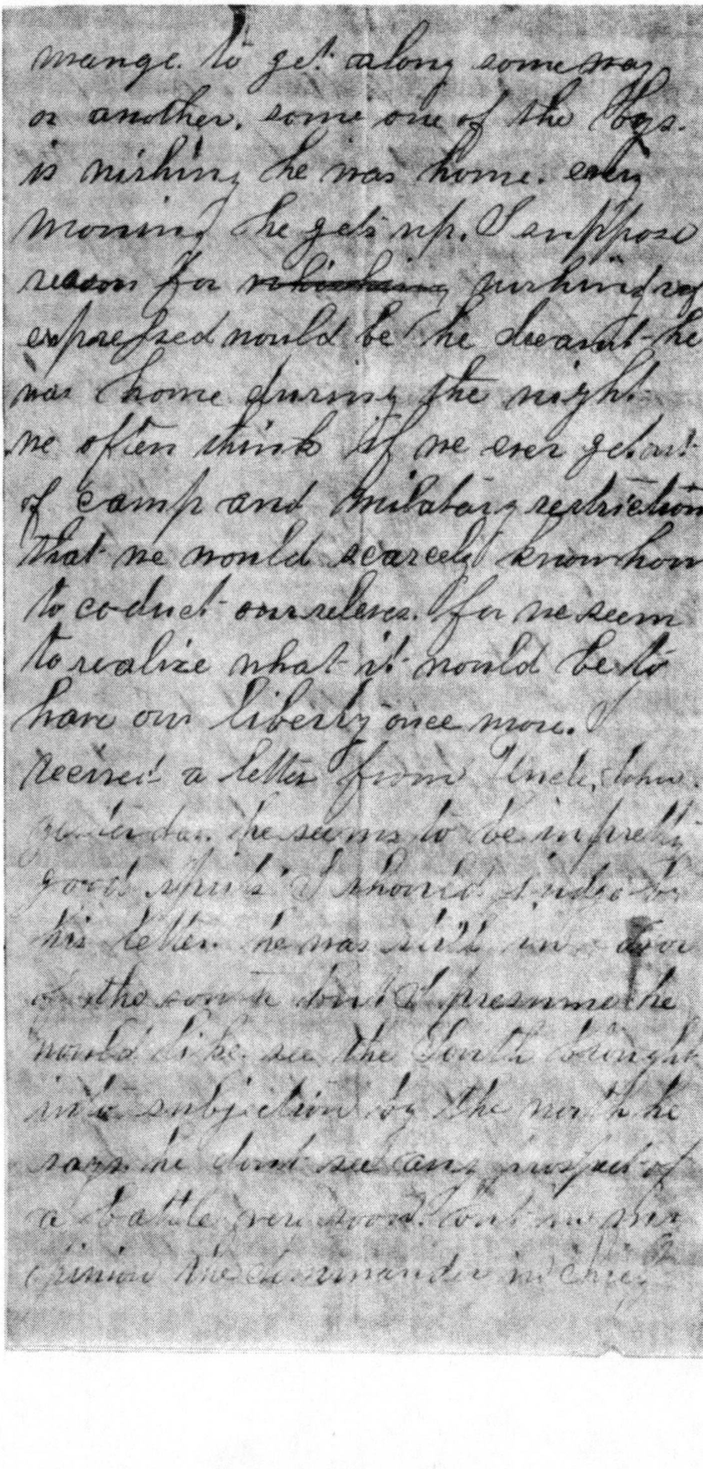

mange to get along someway
or another. some one of the boys.
is wishing he was home. every
morning he gets up. I suppose
reason for ~~whistling~~ wishing so
expressed would be he dreamt he
was home during the night.
we often think if we ever get out
of Camp and Militairy restriction
that we would scarcely know how
to conduct ourselves. for we seem
to realize what it would be to
have our liberty once more. I
Received a letter from Uncle John
yesterday. he seems to be in pretty
good spirits. I should judge by
his letter. he was still in favor
of the course but I presume he
would like to see the South brought
into subjection by the north he
says he dont see any prospect of
a battle very soon. but in his
opinion the Commander in Chief

is about ready to make a strike
that will be a death blow to
secesh. There is a very large ex
pedition fitting up here under
Gen. Burnside. I presume Mr.
Andrews is in the expedition
if I had known he was about
here I might have seen him. The
Infantry camp is about a
mile from us. I would like to have seen
him very much indeed. I suppose
he holds some office for I don't
suppose he would went out as
a private. he may have went as
a musician for they have got
some splendid bands. I was
very glad to hear the good news
from home. it seems as though
it be a great benefit to the
church. for I think the members
will become more united with their
Pastor. I should like to be at home
very much indeed but when I

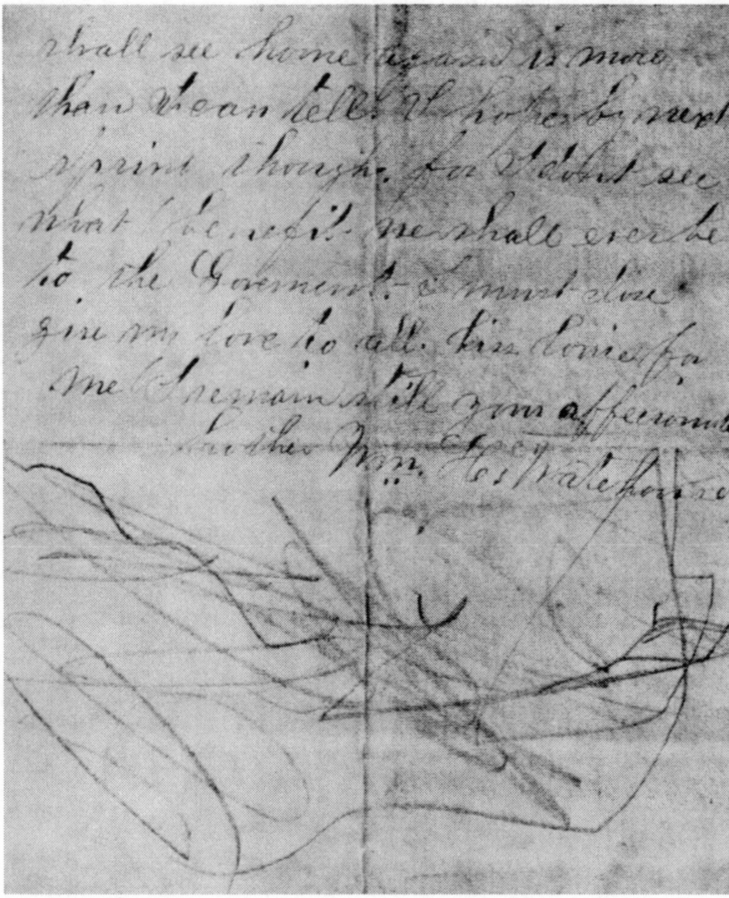

shall see home again is more
than I can tell. I hope by next
spring though. for I don't see
what benefit we shall ever be
to the Government. I must close
give my love to all. kiss Louisa for
me. I remain still your affectionate
brother
Wm. H. Waterhouse

Please Note: The word 'secesh' which I use in several of my letters was invented in 1861 and used for the first two years during the Civil War. We Yankees created it as a slang word to describe the Southerners who preferred succession to remaining a part of the Union. It was a derivation of 'succession'. It was not meant to have a nice connotation.

February 7, 1862 letter to Sister Cinty:

Camp St. Vrain Feb. 7th 1862

My Dear Sister

I received your welcome letter after a long time but though it was after so long delay I was very glad to hear from you. I had begun to think you had forgot me. I had made a move to some place another but we will remain in the old camp and we are likely to for aught I see. We have been again inspected by a U. States Medical Officer a great many of the Regiment will undoubtedly be discharged and I suppose they will reduce the Regiment to 8 companies it now consists of 12 There is a report current that we go to New Mexico as soon as the ground becomes more settled. Our General wants this Brigade should go there on account

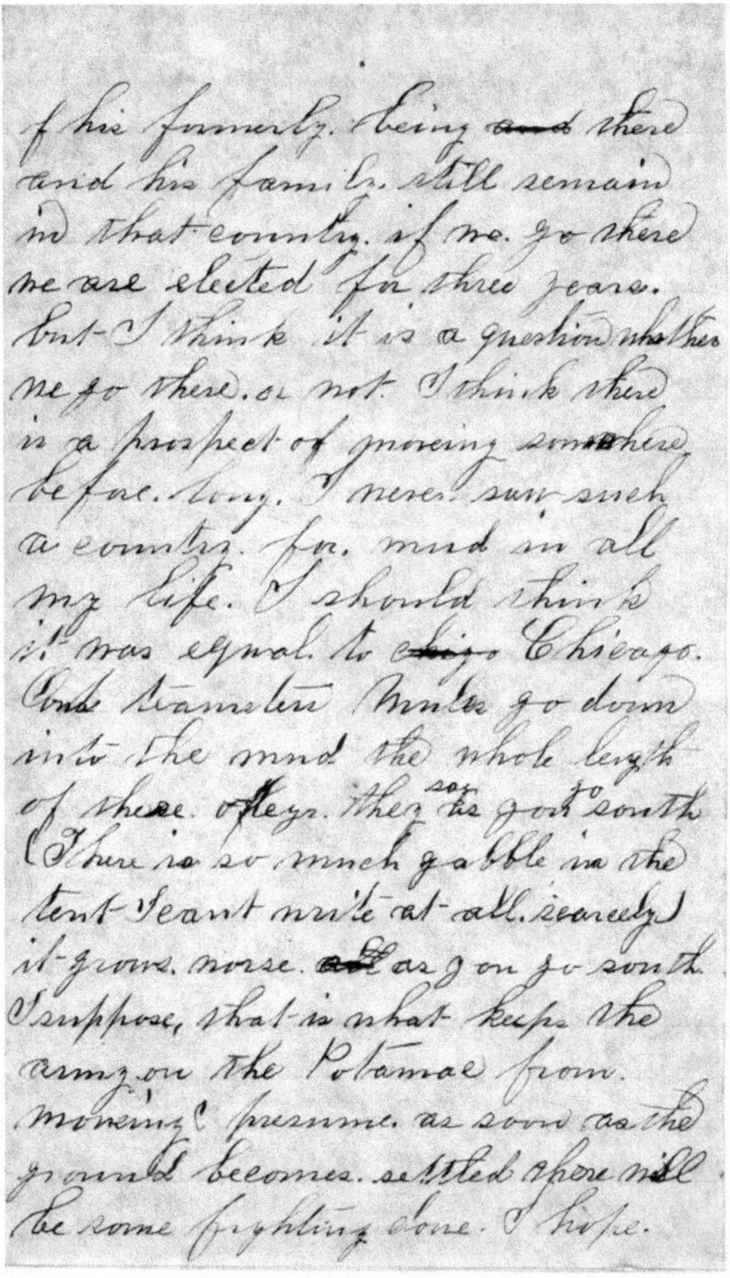

f his formerly. being ~~and~~ there
and his family. still remain
in that country. if we go there
we are elected for three years.
but I think it is a question whether
we go there. or not. I think there
is a prospect of moving somewhere
before long. I never saw such
a country for mud in all
my life. I should think
it was equal to ~~Chicago~~ Chicago.
Our teamsters mules go down
into the mud the whole length
of these legs. they say its got to south
(There is so much gabble in the
tent I can't write at all scarcely)
it grows worse ~~and~~ as you go south.
I suppose, that is what keeps the
army on the Potomac from
moving I presume as soon as the
ground becomes settled there will
be some fighting done. I hope.

it will soon bring the war to a
close. I guess the Burnside Expedition
will not make out much I am
sorry for it has cost the Goverment
an imense sight of money I pity
Mr. Andrews. if he is with it I suppo
he is for the regiment he was connecte
with ~~it~~ has gone. There some
fine soldiers in that Expedition
for I seen them drill and I know
the material that regiments are
made of. of all the soldiers I have
seen I think they were. the best.
I think the Expedition on the Miss
must be a pretty big thing I hope
it will be more successful. than
the Burnside. I received letter from
home. the same day rec yours. that
was in the 5th. she wrote that additi
to the church almost every Sunday
she seems to think Mr. Lucas will
not stay there another year. I don't

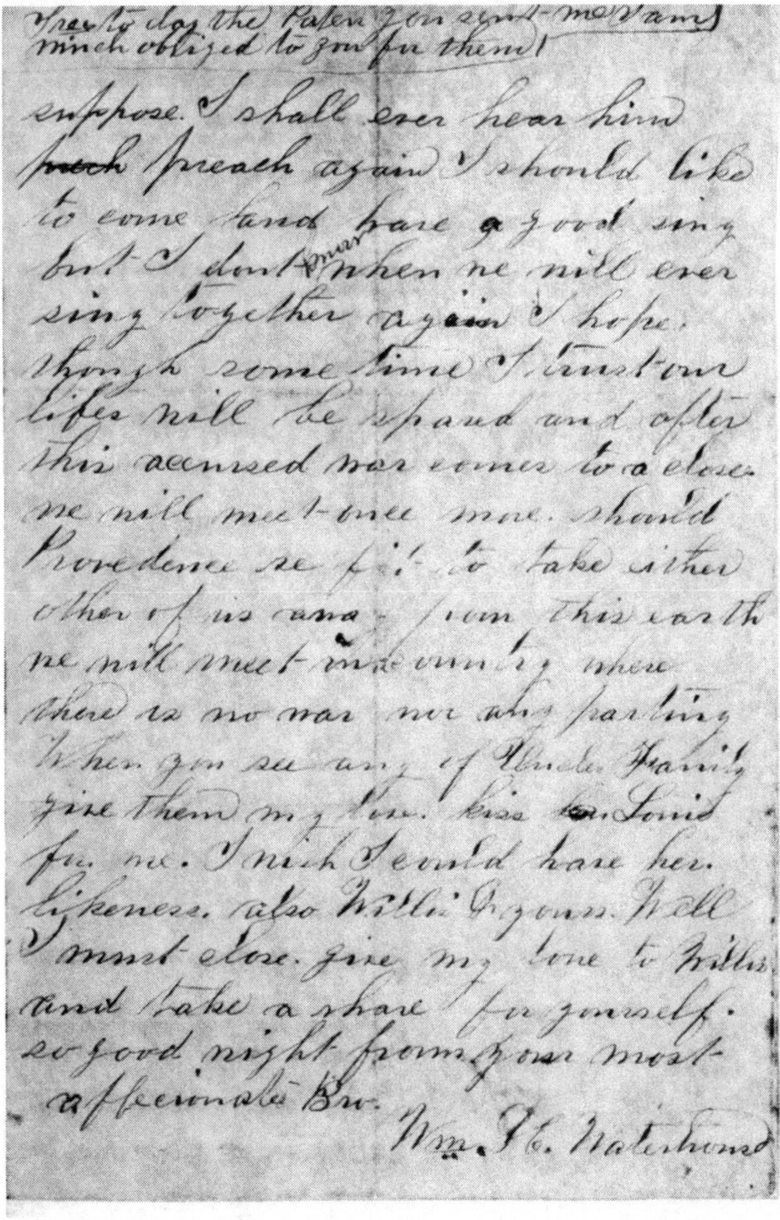

Recd to day the Paper you sent me I am much obliged to you for them

suppose I shall ever hear him
preach again I should like
to come and have a good sing
but I dont know when we will ever
sing together again I hope
though some time I trust our
lifes will be spared and after
this accursed war comes to a close
we will meet once more. should
Providence see fit to take either
other of us away from this earth
we will meet in a country where
there is no war nor any parting
When you see any of Uncles Family
give them my love. kiss Louis
for me. I wish I could have her
Likeness also Willie & yours. Well
I must close. give my love to Willie
and take a share for yourself.
so good night from your most
affectionate Bro.

Wm. H. Waterhouse

In February, we heard about General Burnside Expedition's losses and wondered if the mud had anything to do with it, as I had been much impressed with their strength when I saw that huge regiment drill. Then in late March, we had better reports of his recent victory. All this time we waited and even believed that there was no place or need for us. Early March, we were put on alert to move within forty-eight hours, but nothing transpired. We even lost our general as he took the Vermont Regiment to join the battles on the Potomac. It was rumored, we would be dismissed and sent home without ever seeing the rebs!

March 20, 1862 letter to Sister Cinty:

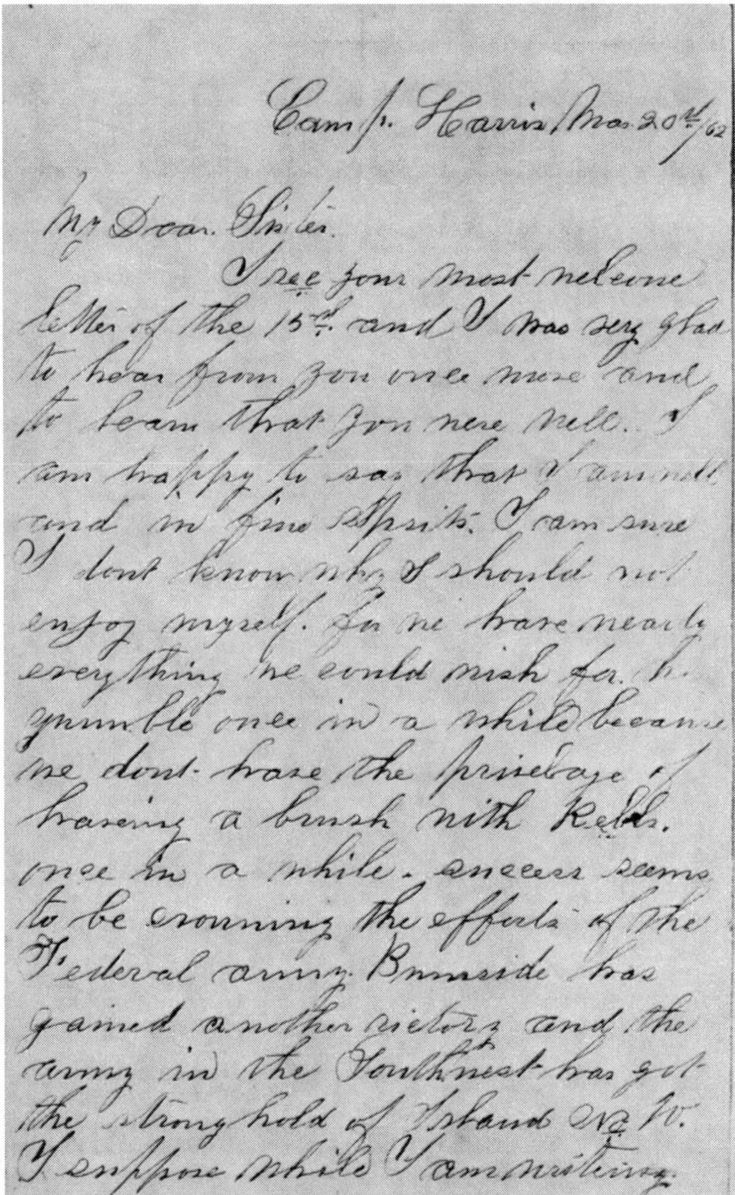

Camp H. Harris Mar 20th/62

My Dear Sister

I rec your most welcome letter of the 15th and I was very glad to hear from you once more and to learn that you were well. I am happy to say that I am well and in fine spirits. I am sure I dont know why I should not enjoy myself. for we have nearly everything we could wish for. We grumble once in a while because we dont have the privelage of having a brush with Rebs. once in a while. success seems to be crowning the efforts of the Federal army. Burnside has gained another victory and the army in the Southwest has got the stronghold of Island No 10. I suppose while I am writing

these same noble men are fighting
at Memphis I am afraid I shant
see any active service though one
week ago I thought I would smell
Rebel gunpowder before this time
for we were ordered to pack up and
be ready start at a moments notice
but since that time things have
taken a different turn from
what we expected. The Vermont
Regiment that formed a part
of this Brigade has marched and
our Gen it is said has left us
and if it is so I dont see but what
we are all afloat just as we were
8 months ago but the govement
may find a place for us yet if
it dont we will be sent home
before long I suppose. Since I wrote
you last Mrs Pratt has been
here and spent a few days when
she left here she went on to

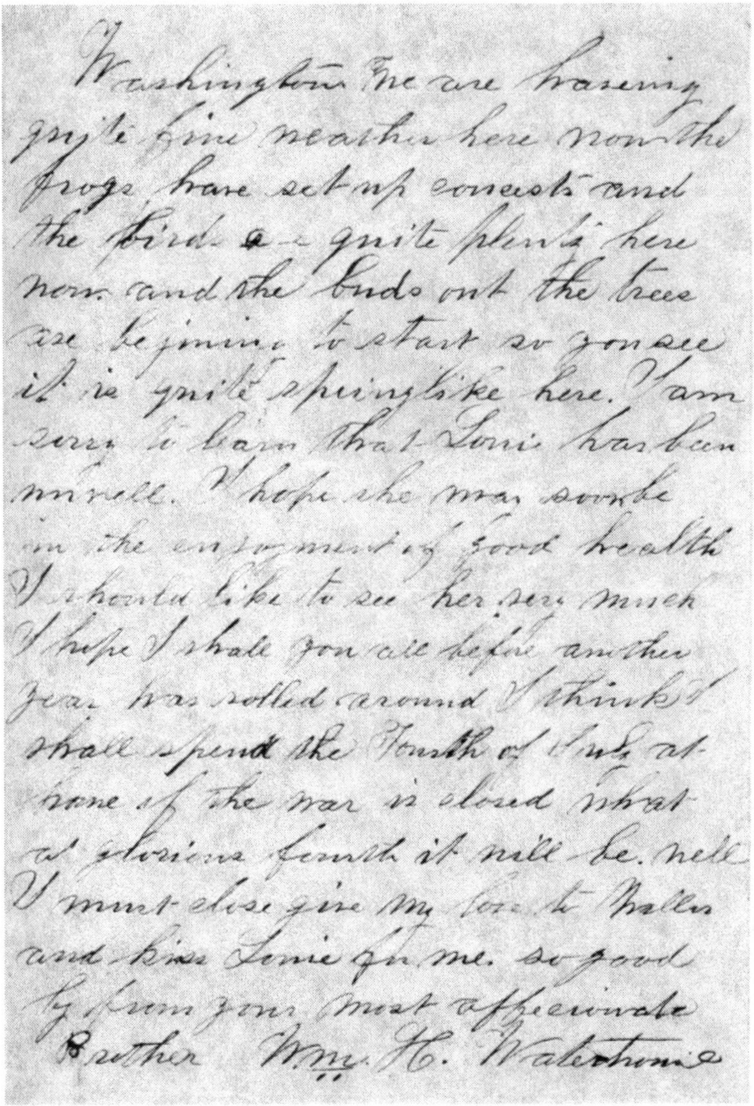
Washington. We are haveing
quite fine weather here now the
frogs have set up concerts and
the birds are quite plenty here
now and the buds out the trees
are beginning to start so you see
it is quite springlike here. I am
sorry to learn that Lonie has been
unwell. I hope she may soon be
in the enjoyment of good health
I should like to see her very much
I hope I shall you all before another
year has rolled around I think I
shall spend the Fourth of July at
home if the war is closed what
a glorious fourth it will be. Well
I must close give my love to Walter
and kiss Lonie for me. so good
by from your most affecionate
Brother Wm. H. Waterhouse

The first death of our regiment came on March 6, but not from war, but illness. It removed the light-heartedness we had before, but perhaps made us better minded for war when we received immediate orders that we would march in a day or two to join General Banks Army and his campaign.

March 28, 1862 letter to Mother:

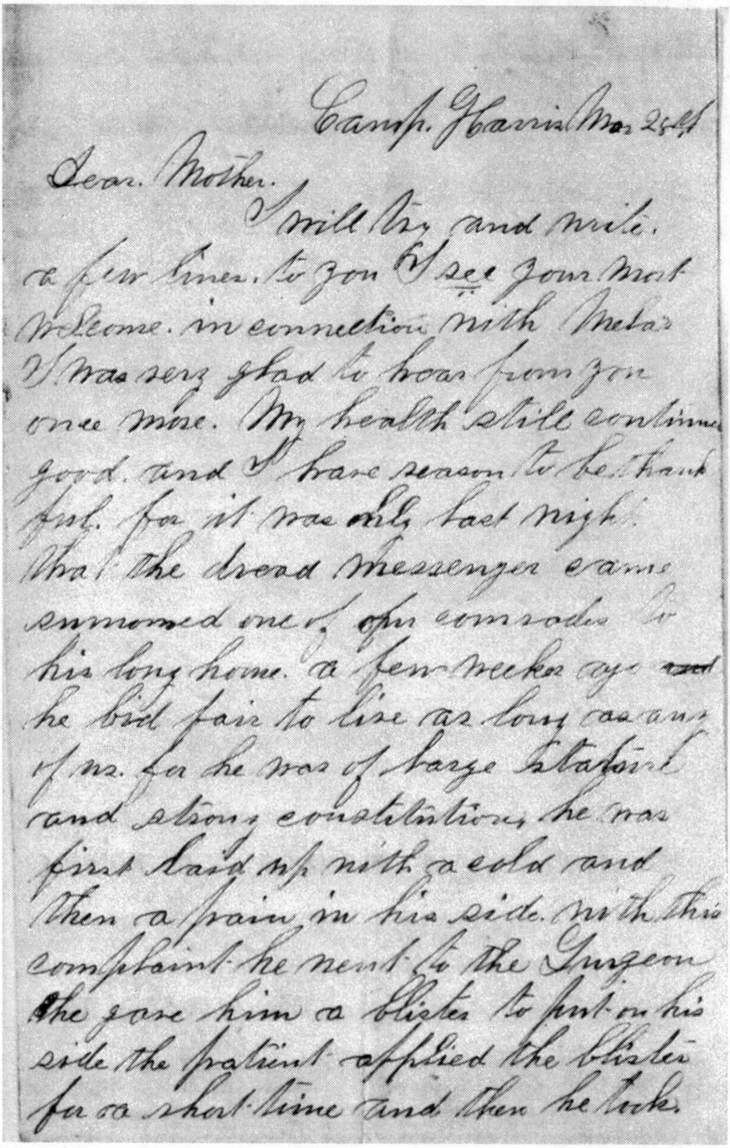

Camp Harris Mar 28th

Dear Mother

I will try and write
a few lines to you I see your most
welcome in connection with Metas
I was very glad to hear from you
once more. My health still continues
good and I have reason to be thank
ful for it was only last night
that the dread messenger came
summoned one of our comrades to
his long home. a few weeks ago
he bid fair to live as long as any
of us for he was of large stature
and strong constitution he was
first laid up with a cold and
then a pain in his side with this
complaint he went to the Surgeon
the gave him a blister to put on his
side the patient applied the blister
for a short time and then he took

took it of for he did not like to have
a blister on him while in camp.
again on the next day he reported
and he told the Doct his medicine
did him no good this made Surgeon
rather angry. and so he put one
another plaster himself and told
him to keep it on till the next
morning and if he did not he
would put him in the guard house
and the next morning it was
removed after remaining 24 hours.
and such a side I never saw
he was laid up for four weeks.
after this he began to get a little
better. after we got marching orders
he applied for a furlough. which
favor was granted him. this seemed
to excite him so that he taken
down and in a day or two after. this
fresh attack he died I think the
cause of his death was the blister

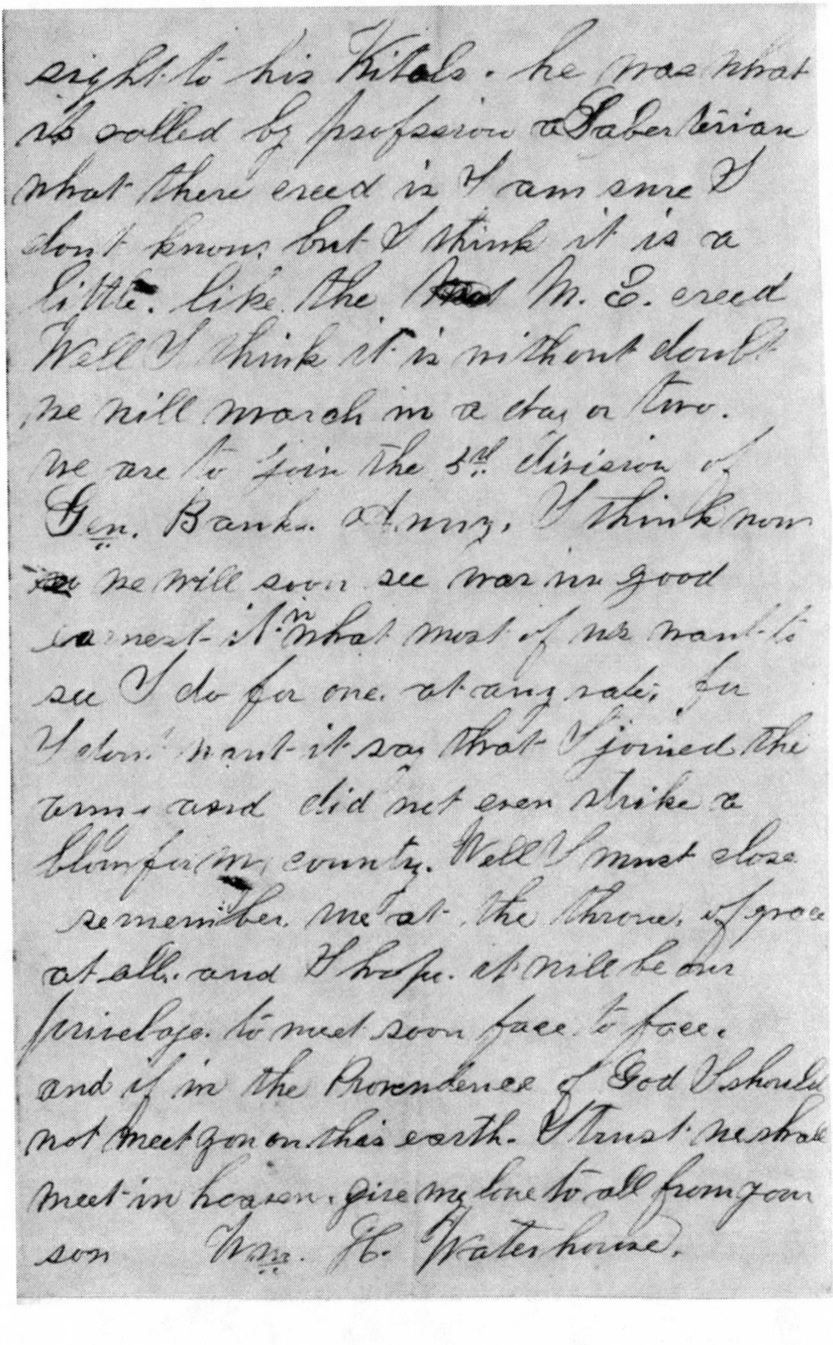

sight to his Vitals. he was what
is called by profession a Baberterian
what there creed is I am sure I
dont know but I think it is a
little like the M. E. creed
Well I think it is without doubt
we will march in a day or two.
we are to join the 5th division of
Gen. Banks Army. I think now
we will soon see war in good
earnest. It is what most of us want to
see I do for one at any rate, for
I dont want it say that I joined the
army and did not even strike a
blow for my country. Well I must close
remember me at the throne of grace
at all and I hope it will be our
privelege to meet soon face to face.
and if in the Providence of God I should
not meet you on this earth. I trust we shall
meet in heaven. give my love to all from your
son Wm. H. Waterhouse.

March 7, 1862 letter to Sister Mela (date is wrong- should be 28th-same date as letter to mother):

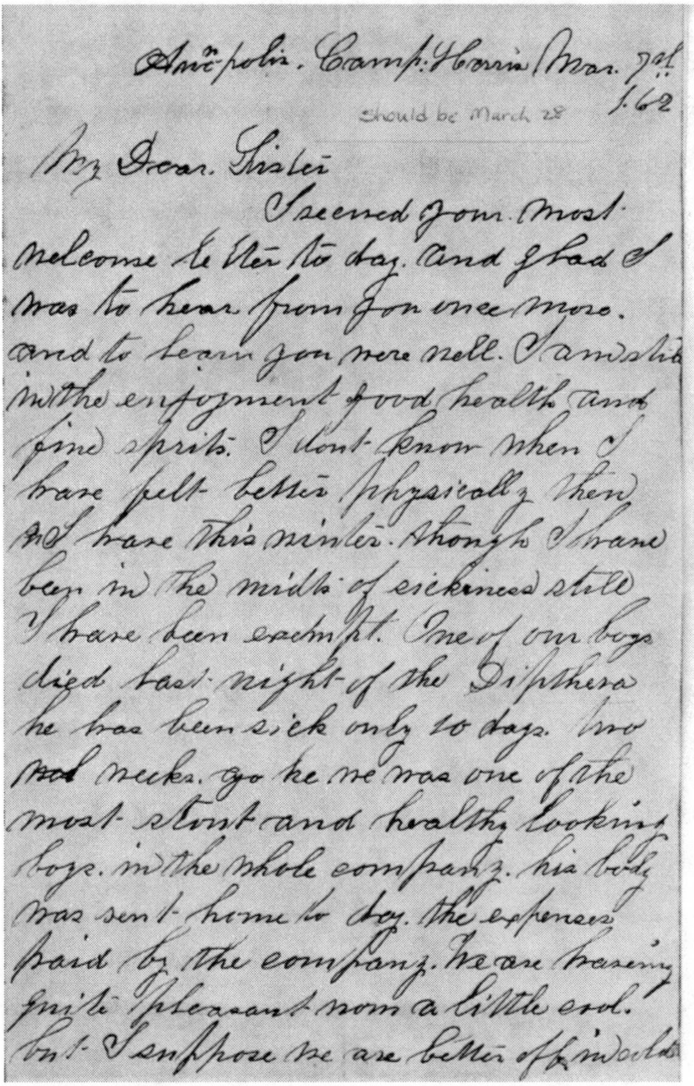

Annapolis. Camp. Harris Mar. 7th.
1.62
should be March 28

My Dear. Sister

I received your most welcome letter to day. And glad I was to hear from you once more. and to learn you were well. I am still in the enjoyment good health and fine sprits. I dont know when I have felt better physically then as I have this winter. though I have been in the midst of sickness still I have been exempt. One of our boys died last night of the Dipthera he has been sick only 10 days. two weeks. ago he was one of the most stout and healthy looking boys in the whole company. his body was sent home to day. the expenses paid by the company. We are having quite pleasant now a little cool. but I suppose we are better off in cold[illegible]

than in warm. Last week we had quite
a severe gale. three of our tents were blown
some of the other companies had
roofs two there stables were blown
off. and the camp decorations
were blown round rather promiscuously
I don't think I ever saw it blow
quite so hard ~~fo~~ before in my life.
we have our camp trimmed up very
nicely. Most of the Field Officers
have there ~~wifes~~ wives here Mr. Chaplain
has got his better half here. she is
a Long Island Lady formerly of
Glen Cove. they kindly invited me
to spend the evening with them
I did so. I found them to be very
agreeable and passed the time I
spent with them very pleasantly
indeed. Mrs. Tompson (that his her
name) is quite a fine singer. and
I should think well educated.
There has been an man here lecturing

on temperance so you see we are
well provided for as soldiers for a
change to ~~bear~~ break the monotiny
of this drill day after day that a
soldier is obliged to go through I am
glad that our armies have been
so successful both east and west.
I hope the army on the Potomac
will be able to make a move
before long we are now under orders
to hold ourselves in readiness to
march under 48 hours notice. if
we move I suppose we will reinforce
Gen Banks division on the Potomac
I would like to go down there and
make one charge on the Rebels. I
dont want to go home. have it to
say I did not even smell gunpowder
but I dont know but we shall.
I dont suppose we would be very
effective in an open battle. but
we could do picket duty for hold

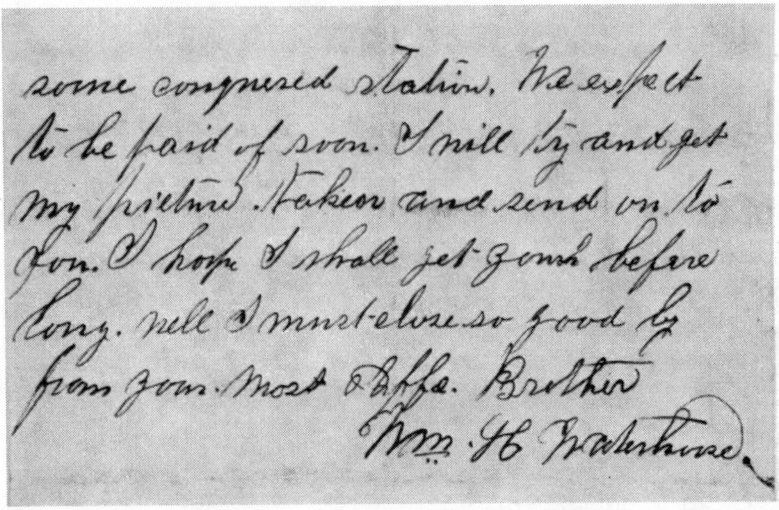
some conquered Station. We expect
to be paid of soon. I will try and get
my picture taken and send on to
you. I hope I shall get home before
long. well I must close so good by
from your Most Affe. Brother
Wm. H. Waterhouse

March, 1862, McClellan submitted his proposed plans to the War Department. Using Fort Monroe as the first base of operations, they would concentrate their strength between Yorktown and West Point, Virginia and with help from the naval forces would set up a new base only twenty-five miles from Richmond. Burnside's Expedition with the federal gunboats was underway in North Carolina. All this left the remaining Potomac troops quietly protecting Washington, but wanting to be in the fight.

In early March, 1862, the Federal army heard news that the Confederate army was retreating from Bull Run and Manassas to reposition itself in defense of Richmond. McClellan, with some of his Army of the Potomac, made their way on March 10 to hopefully be able to fire on the retreating ranks, but missed them by two days. General Banks' troops had been ordered to be ready, but were not called until the end of March to go to Harper's Ferry, thus missing skirmishes with Jackson in the Winchester and New Market area.

Harper's History of the Civil War tells us: "When Jackson fell back in the valley from Winchester toward Staunton, he was followed by Union Shields, with a division of Banks' Fifth Corps. This retreat, which was kept up as far as New Market, brought Jackson within fifty miles to joining Johnston. Shields undertook to decoy Jackson from doing this. He made a feigned retreat back to Winchester, marching his whole force thirty miles in one day. The ruse was successful. Jackson turned to pursue.

Banks, who thought it impossible that Jackson would venture to attack him, marched his whole corps, with the exception of Shields' division, toward Centreville. Shields, who still hoped that Jackson would venture an attack, secretly posted the bulk of his division in a secluded position two miles from Winchester. Not knowing this, the people of the town reported to Jackson that the place was evacuated except by a small rear-guard.

On March 22, Jackson's cavalry made a dash into Winchester, driving into Shield's pickets. The attack was repulsed after a sharp skirmish, in which Shields was severely wounded, his arm being broken by the fragment of a shell. Confident that Jackson would not renew the engagement, Banks left for Washington. Shields, anticipating a strong attack, even with his wound, prepared for it. The assault began at noon with a sharp artillery fire, which met with a strong reply. At three o'clock Tyler's brigade charged upon the Confederate batteries on the left and captured them.

The Confederates retreated, leaving their dead and wounded behind. Banks returned next morning, and pursued the retreating enemy thirty miles to Woodstock, ceasing the pursuit only when his men were thoroughly exhausted. The Federal loss in this engagement was 103 killed and 441 wounded. Of the Confederates, 270 were reported to have been buried on the battle-field and many others by the inhabitants. Their entire loss was estimated at 500 killed and 1000 wounded. The Federals call this the Battle of Winchester, while the Confederates call it the Battle of Kernstown.

Thanks to a glowing report from General Kimball, Shields was made a Brigadier General and again took command on April 30.

5

HARPERS FERRY, WEST VIRGINIA AND WOODSTOCK, VIRGINIA -APRIL STRASBURG & TOM'S BROOK, VIRGINIA - MAY, 1862

Finally, the last of March, 1862, we were ordered to the Shenandoah Valley to report to our own General Hatch, commanding the cavalry under General Banks. We struck our tents in Annapolis April 6 and moved via Washington to Harper's Ferry by train. It took almost twenty-four hours and when we arrived, the Provost Marshall had no knowledge of our existence, so we had to stay on the train overnight. The next morning, we unloaded the horses, fed them and took them to their temporary quarters in a fine dwelling with cornices on the wall. During that day, the worst snow storm in eight years came leaving about eight inches of snow on the ground. It took awhile to dry both horses and us back to normal. Our six day's stay in Harpers Ferry couldn't have been nicer as even the house where we stayed was lovely; the horses' house better than ours. Beautiful country between the Potomac and the Shenandoah Rivers. Before the war it had to have been wonderful, but now there were many completely destroyed places both in town and in surrounding areas.

Battles had happened here. The rebels still raided the town frequently. Eleven were caught and imprisoned in John Brown's building just a day or two before we arrived.

History tells us: On October 16, 1859, John Brown, a radical abolitionist led a group of twenty-one men in a raid on the Arsenal. Five of the men were black: three being free blacks, one a freed slave, and one a fugitive slave. During this time, assisting fugitive slaves was illegal under the Dred Scott decision. Brown attacked and captured several buildings; he hoped to use the captured weapons to initiate a slave uprising throughout the South. The first shot mortally wounded Heyward Shepherd, a free black man working as a night baggage porter for the B&O Railroad that ran through Harpers Ferry near the armory.

That shot aroused a Dr. John Starry from his sleep shortly after 1:00 a.m. When he walked from his home to investigate the shooting, he was confronted by Brown's men. Starry stated that he was a doctor but could do nothing more for Shepherd, and Brown's men allowed him to leave. Instead of going home, Starry went to the livery and rode to neighboring towns and villages, alerting residents about the raid. When he reached nearby Charles Town, they rang the church bells and aroused the citizens from their sleep. John Brown's men were quickly pinned down by local citizens and militia, and forced to take refuge in the engine house adjacent to the armory.

The Secretary of War asked for the assistance from the Navy Department for a unit of United States Marines, the nearest troops. Orders had Lieutenant Israel Greene to take a force of eighty-six Marines to the town. In need of an officer to lead the expedition, U.S. Army Lieutenant Colonel Robert E. Lee was found on leave nearby and was assigned as commander along with Lieutenant J. E. B. Stuart as his *aide-de-camp*. The whole contingent arrived by train on October 18, and after negotiation failed, they stormed the fire house and captured most of the raiders, killing a few and suffering a single casualty themselves.

Brown was tried for treason against the state of Virginia, convicted, and hanged in nearby Charles Town. Starry's testimony was integral to his conviction. Andrew Hunter of the prosecution said, "John Brown captured the attention of the nation like no other abolitionist or slave owner before or since." The Marines returned to their barracks and Colonel Lee returned to finish his leave. The raid was a catalyst for the Civil War..

April 10, 1862 Letter to Mother: see next page:

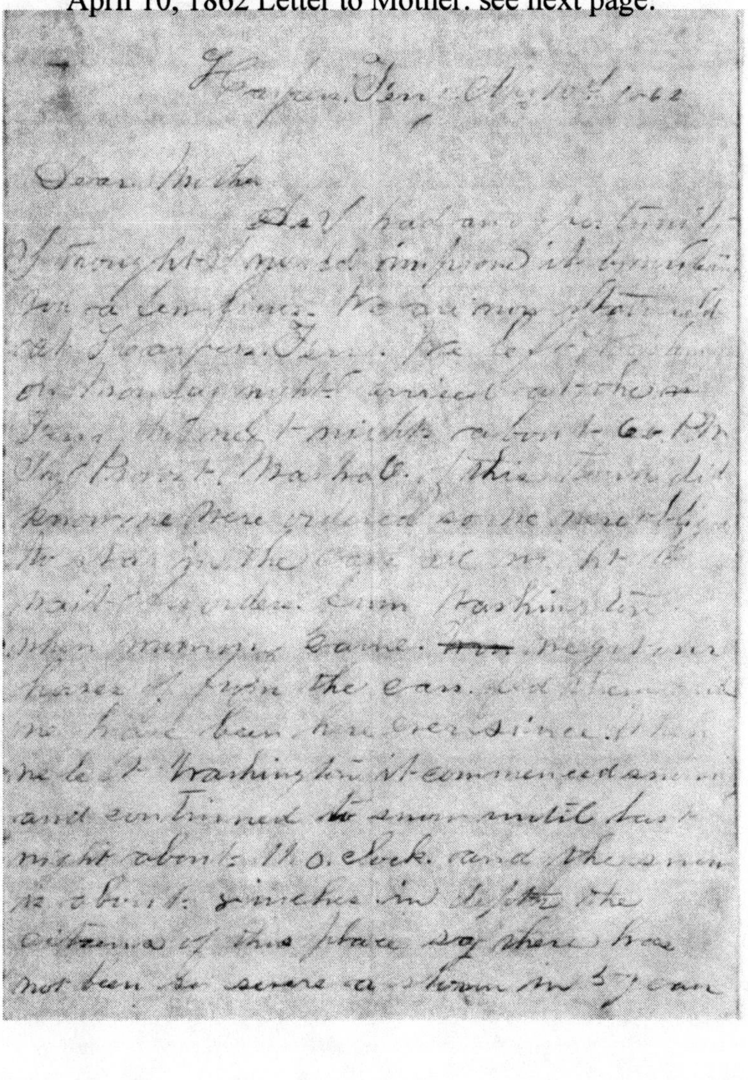

Harpers Ferry Apr 10th 1862

Dear Mother

As I had an [illegible] I thought I would improve it by writing you a few lines. We are now stationed at Harpers Ferry. We left Washington on Monday night [illegible] about 6 o'clock [illegible] when morning came. We got our horses off from the cars. And there [illegible] we have been here ever since. When we left Washington it commenced snowing and continued to snow until last night about 11 o'clock and the snow is about 8 inches in depth. The citizens of this place say there has not been so severe a storm in 5 years

Transposition of first two pages of April 10 letter due to the condition of the letters:

Harpers Ferry, Apr. 10, 1862

Dear Mother

As I had an opportunity I thought I would improve it by writing you a few lines. We are now stationed at Harpers Ferry. We left Washington on Monday night arrived at the Ferry the next night, about 6 P.M. The Provost Marshall of this town did (not) know we were ordered so we were obliged to stay in the cars all night to wait for orders from Washington. When morning came, we got out horses of(f) from the cars, fed them and we have been here ever since. When we left Washington it commenced snowing and continued to snow until last night about 11 o'clock and the snow is about 8 inches in depth the citizens of this place say there has not been so severe a storm in 5 years We all pretty well soaked when we left Washington and when we took our horses of(f) the cars, we got wet over again. We have our horses in a fine large Brick dwelling house that must have 2 or 3000 dollars they are finished of(f) with a nice cornice on the walls on the lower floor, and the house we occupy is as good an house as any one could wish. how long we shall stay here I dont know our Colonel told us yesterday we would camp about five miles from here. I had as likes stay as any where, and we will have some scouting to do here for the rebels come right into the city a day or two ago 11 were taken prisoners. they are confined in John Browns old building, some of them say they were forced into the rebel service. it is sad to see...

Page 3 follows in original letter form:

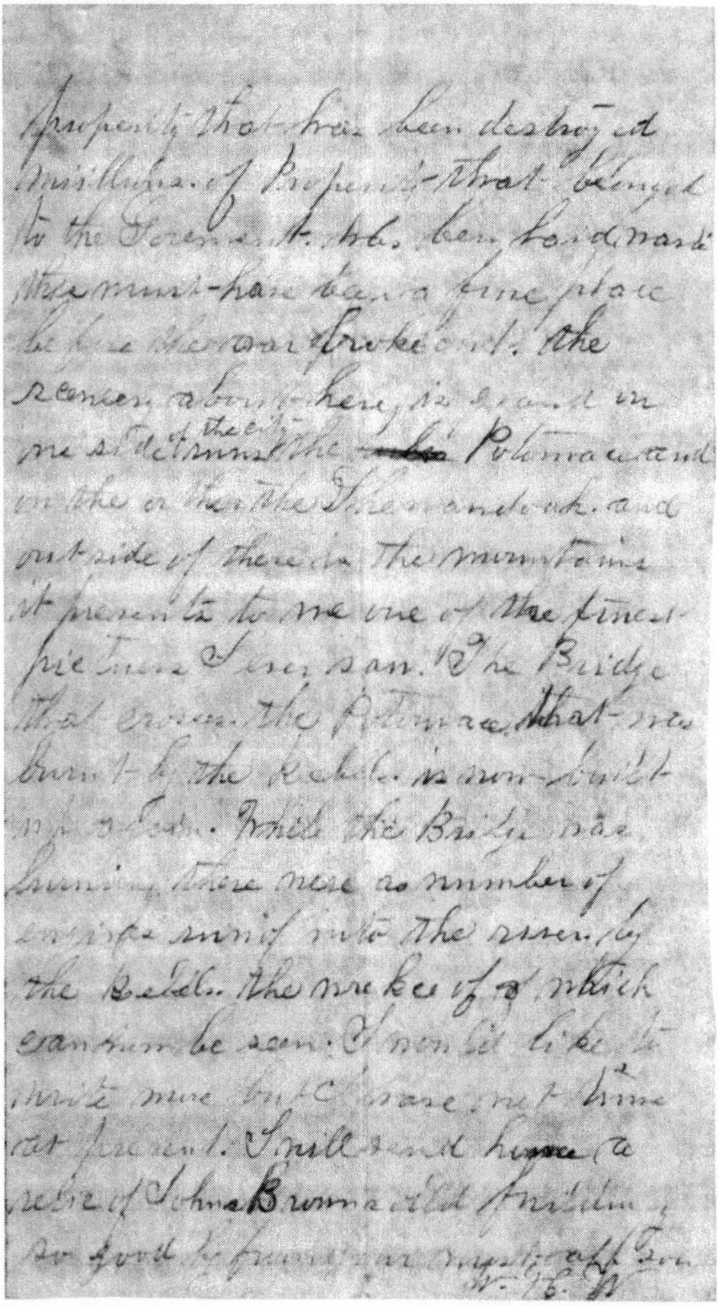

property that has been destroyed
millions of Property that belonged
to the Government. has been laid waste
they must have been a fine place
before the war broke out. The
scenery about here is grand on
one side of the city runs the Potomac and
on the other the Shenandoah. and
outside of these is the mountains
it presents to me one of the finest
pictures I ever saw. The Bridge
that crosses the Potomac that was
burnt by the Rebels is now built
up again. While the Bridge was
burning there were a number of
engines run into the river by
the Rebels. the wrecks of which
can now be seen. I would like to
write more but I have not time
at present. I will send home a
relic of John Browns old building
so good by from your affectionate Son
W. B. W

The following reads:

Direct to Harpers Ferry
5th N. Y. V. C. Co. E. care of
Capt. Pratt

Will you please to send me a
few Postage Stamps for we are
not yet paid of (please note a lot of the f's are ff.)
and I am short of money.

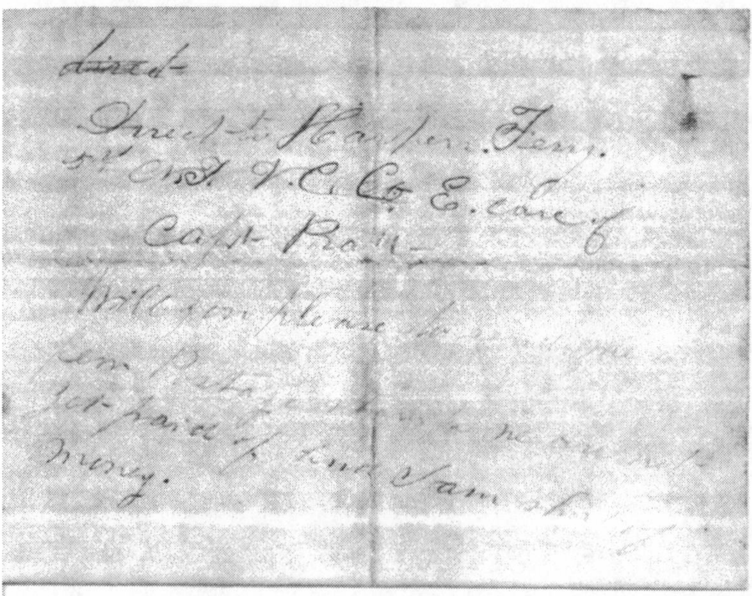

Note: after 1st page of next letter, a transposition follows.

April 26, 1862 to Mother:

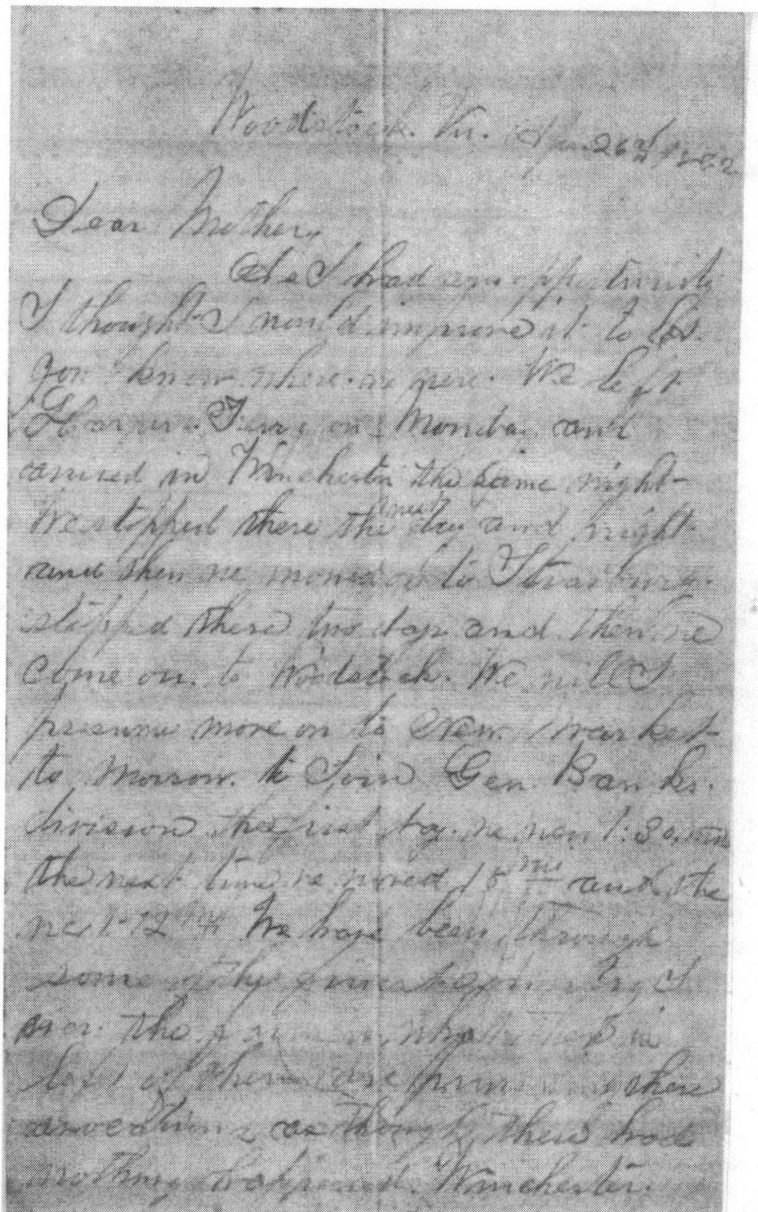
Woodstock. Va. April 26th 1862

Dear Mother

As I had an opportunity I thought I would improve it to let you know where we are. We left Harpers Ferry on Monday and arrived in Winchester the same night. We stopped there the next day and night and then we moved to Strasburg. stopped there two days and then we came on to Woodstock. We will I presume move on to New Market to morrow to join Gen. Banks division the first day we went 30 m the next time we went 15 m and the next 12 m. We have been through some of the [illegible] I ever saw. the [illegible] of them [illegible] are [illegible] as though there had nothing [illegible] Winchester.

Transposition of pages of April 26 letter:

Woodstock, Va Apr. 26, 1862

Dear Mother

As I had an opportunity I thought would improve it to let you know where we were. We left Harpers Ferry on Monday, and arrived in Winchester the same night We stopped there the next day and night and then we moved on to Strasburg. stopped there two days, and then we come on to Woodstock. We will I presume move on to New Market tomorrow, to join Gen. Banks division. the first day we went 30 miles the next time we moved 18mi. and the the next 12mi. We have been through some of the finest country I ever. the farmers, what there is left of them are pursuing there avocations as though there had nothing happened. Winchester is quite a fine place, though a great many of the buildings are vacated every man woman and child are all secesh. they seem to hate the Yankees, as they call us very much indeed. Strasburg is a lonesome, dreary dull place. the 66th Ohio infantry are putting fortification. I think it will be held as a sort of Military Post. Woodstock is a pretty little place. it has been quite a busy little town I should think. We occupy a building that was a store house. the steeple on the old Court House is shattered by a shell that was fired by our troops into the rebeles. The Rebles run here like a flock of scared sheep. Thre is mo Property destroyed here, and Harpers Ferry except Railroad bridges. We expect to join Banks, just as soon as we can get there. Jackson is on the

... *Remainder of this letter is missing.*

We were called quickly to go to New Market and Harrisonburg for our first time to meet our enemy; reporting to Banks at Harrisonburg on May 3d after having our first skirmish at Port Republic on May 2. Port Republic was a forlorn village situated in the delta formed by the North and South Rivers, affluent of the South Fork of the Shenandoah. Because of its geological position, it was used by both sides and changed hands many times. On the 2nd we ran into the

Confederate pickets from Harrisonburg where Jackson had been for three weeks. From this time on until the close of the war we would see continuous active service.

Although we lost our general when sent farther south, Captain Pratt stepped up to do a fine job. We were to join General Banks division as soon as we could arrive there. We moved from Harper's Ferry to Winchester (thirty miles) the same day and stayed two days; then on to Strasburg (eighteen miles) and stayed two days; and then to Woodstock (12 miles). This whole countryside was the finest I had ever seen. The people still left in the area were all for the rebels; actually hated us 'yankees,' as they called us. We called them 'secesh.'

General Nathan Kimball wrote: "The end of April, General Banks directed a forward movement to force a passage across the river. The river was much swollen by rains, rendering it impossible to ford. There being only one bridge, it became the center of contest. The enemy having failed to destroy it, although had set it on fire.

A splendid dash by a detachment of our cavalry through the bridge drove the enemy away and extinguished the flame. In this seven day battle, the regiments were the 1st Ohio, 1st Michigan and 5th New York." The statistics for the 5th NY were 2 killed, 5 wounded, and 7 missing.

Note: after 1st page of next letter, a transposition of entire letter follows.

May 15, 1862 to Mother:

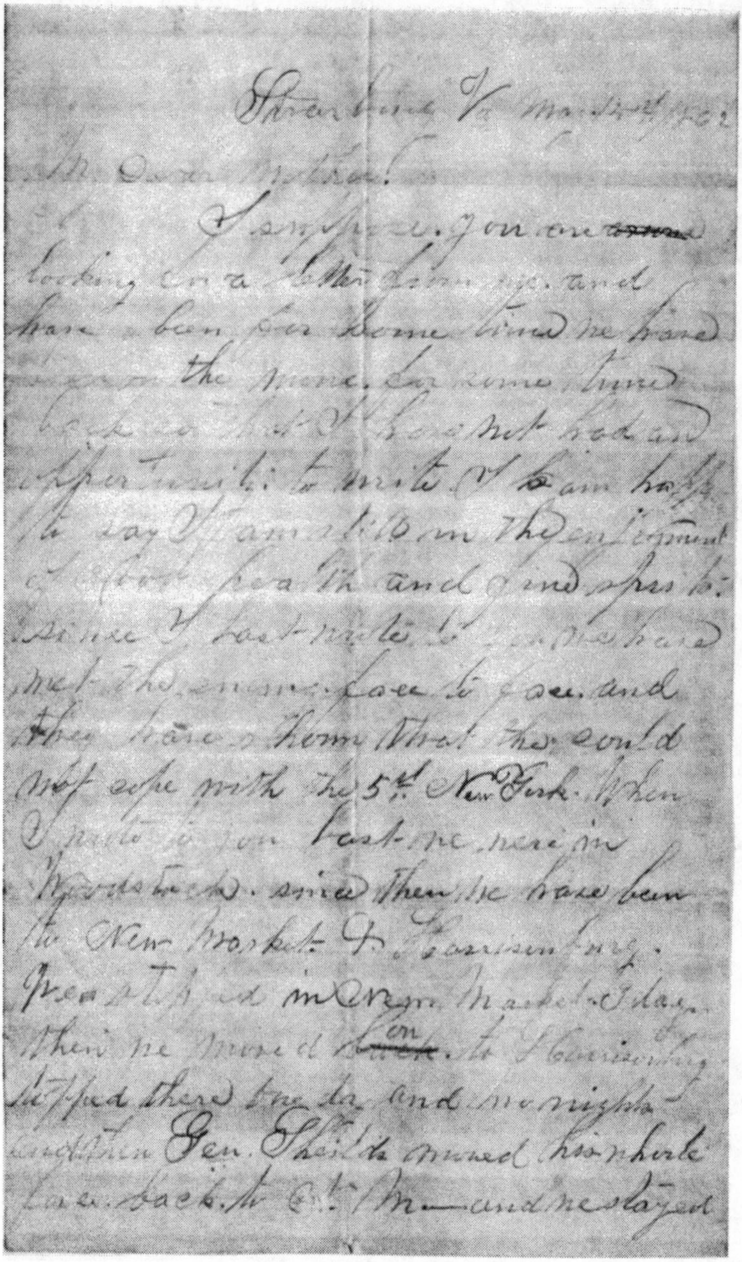
Strasburg Va May 14th 1862

My Dear Mother!

I suppose you are looking for a letter from me and have been for some time we have been on the move for some time back so that I have not had an opportunity to write & I am happy to say I am still in the enjoyment of good health and good spirits. Since I last wrote to you we have met the enemy face to face and they have shown them that they could not cope with the 5th New York. When I wrote to you last we were in Woodstock. since then we have been to New Market & Harrisonburg. We stopped in New Market 3 days. Then we moved on to Harrisonburg stopped there one day and two nights and then Gen. Shields moved his whole force back to [illegible] and we stayed

Transposition of all four pages (as written) of May 15 letter: *Strasburg, Va, May 15th 1862*

My Dear Mother

I suppose you are looking for a letter from me, and have been for some time we have been on the move, for some time back so that I have not had an opportunity to write. I am happy to say I am still in the enjoyment of good health and fine spirits. since I last wrote to you we have met the enemy, face to face, and they have shown that the could not cope with the 5th New York. When I wrote to you last we were in Woodstock. since then we have been to New Market, & Harrisonburg then we moved on to Harrisonburg stopped there one day and two nights and then Gen Sheilds moved his whole force back to N.M. - and we stayed there something like a week. We have been skirmishing and doing picket duty. our first skirmish was quite severe. We left camp about 10 o'clock in the morning with a force of about 150 men and two pieces of Artillery after going about 8 miles on a quick trot we met the enemy's pickets. We drove them and were ordered to charge. We did so, and such a charge. We put our horses on the dead run, for about four miles. When we met a force of Ashby's Cavalry of about 400 strong. as long as there powder lasted they stood but when we come to use sabers, they ran like cowards. our boys done nobly. one of our company had the leg to his horse broken and the enemy rushed him and told him to surrender but he told them no he would not. he fought bravely so long as he could stand, until they shot him through, but we got him before he died. he died in about an half an hour. after we got him we had our Adjutant taken prisoner. We took 4 prisoners killed it is said 10. We have been reconnoitering ever since but the rebls dont show themselves yesterday we moved back to Woodstock and today we have come back to Strasburg. I suppose the object in our retreating back is to draw Jackson's Army into the Valley. Where we are now stationed the valley is quite narrow and we could oppose any force that could meet us and I think Fremont will also come up in his rear. I dont think

Jackson will hold out much longer. almost daly deserters come in and state that the army is very much demoralized the citizens that is some of them say our vacateing the Valley is the worst thing we could do for them, for there are a great many secreted in the mountains that will be ferreted out and pressed into the army Whether there is any truth in it or not I dont know. I rec your letter some time since I hope if you hear from me you will continue write, for we are where we cannot write very often but the letters come to us I would like the Examiner to for we get but very little reading matter but I must close. remember me at the throne of grace that my life may be spared and should my life be taken, I trust I shall get to that abode where there is no wars no sin give my love to when you write to Cynthia tell she must if she dont hear from me. so good by from your most affectionate Bro.

Wm. H. Waterhouse

After this, each force rechecked their positions and their strategies. Jackson was reinforced with Ewell's division at the south fork of the Shenandoah near Gordonsville. Meanwhile the Federal army had created a new Department called the Rappahannock with McDowell in command.

Shields, having been made a Brigadier General, thanks to Kimball, was ordered with McDowell to join McClellan before Richmond leaving Banks stripped down to only a 6000 men force. Banks had followed Jackson to Harrisonburg, but then was ordered to fall back fifty miles to Strasburg to fortify his regiment.

May 1, Jackson threatened and entered Harrisonburg for three weeks but after May 8, the rest of the valley was in possession of the Union forces because Jackson's army was held in check beyond Shenandoah by Banks and Shields. Then an order came for Shield's division to join General McDowell's at Fredericksburg, which proved to be unfortunate.

General Burns wrote on seeing this order: "Results are not for us to consider, and orders are received to be obeyed. I regret it because I feel that the policy, of which this order is a part, is to end in allowing the grand army of the rebels to escape unharmed from Virginia, and add another year to the war. It is impossible to anticipate what work lies before us. I feel the imperative necessity of making preparation for the worst."

Note: after 1st page of next letter, a transposition of entire letter follows.

May 21, 1862 letter to Sister Cinty:

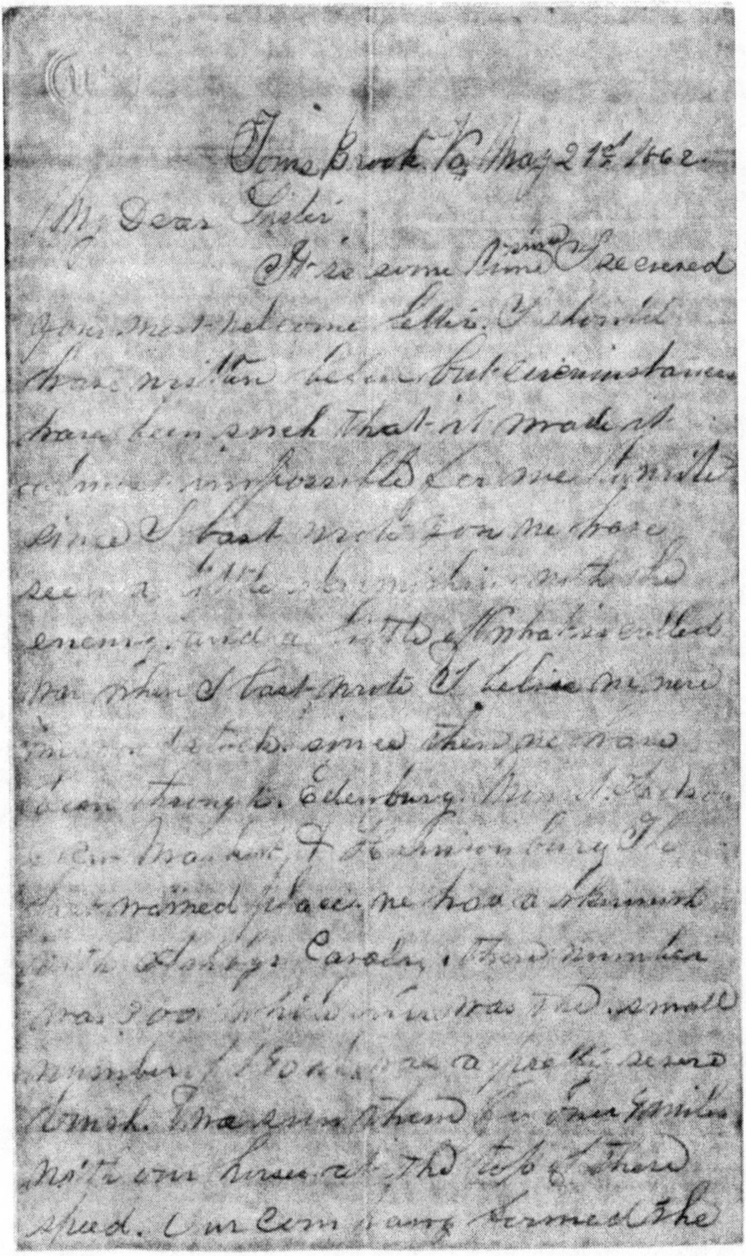

Toms Brook Va May 21st 1862

My Dear Sister

It is some time since I received your most welcome letter. I should have written before but circumstances have been such that it made it almost impossible for me to write since I last wrote you we have seen a little skirmishing with the enemy and a little of what is called war when I last wrote I believe we were [illegible] since then we have been through Edenburg. Mt. Jackson New Market & Harrisonburg the last named place we had a skirmish with Ashby's Cavalry. Their number was 900 while ours was the small number of 150 [illegible] a pretty severe brush. Chasing them for four miles with our horses at the top of their speed. Our Company formed the

Transposition of all four pages (as written) of May 21,1862 letter to Sister Cinty:

(Possibly some of the stationery was furnished by the government or army, as several sheets have the letters U S in an oval, embossed or in raised letters)

U S

Tom's Brook, VA May 21st 1862

My Dear Sister

It is some time since I received your most welcome letter. I should have written before but circumstances have been such that it made it almost impossible for me to write since I last wrote you we have seen a little skirmishing with the enemy, and a little of what is called war when I last wrote I believe we were in Woodstock. since then we have been through Edenburg, Mount Jackson New Market and Harrisonburg. The last named place we had a skirmish with Ashby's Cavalry. there number was 300, while ours was the small number of 190 it was a pretty severe brush. we run them for over 9 miles with our horses at the top of there speed. Our company formed the advance guard consequently we had the most fighting one of our company had his horse shot and after he was dismounted the rebles shot him through and then cut him with there Sabre. we succeeded in getting him before he died. I assisted in carrying him to the ambulance wagon he died in about 30 minutes after he was wounded. he has no father he leaves a widowed Mother a Sister and brother. The boys got up a subscription and sent home quite a sum of money. A moment before he died he said to one of his comrades (whose name was Matthew) good by Matt I am going to die now. tell Mother I am (scratched out) how I died he then bade us all good by. it was sad to see one of our boys die by the wounds received by the rebles. we also lost one of our Battalion Adujddnt (scratched out)_Adjudant. When we last heard from his he was in Richmond we took seven 7 prisoners and killed 10 the(y) run like cowards. Since then the whole of Banks division have been moved within 4 miles of Strasburg. our regiment forms the advance of the whole Army.

we on Picket Duty once or twice a week. Some of Ashby's Cavalry will dash out and as soon as our reserve moves up they will run like a flock of wild sheep. we are now having fine weather the Scenery of this Valley beautiful beyond description I hope the time is not far distant when this unholy war will be at an end. deserters are continually coming in from Jackson's army they state quite a deplorable state of affairs are existing in their ranks. I am afraid our forces will be defeatded at Corinth but we must hope for the best. Confederate Temp (?). is quite plenty here in the valley. I will send you a note well I must close. give my love to all. kiss Louis for me. so good by dont hesitate to write if you dont hear from me, for your letters will reach me direct to Washington D. C. or elsewhere. 5th N. Y. V. Cavalry Comp. E care of Capt. Pratt, Banks Division Department of the Shenandoah good by from your Bro. Wm. H. Waterhouse P. S. I see by the New York papers that Elder Knapp is dead. I wish you would send me your pictures. Good by.

Union Fremont's Mountain Department led by Milroy approached Jackson from the direction of Romney to the village of McDowell, forty miles southwest of Harrisonburg. Here Milroy was attacked on May 8, 1862, by Jackson. In this action, sometimes called that of Bull Pasture, the Confederates sustained the heavier loss, but gained their point by driving Milroy from the field and capturing a substantial amount of stores.

May 12, Banks moved to Strasburg, thus opening the way for Jackson. This scattered the Federal forces, leaving Banks the most vulnerable and open for Jackson to attack, which came from New Market. If he stayed in Strasburg, Banks knew it meant he would be starved out or beaten. All that remained for Banks was to retreat down the Valley, as Burns said, "entering the list with the enemy in a race or a battle, as he should choose, for the possession of Winchester the key or the Valley."

Jackson's idea was to push towards Winchester to gain the rear of Banks. Westward over the mountains was not a choice for Burns. He had to retreat down the valley and rush for possession of Winchester. Three days of hard fighting at Front Royal, Jackson forced the heroic soldiers of Banks' divisions from the Valley. Jackson pushed from Front Royal to Middleton and May 23, Jackson with 1500 dashed down upon Banks with 9000, mostly stationed in detachments at Strasburg and Front Royal, nearly twenty miles apart by the route Banks was forced to take.

At 9:00 am on May 24th, the retreating column was on its march, the train in front. The rear had hardly gone three miles when reports came from the front that the enemy held the roads. The train was sent to the rear, and the troops moved to the front. After a short encounter, the head of the Confederate column was beaten back, and Banks succeeded in reaching Winchester.

After that small encounter, but before daybreak on 25th, Jackson assailed him with superior and constantly increasing force. After a five hour battle, Banks began to retreat hurriedly toward Martinsburg where he rested a couple of hours, then pushed for the Potomac reaching Williamsport by sunset.

The ferry barely took the ammunition train, the ford was occupied by wagons, the cavalry waded and swam the river, but there was no way to get the infantry across. With the help of pontoon train brought from Strasburg, the infantry crossed by noon the next day.

"Never," said Burns, "were more grateful hearts

in the same number of men than when, at midday on the 26th, we stood on the opposite shore." In this retreat of fifty-three miles, Banks lost six to eight hundred men, of whom the greater part were captured. Of his train of five hundred wagons, he lost fifty-five besides considerable stores. A few days later he estimated his loss at nine hundred of whom thirty-eight were killed, one hundred fifty-five wounded and the rest missing. This retreat caused a panic in Washington. It also caused us individual men to lose all our personal belongings.

Jackson reached the river just in time to see his enemy safe on the Maryland side.

Harper's History of the Civil War tells us as do my letters of June 15 and 16, 1862: this did give Stonewall Jackson the opportunity to display his peculiar strategic ability.

It is especially hard to accept the first death of a comrade in battle. Even when the first of our company died of an illness, we all felt a great loss, but nothing like the shock of our first in war. Perhaps it was that loud message that it could have been me that shook my boots, the very boots and words from my father. All of us could not believe how courageous Spencer had fought, not surrendering, right to his death. Again Pa's exact words. I think we each took on a new dedication to make this young man's death not be in vain and to fight as nobly as he had done. This loss of gallant Spencer would remain with each of us forever.

6

CAMP IN THE WOODS NEAR WINCHESTER, VIRGINA - JUNE, 1862

Harper's Pictorial History of the Civil War continues: Jackson celebrated his victory of chasing 'the Union Army out of Virginia, but only rested for one day. Realizing he was cut off from his supplies and support forces. He quickly started his retreat back, but masked it with a feigned attack on Ewell's division at Harper's Ferry.

McDowell never thought that Jackson would follow Burns all the way to the Potomac, thus placing himself two times farther away from friendly forces than either McDowell or Fremont were from him. Thus he did not carry out orders to join with Fremont and cut Jackson off. Nine days after Jackson on his retreat passed through Strasburg, just before the junction of Fremont and Shields (sent by McDowell) was to have been effected. If either of these commands had marched with only half of the celerity of Jackson in his advance and retreat, the Confederate force would have been cornered in the lower part of the Valley with no hope or chance for escape.

Jackson passed one point near Strasburg only a few hours before Fremont, who caught Jackson's rear flanks. A skirmish ensued and checked Fremont, allowing Jackson into Strasburg. Here he found out Shields had been in Fort Royal and had not joined Fremont. Jackson went down the main road, but sent a detachment to burn all the bridges over the South Fork.

Fremont continued harassing Jackson's rear force, but Jackson was able to cross the river and destroy the bridge immediately, which put him a full day ahead, due to the time for rebuilding the bridge. Jackson was able to join Ewell at Port Republic. Jackson decided to throw his whole force across the east side of the river against Shields' advance unit, led by Tyler, of only 3000 men and six guns. Jackson burned the bridge behind him so Fremont could not help.

Tyler had a commanding post and fought off the Confederate assaults with heavy loss to the South. Then a Confederate brigade marching through dense forest assaulted Tyler's left flank combined with the front attack forced Tyler to retreat leaving all his guns but one. The loss of life was great for both sides.

Here ended the pursuit of Jackson who remained near Weyers Cave across the South River from June 12 to the 15th, then he set out to join Lee in Richmond. He had fully accomplished the object he had in view. With barely 20,000 men he had neutralized McDowell's 40,000, Fremont's 20,000 and driven Banks' 6,000 beyond the bounds of the Confederacy.

During this exact period but near Richmond, the same bungling of orders and communication between McClellan and McDowell happened. It is said that if these two had joined, Richmond would have fallen, even as late as June 26th orders to join weren't done leaving McClellan exposed.

Note: after 1st page of next letter, a transposition of entire letter follows.

June 16,1962 to Sister Cinty:

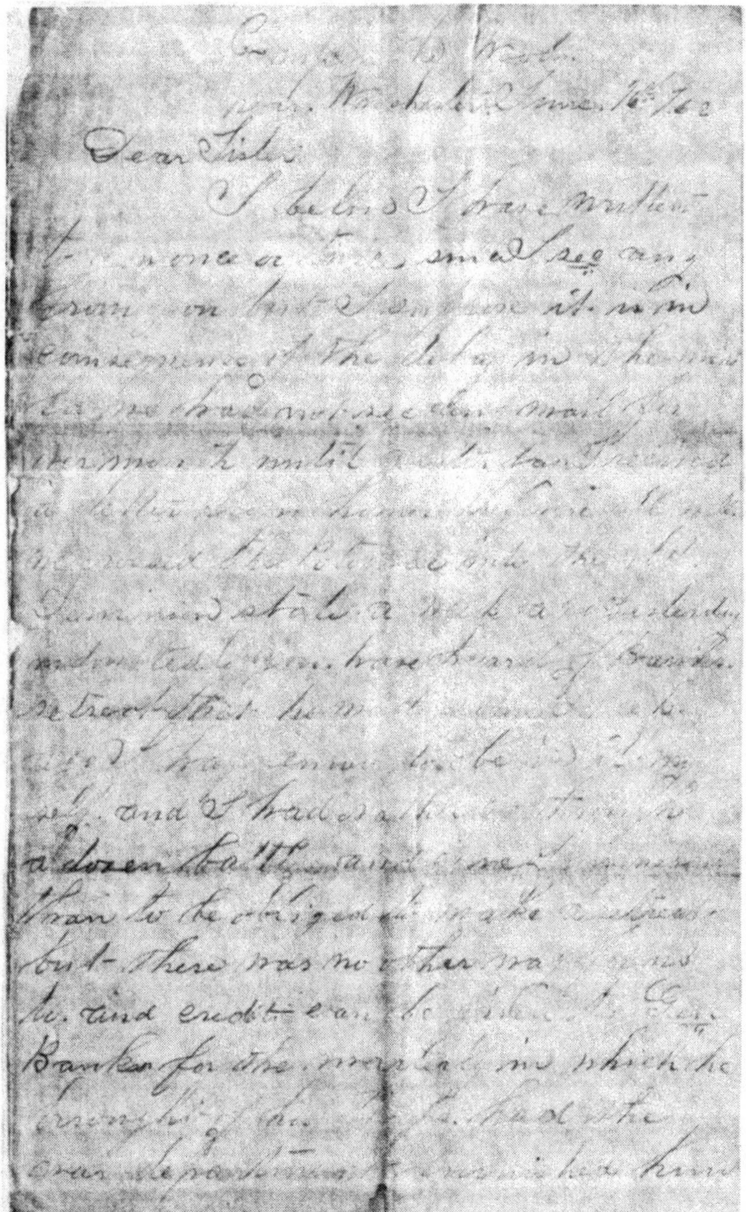

Dear Sister

I believe I have written

Transposition of all four pages (as written) of June 16,1862 letter to Sister Cinty·

Camp in the Woods near Winchester June 16th/62

Dear Sister

I believe I have written to you once or twice since I rec any from you but I suppose it is in consequence of the delay in the mail for we had not rec any mail for over month until yesterday I received a letter from home. They were all well. we crossed the Potomac into the old Dominion state a week ago yesterday undoubtedly you have heard of Banks retreat that he made some 3 weeks ago I happened to be in it my self and I had rather go through a dozen battles and come of(f) conquerors than to be obliged to make a retreat but there was no other way for us to and credit can be given to Gen. Banks for the masterly in which he brought of(out) his troops. had the war department furnished him with troops some(same) as he requested them to do undoubtedly we would not have been routed. Some two weeks before we made the retreat Gen. Banks applied for troops and a few weeks days after he made the application he sent an aid de camp but he rec no troops. consequently (to me a common phrase) we had to skedaddle but old Jackson has been worsted the force that was brought into the Valley by him numbering 25 to 30,000 has been reduced to 5,000 and Fremont has captured a number of his guns. Uncle Sams force now in the Valley is nearly 100,000 and troops are till coming in from by the way of Williamsport & Harpers Ferry. it is said the force is to be raised to 150,000. last accounts stated that Jackson"s force was 75,000 that we new of. undoubtedly this Valley is to be the scene of the summers campaign rumor says Beaureguard I comeing up here to take command of the confederate forces. We also have 150 pieces of cannon. I think we can give a little bit of a rush This city is full of Rebel prisoners they are being sent of(f) to Baltimore daly. we some able Generals here now old (or rather in years young) but old in renown is Gen. Sigel, also Banks, Fremont and Shields we also have Gen. Crawford of Sumter fame, then Surgeon of the U.S. Army. Our regiment has lost by disaster sickness, desertion and discharged 550. when we come (came)into (into) Annapolis we had 1000 men now 450 Our Col. it_is has gone to Washington to get recruits. a_ great many of the officers now we have come into active service have resigned we have no Major's two of them haveing resigned and the third has been attached to Gen. Sigel's Staff. one of our company Lieutenants has been promoted to captain so we are minus one officer. Mother wrote that Bet. Wiggins was to be married soon I hope all these young lasses wont step into the bonds of Matrimony before I get home for I may want one myself some(same) time she wrote that Dan Welsh heard from Hen Christian he said he was all right I expect he has seen some hard fighting the Rebles are death on our men that wear the Zouave uniform they will give them no quarter. Henry's Uniform is a very conspicuous one being a bright crimson red, with leggings there cap is part white also I bet he makes a good soldier Mother wrote that (that) they had no Minester yet I should think it be quite a pull back to the church but I must close remember me as you approach the throne of grace that I may be kept from temptation and that success may attend all our efforts put forth in behalf of our country give my love to all kiss Louis for me. good by from your most aff brother

Wm. H. Waterhouse

(Write soon)

Note: **ZOUAVE** (zoo-ahh-vah) was the name given to native North African troops employed by the French Army as fighters and mercenaries. Their dash, spirit, and heroic style of warfare caught the fancy of many military observers worldwide in the 1800's, including a young American named Elmer Ellsworth.

Ellsworth organized the "US Zouave Cadets", the first zouave organization in this country, and toured the north where they participated in parades and drill competitions. The popularity of the cadets caught on in other areas of the nation and it was this idea that gave birth to "zouave regiments" during the American Civil War. A number of zouave regiments were organized in the North and South in 1861, modeled after the zouave regiments of North Africa and Ellsworth's Cadets.

The uniforms of these regiments were very distinctive and made them stand out in camp and on the drill field. Regrettably, their bright red trousers and sashes also made them good targets on the battlefield. Never the less, a number of zouave regiments were raised, uniformed, and marched off to war to serve both sides.

The young man who started the zouave craze in America did not live long enough to see the zouave regiments his example inspired march to the battlefield. In 1861, Ellsworth returned to New York (his home state) and organized the 11th New York Infantry, "Ellsworth's Fire Zouaves". The men in the regiment recruited from the many different fire departments in New York City. The 11th New York moved to the defenses of Washington that April where their commander, Colonel Ellsworth, paid a courtesy call on the president. Ellsworth had become an acquaintance of Abraham Lincoln while living in Illinois, and the president was very fond of the dashing 24 year-old officer, viewing him as a symbol of Union and patriotism.

On May 24, 1861, the day after Virginia seceded from the Union, the 11th New York Infantry was ordered to seize Alexandria, Virginia, across the Potomac River from Washington. While securing the city, Colonel Ellsworth personally removed a Confederate flag from the front of an inn known as the Marshall House and was gunned down by the furious innkeeper.

A grief stricken President Lincoln ordered Ellsworth's body to be laid in state at the White House before the body was taken home to New York for burial. Ellsworth's tragic death became a symbol of the Union cause while northern newspapers and politicians eulogized him as one of the North's greatest patriots. Soon after his burial, his old regiment changed their nickname to "Ellsworth's Avengers".

Despite these efforts, a zouave regiment only retained its distinctive dress if the men repaired their clothing and the distinctive zouave uniforms slowly disappeared from the army as time passed. By the time of the Battle of Gettysburg, many of these regiments had lost or worn out their original uniforms and adopted the standard Union uniform. Still, there were a handful of regiments that retained a portion of the zouave uniform- the jacket- such as the 23rd Pennsylvania Infantry and the 95th Pennsylvania Infantry. Even some wore Union uniforms but became zouave regiments.

The 146th New York Infantry did not start the service in zouave uniforms, but adopted them in June 1863 just before the Gettysburg Campaign began. Some of the other regiments in that brigade, including the 140th New York and 155th Pennsylvania Infantry, adopted zouave uniforms later in the war. I know that Hen Christian must have had close times fighting in that brigade.

Note: after 1st page of next letter, a transposition of entire letter follows.

June 25, 1862(labeled 15th, but can't be) to Mother:

Camp in the Woods
near Winchester, June 15th/1862.

Due to happenings described in this letter, date should be 25th

Dear Mother
This morning we rec a mail
for this regiment for the first time in
a month and with it came your letter
I can tell you it done me a heap
of good to hear from home once. How
it seems to put new life into the
men when the mail comes in. Last
[illegible] we crossed the Potomac at
Martinsburg where we stopped over
night and the next day came on to
Winchester where we [illegible]
since we have come here we have been
out on the road to Romeny to a
place called Capper Springs there springs
are mineral and there is a large building
for boarders capable of accommodating
near 200 persons. And the report was
that there was a few Rebels there that
had been sent [illegible] of Gen Banks.

Transposition of all four pages (as written) of June 15,1862 (should be 25th)letter to Mother:

Camp in the Woods near Winchester, June 15th, 1862

Dear Mother

This morning we rec a mail for this regiment, for the fist time in a month and with it come your letters I can tell you it done me a heap of good to hear from home once more. it seems to put new life into the men when the mail comes in. Last Sunday we crossed the Potomace to Martinsburg where we stopped over night and the next day come on to Winchester where we are now stationed since we have come here we have been out on the road to Romeney to a place called Copper Springs. these springs are mineral and there is a large building for boarders capable of accommodating some 200 persons, and the report was that there was a force of rebles there that had been sent to put of(f) Gen. Banks baggage train but did not succeed in doing it and Jacksons Army in turn being obliged to retreat they were cut of(f) from the main force well as I said before we were sent after those fellowes. we rode all night and arrived at the Springs about daylight we dismounted from our horses all the time expected to find some rebles. we surrounded the building and then entered it at all points but nary a rebel did we find they had got wind that we were comeing and left at the early part of the night. Well as it was we some breakfast out of the keepers of the house, and feed for our horses, and then we went a scounting around the country, during the day we destroyed some two or three whiskey distilleries, and got information where we could get grain and horses if needed. The goverment dont find any fault with the army if we do confiscate secesh property it will be hard on the farmers, there for there will all be destroyed there some of the finest wheat fields in this valley I ever saw in my life. Stonewall Jackson sent a message in here this week that he would occupy this town on Saturday, the 14th yesterday, but the old fellow has not got here I reckon old Gen, Fremont is not going to be drove back so easy. I suppose there is no doubt but we have got as many as 20,000 troops here in the , and they are still coming by the way of

Williamsport and Harpers Ferry. I dont think there is any doubt what this Valley will be the scene of the summers campaign if we conquer them in the field it is suppose they will carry on a guerilla warfare. this valley is a very important field to them on account of its richness. it will be long time I think though before the rebles will be able to strengthen there foothold here though for we have got some able Generals in the field here now. I have not had the privelage of seeing old Gen Sigel yet but some of our boys have. they like his appearance. Much Since our regiment got reduced from 1,000 men to about 450 our Col. has gone to Washington it is said to recruit for the regiment and rumor says we will be sent there but we cant tell what will be done. I was in hopes I should get a letter from Cynthia today but I did not. I am sorry you dont get any minister yet it seems as though it would be a great pull back to the church I am obliged to Mrs. Clark for her kind regards to me. I should like be in the Basement very much I think I should enjoy it very much indeed it is a long time since I have heard any preaching from the Bible. but I must close I should like write more give my love to all and pray for at all times so good nite from your most aff son

Wm. H. Waterhouse

The history of the New York 5th Cavalry lists these battles bravely fought during this time: "Ordered to join Banks in the field March 31. South Fork, Shenandoah River, April 19. New Market April 29. Port Republic May 2. Conrad's Store May 2 and 6. Report to Gen. Hatch May 3. Rockingham Furnace May 4. Near Harrisonburg May 6. New Market May 7. Columbia River Bridge May 8. Bowling Green Road near Fredericksburg May 11. Operations in the Shenandoah Valley May 15-June 17. Woodstock May 18. Front Royal May 23 (Cos. "B" and "D"). Strasburg, Middletown and Newtown May 24. Winchester May 25. Defense of Harper's Ferry May 28-30 (4 Cos.). Reconnaissance to New Market June 15. Near Culpeper Court House July 12."

~ ~ ~ ~

Things were happening in Washington that we fighting men could not know. A very young General Pope, a recent graduate of West Point who had done well in the Mississippi arena, suddenly was called in June to take over a newly created "Army of Virginia." General McDowell with 18,500 troops, General Fremont with 11,500 and General Banks with his 8,000 had to report immediately to Pope. All were senior to Pope. Fremont took offense of this and immediately resigned and retired from military duty. General Sigel took over Fremont's troop command.

Pope's entry after examining the cavalry report: "...5000, but most of it is badly organized and armed, and in poor condition for service."

7

MADISON AND ARLINGTON HEIGHTS, VIRGINIA - JULY, AUGUST AND SEPTEMBER, 1862

During the last days of June the heavy and strategic Seven Days' Battles occurred, from Chickahominy Cliffs northeast of Richmond and ending in the Union army retreating to Harrison's Landing on the James River in southern Virginia. Our regiment stayed in Madison, closer to the Rappahannock-Shenandoah area; therefore, we were involved in many skirmishes.

July was a very busy month for the New York 5th Cavalry. The cavalry regiments from both sides were used as reconnaissance units. Our camps were always closest to the enemy and forward from the other forces. We were the eyes and ears of our commanders trying to find out first where the enemy was and what they were doing before they found us. Sometimes we surprised them and other times they, us. In July we were out scouting or picketing daily. We had "skirmishes" July 1 near Woodstock; on the 2nd at Warsaw Ford, both with no casualties, but on July 6that Sperryville, we had one wounded and one missing.

General John Pope had been ordered to protect Washington in the event of a sudden surprise attack by the Confederates, thus his army stayed in the north of Virginia. Pope's initial orders to told us he had been sent to lead us into battle, not retreat. He also listed many orders pertaining to the rules set to deal with the civilians they encountered anywhere, such as anything needed could be taken from them, giving a voucher for it to be paid at the end of the war if on the winner's side; all food and supplies were to come from the population; and the population were to be held responsible for any damage done to bridges, railroad, etc. and could be shot or hung. His General Orders brought a response from the Confederates in Eastern Tennessee to pass equal orders to their soldiers.

On July 12th we were near Culpepper Court House and on the 15th were hit at Orange Court House, where we had five missing. Two days later three more missing at Liberty Mills before our heaviest loss on July 18 at Barnett's Ford: one wounded and 23 missing. On July 28, 1862, I was promoted from Private to Corporal again, probably because we had lost so many from destruction, disease and desertion. We had gone from 1000 to 450 persons in our Regiment since January, 1862. We were pulled back to recuperate the rest of July, 1862.

uly 13, Lee, realizing the strategic importance of the main railroad communication between Richmond and the South located at Gordonsville, sent Jackson and Ewell in that direction, in hopes of striking a portion of Pope's army before it could be re-enforced.

July 14, Union General Banks, who had moved his regiment to Culpepper, was ordered to send Hatch, who commanded the cavalry, to seize Gordonsville. Hatch failed to execute this order twice and was replaced by Buford.

The next two weeks, both forces reinforced their troops in this area. Even General Pope arrived from Washington on the 29th.

August 8,1862(should be 2nd)*to brother-in-law Willis:*

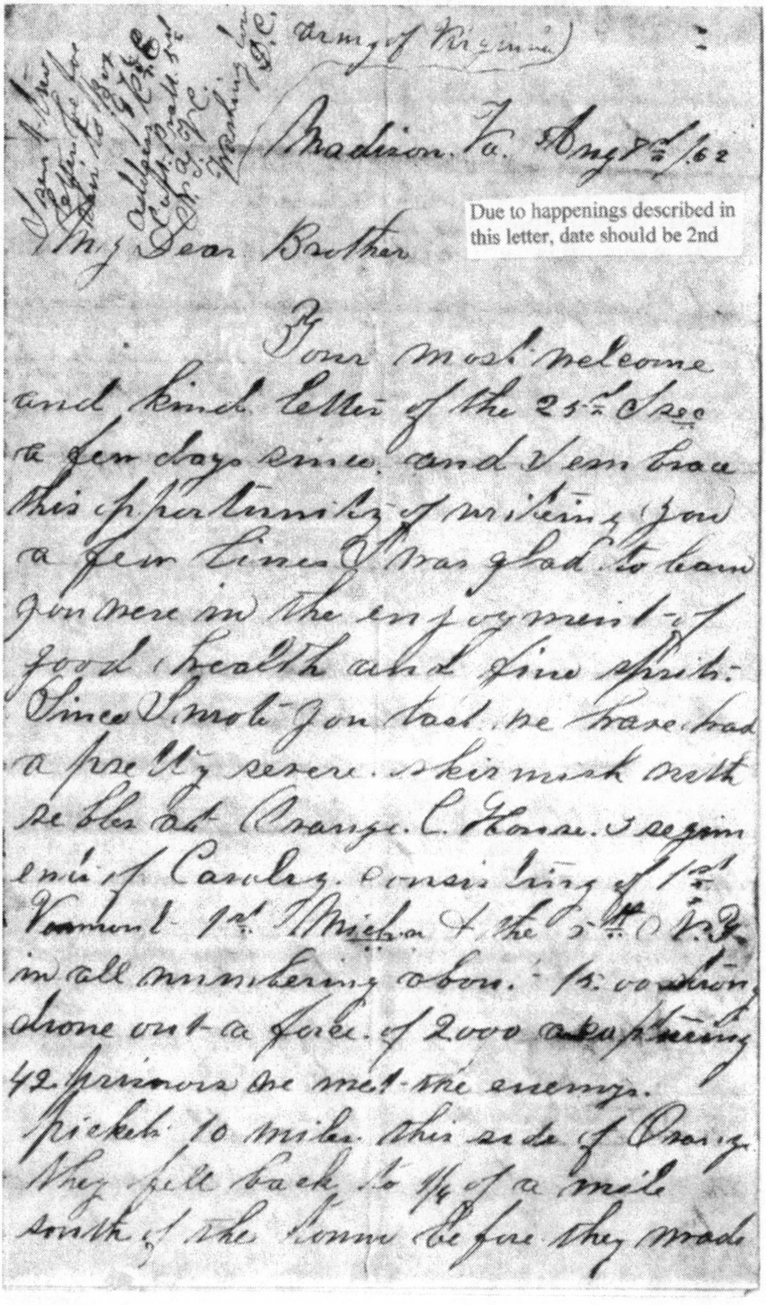
Army of Virginia

Madison Va. Aug 8th /62

Due to happenings described in this letter, date should be 2nd

My Dear Brother

Your most welcome and kind letter of the 25th Recd a few days since, and I embrace this opportunity of writing you a few lines. I was glad to learn you were in the enjoyment of good health and fine spirits. Since I wrote you last we have had a pretty severe skirmish with rebels at Orange C. House. 3 regiments of Cavalry consisting of 1st Vermont 1st Michigan & the 5th N.Y. in all numbering about 1500 men drove out a force of 2000 capturing 42 prisoners. We met the enemy's pickets 10 miles this side of Orange. They fell back to 1/4 of a mile south of the town before they made

a stand our conf. was in the
advance as it always is where
they expect a fight. when we arrived
at the opposite side of the town
from where the rebels were we were
ordered by Gen Crawford to charge
through while two other companies
were sent out to come in on there
rear. no sooner was the order given
to charge than of we went we found
no enemy until we had gone
through town when they began to
file out of a piece of wood that
lay on the side of the road. we then
were puzzled to know whether they
were our men or not for the sergeant
call right come on Capt. Pratt but
we wasn't long finding out who they
were for they began to form line
and sent the bullets after us. we
were not strong enough to charge
down on them so we fell back to the

we could have a better position
they come up ~~to where~~. within close
pistol shot. where one comp. held
them untill our ammunition was
gone. while we were holding them
in check then was the time for the
main body of our force to charge
out. whether Gen. Cranford was
scared out of his sense or what I don't
know for he gave them no command
until our comp having used up our
ammunition and seeing no move was
made on there part we fell back.
When the Gen saw us retreating then
he gave the order for them all to retreat
just then the other two companies
that were sent come in on there rear
come down on the enemy. then we
give it to them had our whole force
been engaged we might captured
a large number of them 3 companies
of the 5th. E. G. H. and 2 of the remain

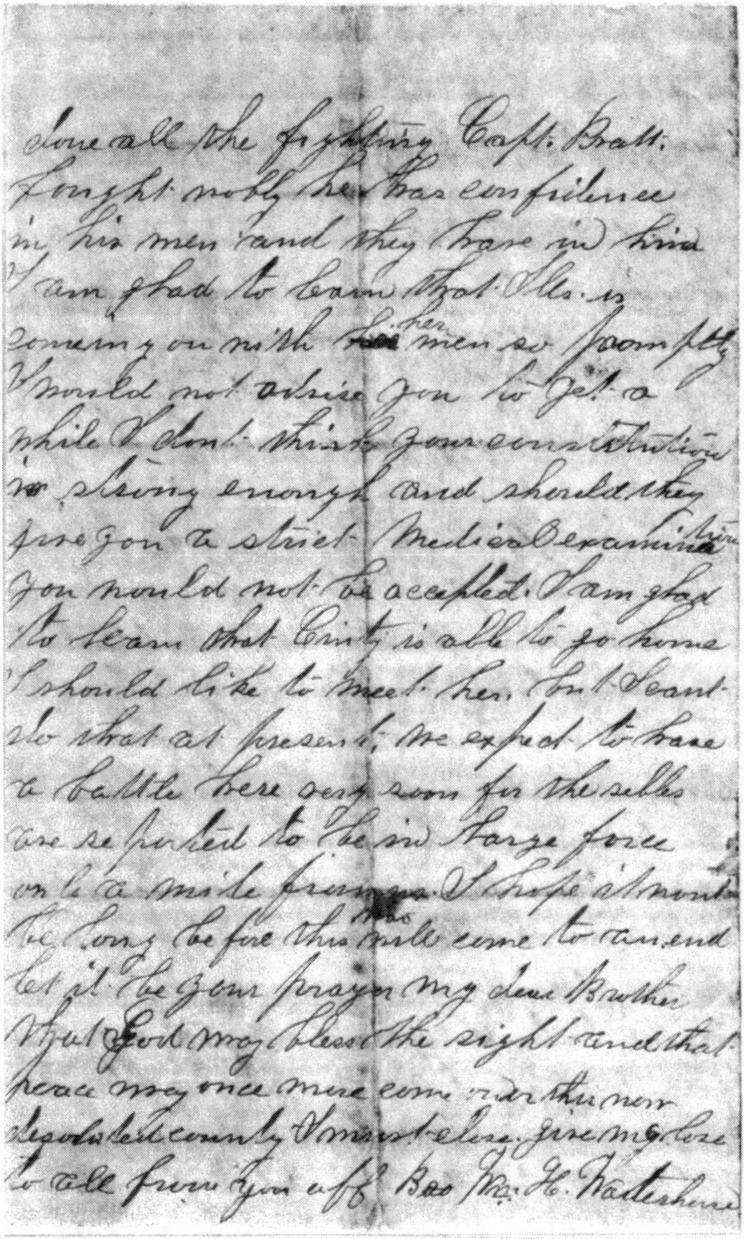
done all the fighting Capt. Pratt.
fought nobly he has confidence
in his men and they have in him
I am glad to learn that Ills. is
coming on with her men so promptly
I would not advise you to get a
while I don't think your constitution
is strong enough and should they
give you a strict medical examination
you would not be accepted. I am glad
to learn that Cinty is able to go home
I should like to meet her but I can't
do that at present. We expect to have
a battle here very soon for the rebels
are reported to be in large force
only a mile from us. I hope it won't
be long before this war will come to an end
let it be your prayer my dear Brother
that God may bless the right and that
peace may once more come over this now
desolated county I must close give my love
to all from your aff. Bro Wm. H. Waterhouse

A description of this battle appeared in a Special Dispatch to the N. Y. Tribune:

"EXPEDITION TO ORANGE C. H. (Court House) OUR TROOPS ATTACKED AND SURROUNDED BY REBEL CAVALRY.

ROUT OF THE LATTER WITH TERRIBLE SLAUGHTER. 30 TO 40 KILLED, 50 TO 60 WOUNDED AND 43 PRISONERS.

OUR LOSS SLIGHT.

WASHINGTON, Aug. 4.

Two hundred of the 5th New York Cavalry and 300 of the 1st Vermont went on a reconnaissance from Culpepper Court House to Orange Court House, 17 miles. They left at 3 o'clock in the afternoon of Saturday last, encamped at night near Raccoon Ford. Early next morning the march was resumed, driving in the enemy's pickets. About 1 o'clock, while marching into the town they were attacked by the enemy, about 600 strong, surrounding our men on all sides. After an hour's severe fighting our force drove them from the town, killing between 30 and 40—21 of their dead lying in one street—wounding between 50 and 60, and taking 43 prisoners; among them one major, two captains and two lieutenants.

The Union party were commanded by Brigadier-General Crawford in person. The enemy were Ashby's Cavalry. Col. Robinson, Co. G. and Co. H. of the 5th N. Y. Cavalry captured nearly the whole of them. Many of the prisoners were badly wounded by saber cuts.

The Major would not surrender, when he was struck a terrible saber blow on the top of his head. One of the captains had one of his ears cut off. The prisoners are now in Culpepper Court House.

The enemy had every advantage over us in position. The following are the names of the killed and wounded of the 5th Cavalry, Ira Harris: Cooley, chief bugler, killed; Lieut. Gear, shoulder; Sergeant Clough, stomach, mortal; Private Quinn, eye; Corporal Charles A. Morris, Co. B; Archibald Frazer, Quartermaster's Sergeant. Three others were slightly wounded, but could not learn their names."

~~~~

By August, action started in the north again after Pope gathered his brigades and made a forty mile line along the Shenandoah, the whole area vacated by the Confederates who were concentrating on the protection of Richmond.

August 7, Pope sent his pickets toward Gordonsville. That same day Jackson moved his command in that direction, in hopes of striking a portion of Pope's army before it could be re-enforced. On the morning of August 9, Banks was pushed six miles forward to a strong position near Cedar Mountain. That afternoon Confederate Ewell, whose division was in advance, came in sight of Banks' position. On the crest of one of the ridges, a body of Union cavalry was seen. Ewell set his battalion across the ridge opposite the Union line. At 4:00pm a fierce fire of artillery had started. The cannonade kept up over an hour. Banks, believing that the enemy was no great force, threw his whole division in two columns across the grain-field between the two ridges. At first, rushed by surprise, the Confederates were confined and suffered losses, but Jackson stepped in to reorganize and the tides turned. The Union advance was checked and forced back across the open field beyond where they had come.

In this accidental engagement, which might be denominated simply an "affair" were it not for the magnitude of the loss on both sides, the Confederates lost, killed and wounded, about 1300; the Union loss was estimated at about 1400 killed and wounded, and 400 prisoners.

Another report from the Civil War Academy: "The Battle of Cedar Mountain also called Slaughter's Mountain and Cedar Run, was fought on August 9, 1862. Although not an extremely well known battle in the Civil War itself, the battle proved to the Union Commanders that Confederate leader Thomas Stonewall Jackson was a force to be dealt with. The style of Stonewall Jackson and Robert E. Lee, new to the Union regimented lines and adherence to discipline on the battlefield, meant that there would be high
~~~~

Union losses from guerilla-style warfare. What the Union General Pope did in response to this was lure the Confederate troops into the open field which made up the eventual Battle of Cedar Mountain. This tactic worked for a little while until a new fighting style was introduced.

As the battle began the Union almost routed the Confederate line, decimating almost 50% of the Rebel troops and pushing Stonewall Jackson to the brink of retreat. Things looked bleak for the Confederates as the Union disposition was one of utter victory. The turn around came when General Stonewall Jackson personally rode in front of his men shouting for them to rally around him. This inspired confidence in his men and they were able to reform their lines and counterattack. Startled and surprised the Union troops fought as well as they could but were eventually beaten back into retreat off the field of Cedar Mountain. The tide had turned towards the Confederates and the North was left wondering if they would even be able to run a defensive position.

This was the first battle of the Northern Virginia Campaign for General Robert E. Lee and Stonewall Jackson. The goal of the Confederates was to free the entire Valley of the Shenandoah, thus paving the way for General Lee's main army, the Army of Northern Virginia, to rage into Maryland and bring the Civil War to a sudden end. One of the main stays of the Civil War was that the Union Army always had the upper hand, at this point in the war, and the year being 1862, victory was in question for the Union troops.

Eventually the Confederates would take up defensive positions in and around the Culpeper Courthouse and eventually fall back to the more protected town of Gordonsville. The two sides would eyeball each other for the next two weeks. The tide of the war had changed a bit; it seemed as if the Confederates were gaining the advantage."

During the next two days, the two armies watched each other. Each having notification that the other had many more forces there or joining them than was actually true. Jackson, knowing he had additional troops on way to meet him, pulled back hoping Pope would follow him. Almost a week passed, both armies being reinforced by Lee from Confederates, and McClellan from the Union forces. On the 22nd Pope had decided that the next day he would cross the river and meet Lee's army face to face, but a fierce rainstorm that night raised the waters of the river six to eight feet, erasing any chance to cross.

That same night, Confederate Stuart, looking for the Union stores, found himself in the midst of Pope's headquarters. He found a black man whom he had known before, who offered to guide him to the spot occupied by Pope's staff. Stuart's men went up to one tent and captured two of the staff members, but the true prize found was Pope's dispatch book, which revealed the situation of his army, his imminent need of re-enforcements and his expectation of the time when they would reach him. Stuart delivered this to General Lee. When that black man led them to the tent, he was potentially fighting the battles of Groveton and Antietam.

By the 27th, Jackson had moved to Manassas and a considerable number of the Union army had come toward Manassas along the railroad. If Pope had moved there one day earlier, Jackson would have been trapped, but still he was in peril. He had to retreat, but which way? McDowell was to his right at Gainesville moving toward Warrenton; if he went north toward Aldie, it would cut him off further from Lee's army; He chose the only one that could save him, even though the chances were heavily against him. Jackson fell back toward where Longstreet was advancing; at the same time deceiving his opponent as to the direction of his retreat. His division moved from Manassas directly north and the cavalry moved northeast as if heading toward Washington. At Centreville they turned sharply west close to the 1861 battlefield of Bull Run. The ruse succeeded.

Pope moved McDowell from Gainesville straight toward Centreville and ordered other units to do the same. McDowell's line of movement took him close by the right of Jackson's secure position, exposing McDowell to a flank attack, which was made by Jackson just before sunset. Both sides suffered heavy loss.

Again, Jackson sternly held his ground beyond Bull Run, on almost the very spot where a year, a week and a day before he had won the title of "Stonewall" at the 1st Bull Run when Bee had said to him, "They are beating us back."

Jackson replied, "Sir, we will give them the bayonet."

Bee cried to his men, "Here is Jackson standing like a stone wall!" The word fitted the moment. "Stonewall! Stonewall!" was passed from man to man.

On August 28th 1862, Pope now felt his army had Jackson surrounded and that Longstreet couldn't arrive to aid Jackson before the 30th. He even wrote: "to gain so decisive a victory over the army under Jackson, before he could have been joined by Longstreet. That the army of Lee would have been so crippled and checked by the destruction of this large force as to be no longer in condition to prosecute operations of an aggressive character."

This plan utterly failed through the determined resistance of Jackson and that Longstreet arrived at noon on 29th. Also, there was inner maneuvering between McClellan, Halleck and Pope, with Pope asking for more troops and the other two not sending. Pope not realizing Longstreet's arrival ordered an attack on what he believed was the extreme right and weak wing of the Confederate army. It was the center. Instead of meeting a retreating army, he was confronted by a strong force. All through the day there many hard fought battles, with extensive loss of life on both sides, in the whole area.

Pope, at one point on the morning of 30thsent a message to Washington: "We fought a terrific battle here yesterday...which lasted from daylight until after dark...The enemy is still on our front, but badly used up..." Thinking Jackson had suffered a defeat, he claimed victory.

Even McDowell wrote, "I have gone through a second battle of Bull Run.....The victory is decidedly ours."

Then a dispatch came into Pope saying the supplies and rations due in from Alexandria could not be sent unless some cavalry came to escort it. There was no cavalry left. Pope still certain Jackson was retreating, ordered all units to attack at noon. There began a day of carnage for both sides, with the Union army giving the order to retreat at 8:00 pm and doing so in order, they were defeated again at Bull Run.

Here again we have another view given by History of Civil War battles: " The battle of Second Bull Run was a result of the Union army suffering a devastating loss at The Battle of the Shenandoah; Union General John Pope assumed command of a combination of three armies. The armies were gathered together and the plan of attack was to engage Richmond from the north. Before Pope could attack he needed to be patient and wait on the arrival of reinforce-ments from the Army of the Potomac.

The Union reinforcements were located on the Virginia Peninsula regrouping after taking heavy losses at the hands of the Confederates. In a speech made before the battle, General Pope showed his confidence that his offensive would be an easy task by stating to his troops that they need not concern themselves with a retreat plan.

The plan for Second Bull Run weighed uneasy on the Confederates leader, General Robert E. Lee. Lee understood the dynamics of battle and easily figured out that he would be outnumbered at least two to one if the Union armies were to unite. Confident and assured, Lee was still a man of extreme reason and did not wish to see his troops needlessly lost. Lee needed a plan and soon he had just the idea that would hopefully salvage what was rapidly becoming a bad situation.

Many Civil War historians deemed what Lee did as a great military tactical maneuver. General Lee decided that it would to his advantage if he left a small but battle hardened force to defend Richmond. Lee then would move the remainder of his army to join

General Stonewall Jackson at Cedar Mountain. Lee's plan was to destroy Pope's army before he had time to receive the reinforcements. The plan was set in motion and Lee hoped that he would get there fast enough to cut off the Union supplies and the reinforcements. He knew that time was of the essence and made great haste.

Lee divided his army into two groups and faced Pope directly at Bull Run. Meanwhile, General Longstreet faced General Pope from across the Rappahannock River. A force of 25,000 men marched around the right flank of the Union army and effectively cut off the supply chain from the Orange Railroad. After Jackson accomplished his attack, Longstreet marched 50 miles in under two days and joined him.

Not only did General Longstreet make it in time but along the way he found the time to capture several hundred Federal troops and a massive amount of supplies from the Manassas Junction. A bewildered Pope marched his troops to and fro in a disorderly show of force in hopes of locating General Jackson. This was to no avail. The crafty Jackson had hidden his troops in an old abandoned railroad cut to the north.

The Confederate plan was working and Lee was moving his two armies into position. Jackson then was ordered to reveal his position and attacked a Federal division to a draw at Groveton. As the Federals tried to break through Jackson's staunch defensive line, they failed and the beginning of the end for the Union forces at Bull Run was at hand. Longstreet then began his strong direct attack on the lightly defended Union left flank.

The assault lasted only a few hours but Longstreet had destroyed the Union forces and had sealed the Confederate victory for Lee. Second Bull Run was a decisive victory for the Confederates and solidified Lee as a brilliant war commander."

In these three days of fighting, the Confederate lost 1400 killed and 7000 wounded; the Union was much higher, around 11,000.

The statistics for the 5th New York Army was 79 dead, 170 wounded and 48 missing out of 480 men. The 5th New York Cavalry only had 1 killed, 5 wounded and 5 taken prisoners.

The bloody battle of Cedar Mountain mentioned in a letter of September 16 has its totals for Crawford's Brigade as 97 killed, 397 wounded and 373 missing and for the whole Union army as: 314 killed; 1445 wounded and 622 missing or captured for a total of 2381.

And for the horrendous Second Battle of Bull Run, which the Union had good success in the first two days and would have won on third day except for the 'treacherous McDowell,' the numbers tell the disaster. For the cavalry: 15 killed; 35 wounded; 150 missing or captured; total 200. For the Union army in total: 1747 killed; 8452 wounded; 4263 missing or captured for a total of 14,462.

September 6, 1862 Letter to Sister Cinty:

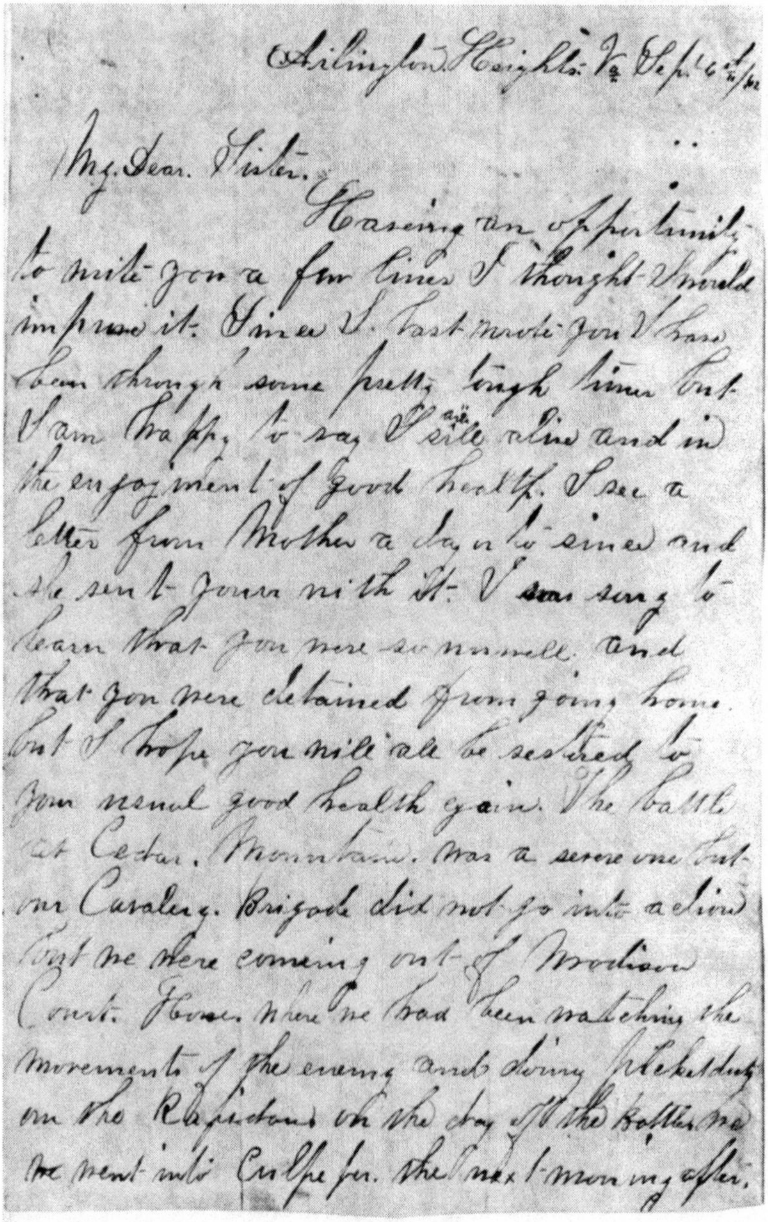

Arlington Heights Va Sept 6th /62

My Dear Sister
Having an opportunity
to write you a few lines I thought I would
improve it. Since I last wrote you I have
been through some pretty tough times but
I am happy to say I still alive and in
the enjoyment of good health. I see a
letter from Mother a day or two since and
she sent yours with it. I was sorry to
hear that you were so unwell. and
that you were detained from going home.
but I hope you will all be restored to
your usual good health again. The battle
at Cedar Mountain was a severe one but
our Cavalry Brigade did not go into action
but we were coming out of Madison
Court House where we had been watching the
movements of the enemy and doing picket duty
on the Rapidan on the day of the battle we
we went into Culpeper the next morning after.

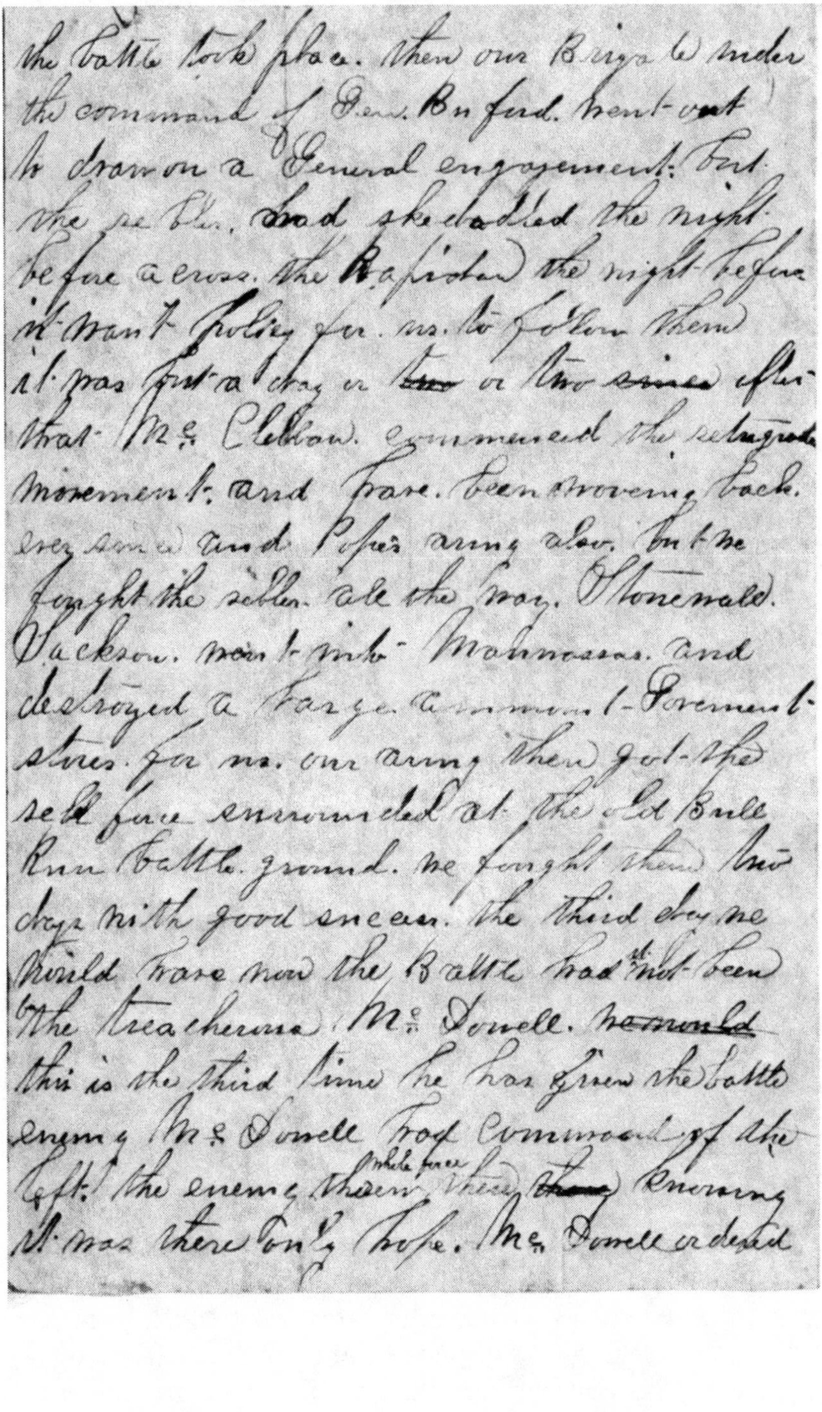
the battle took place. then our Brigade under
the command of Gen. Buford. went out
to draw on a General engagement. but
the rebels had skedaddled the night
before across the Rapidan the night before
it wasn't policy for us to follow them
it was just a day or ~~two~~ or two ~~since~~ after
that McClellan commenced the retrograde
movement. and have been moving back.
every since and Pope's army also. but we
fought the rebels all the way. Stonewall.
Jackson. went into Manassas. and
destroyed a large amount Government
stores for us. our army then got the
rebel force surrounded at the old Bull
Run battle ground. we fought them two
days with good success. the third day we
would have won the Battle had it not been
b the treacherous McDowell. ~~we would~~
this is the third time he has given the battle
enemy McDowell has command of the
left. the enemy threw their whole force there ~~them~~ knowing
it was there only hope. McDowell ordered

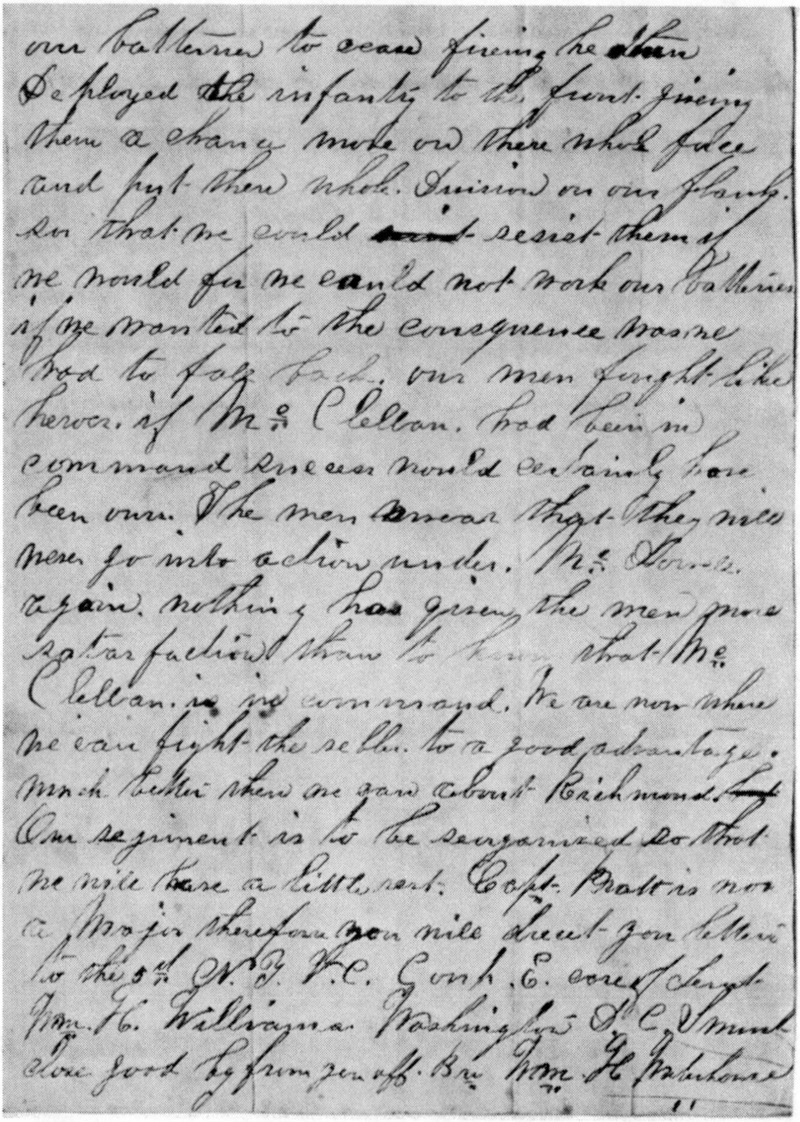

our batteries to cease firing he then
Deployed the infantry to the front giving
them a chance to move on there whole force
and put there whole Division on our flank.
so that we could resist them if
we would for we could not work our batteries
if we wanted to the consequence was we
had to fall back. our men fought like
heroes. if McClellan had been in
command success would certainly have
been ours. The men swear that they will
never go into action under McDowell
again. nothing has given the men more
satisfaction than to hear that Mc
Clellan is in command. We are now where
we can fight the rebels to a good advantage.
much better than we can about Richmond.
Our regiment is to be reorganized so that
we will have a little rest. Capt. Pratt is now
a Major therefore you will direct your letters
to the 5th N.Y. V.C. Comp. E. care of Sergt.
Wm. H. Williams Washington D.C. I must
close good by from your affc. Bro Wm H Waterhouse

I could not have known at the time, but now I take away the blame I put on McDowell since I found that it was Pope who had led us into defeat, not McDowell, who was carrying out Pope's orders. In the battle we were picked up by Porter, who three times during the battle didn't carry out orders, from McDowell once and Pope twice, and was court-marshaled for these later. When he, aided by Reynolds, finally made it into the battle, both fearlessly fought with the odds three to one against us. At the end we retreated, but history now tells us what General Warren said: "...desperate stand had not, however, been unavailing. To all seeming, it saved the defeat from being a rout."

And what Longstreet wrote: "This threw more than its proper share of fighting upon the infantry and enabled the enemy to escape with many of his batteries, which should have fallen into our hands."

This battle is sometimes labeled the 'Second Bull Run Battle,' 'Battle of Manassas plains,' 'Second Manassas Battle,' and 'Battle of Groveton'. The latter probably is the most appropriate due to the small town of that name in middle of the warring fields.

Note: As soon as the 2nd Bull Run ended, Pope requested to be relieved of his command in Virginia, so on September 7, 1862, he departed Washington. The Army of Virginia ceased to exist as such, and the whole force, resuming its old name of the Army of the Potomac, again was placed under the command of General McClellan

Note: after 1st page of next letter, a transposition of that page follows.

8

ARLINGTON HEIGHTS, VIRGINIA -OCT/NOV, 1862 - CAMP NEAR FORT SCOTT ON THE POTOMAC

October 19, 1862 Letter to Sister Mela:

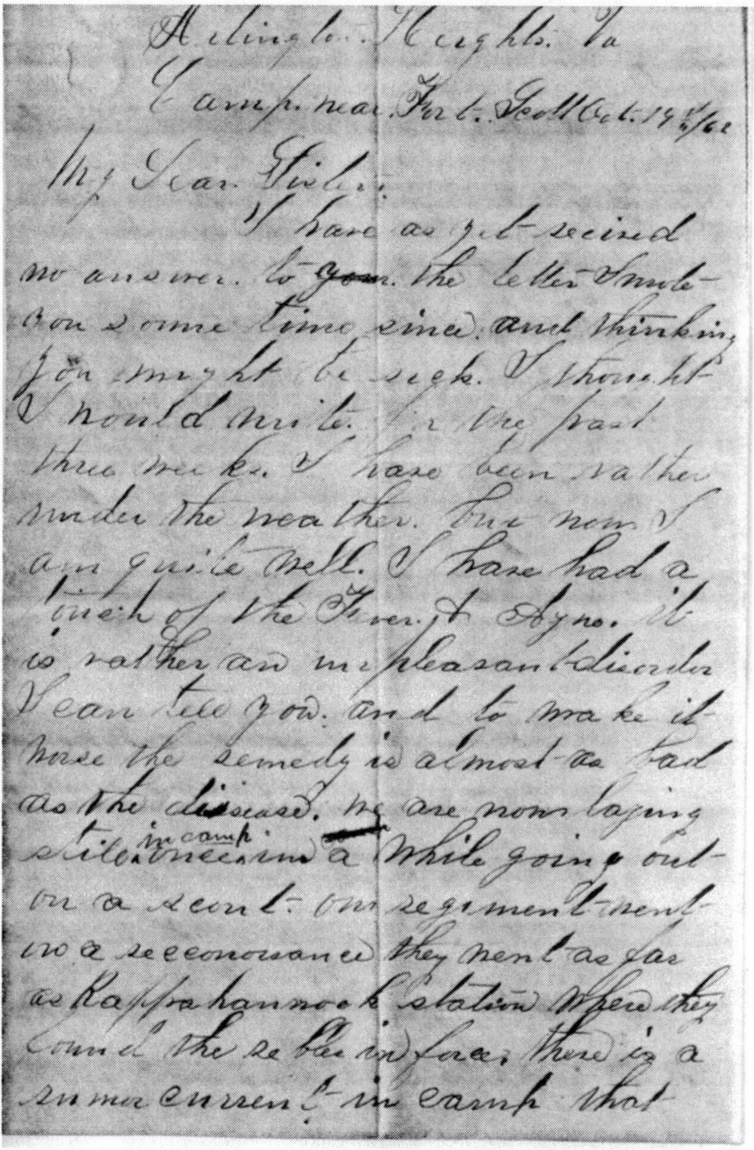
Arlington Heights Va
Camp near Fort Scott Oct. 19th/62
My Dear Sister
I have as yet recived
no answer to ~~your~~ the letter I wrote
you some time since and thinking
you might be sick. I thought
I would write. For the past
three weeks I have been rather
under the weather but now I
am quite well. I have had a
touch of the Fever & Ague. It
is rather an unpleasant disorder
I can tell you. and to make it
worse the remedy is almost as bad
as the disease. We are now laying
still in camp once in a While going out
on a scout. our regiment went
on a reconnoisance they went as far
as Rappahannock station where they
found the rebels in force. there is a
rumor current in camp that

Arlington Heigfhts. Va

Camp. near. Fort Scott Oct.

19th/62My Dear Sister (Amelia or Mela)

I have as yet received no answer to (your) the letter I wrote you some time since. and thinking you might be sick. I thought I would write. for the past three weeks. I have been rather under the weather. but now I am quite well. I have had a touch of the Fever. & Ague. it is rather an unpleasant disorder I can tell you. and to make it worse the remedy is almost as bad as the disease. we are now laying still in camp once in a while going out on a scout. our regiment went on a recconoisance they went as far as Rappahannock station where they found the rebles in force. there is a rumor current in camp that

there will be another battle at
Bull Run before long. but we can
tell for certain. there don't seem to
be much motion in the Army of
the Potomac lately. I hope they will
fight if they are a going to and
have it done with. I hope by next
spring the war will be at an
end. I rec a letter from Horace
a day or two since he wrote me an
excellent letter. he has been at
Washington in the [illegible]
when he wrote to me they were laying
at anchor of Jersey City. were to load
for Fortress Monroe. Ec writes and
says Just peep into the back kitchen
a minute and you will see Amelia & myself
sitting by the west door. a peeling
apples for Pa to dry or Ma to make
into pies. Ma is by the stove getting
dinner. Aunt Fan is in the wash room
washing my "Sunnrayes" as she calls
~~my~~ my clothes say I have got to

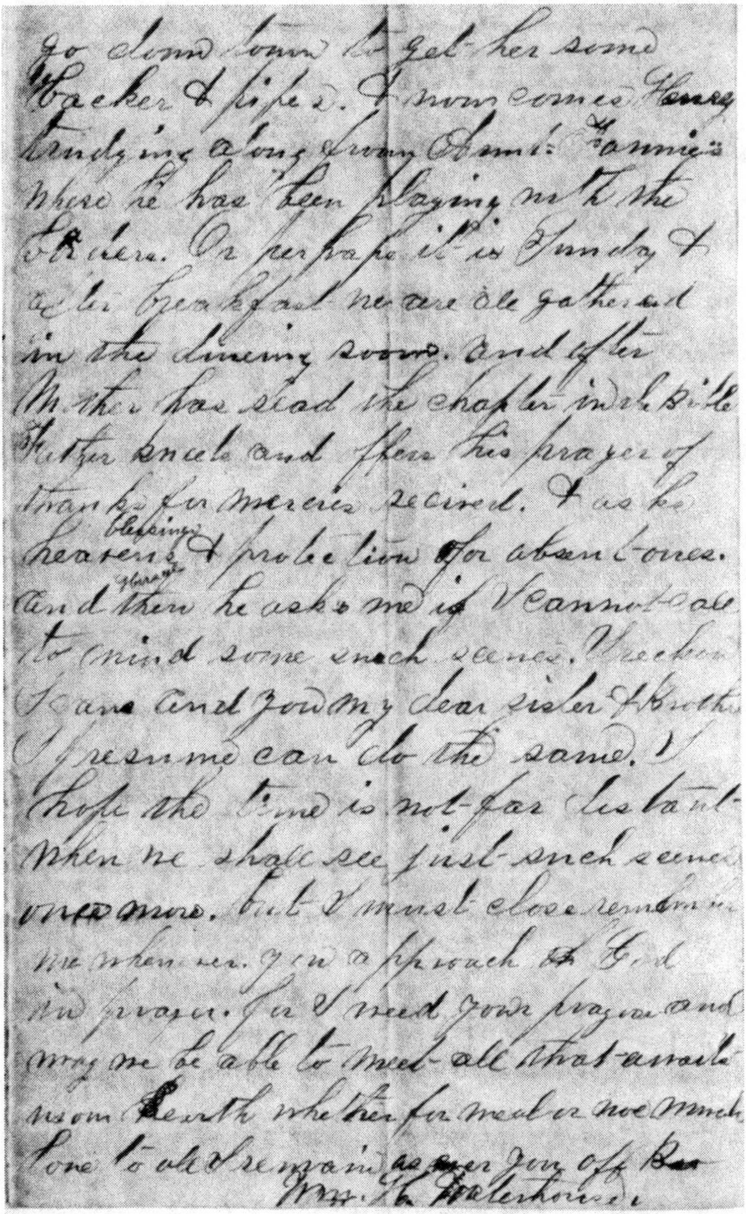
go down town to get her some
Tobacker & pipes. & now comes Henry
trudging along from Aunt Fannie's
where he has been playing with the
Children. Or perhaps it is Sunday &
after breakfast we are all gathered
in the dineing room. And after
Mother has read the chapter in the Bible
Father kneels and offers his prayer of
thanks for mercies recived. & asks
heavens blessings & protection for absent ones.
And then he asks me if I cannot call
to mind some such scenes. Brother
Sam and you my dear sister & Brother
I presume can do the same. I
hope the time is not far distant
when we shall see just such scenes
once more. but I must close remembering
me whenever you approach to God
in prayer. for I need your prayers and
may we be able to meet all that awaits
us on earth whether for weal or woe. Much
love to all I remain as ever your aff Bro
Wm. H. Waterhouse.

I had been so lucky with my health for the first year of duty as a member of the 5th NY Cavalry, but in October I came down with the Fever and Ague

October 22, 1862 Letter to Mother:

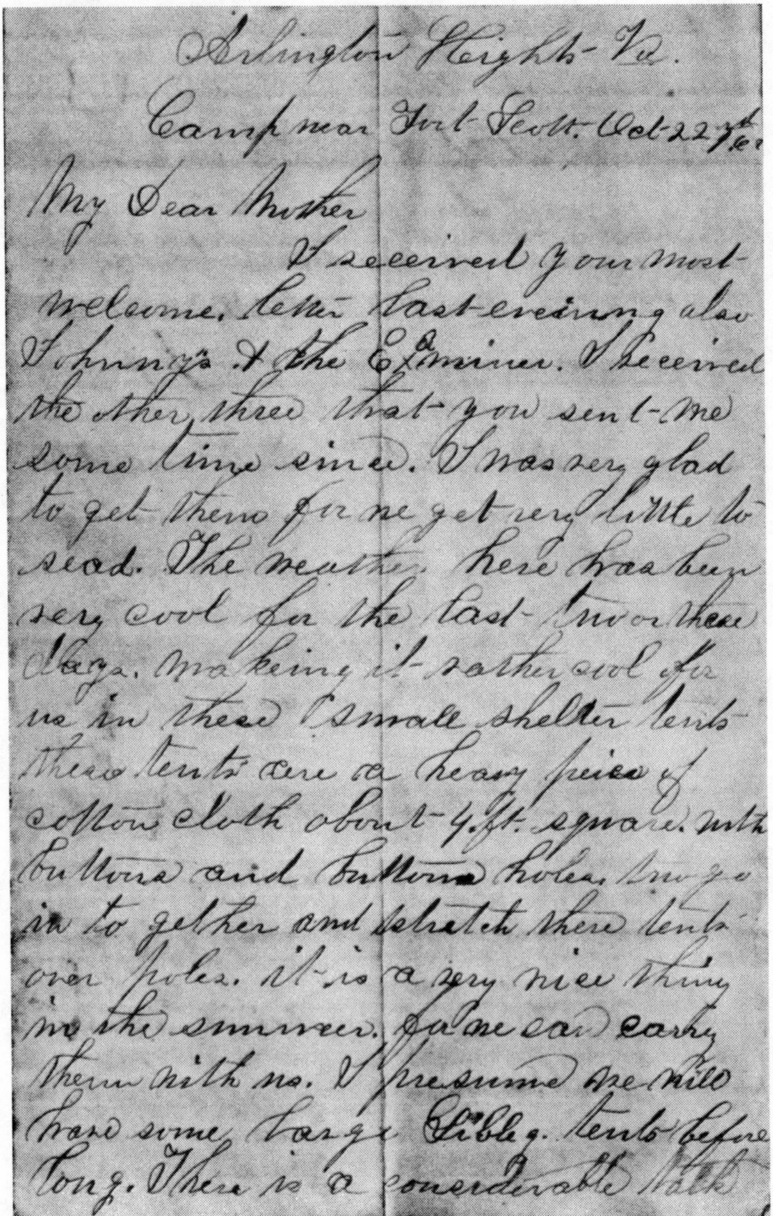

Arlington Heights Va.
Camp near Fort Scott. Oct 22nd /62
My Dear Mother
I received your most
welcome letter last evening also
Johnny's & the Examiner. I received
the other three that you sent me
some time since. I was very glad
to get them for we get very little to
read. The weather here has been
very cool for the last two or three
days. making it rather cool for
us in these small shelter tents
these tents are a heavy piece of
cotton cloth about 4 ft. square with
buttons and button holes. two go
in together and stretch there tents
over poles. it is a very nice thing
in the summer. as we can carry
them with us. I presume we will
have some large Sibley tents before
long. There is a considerable talk

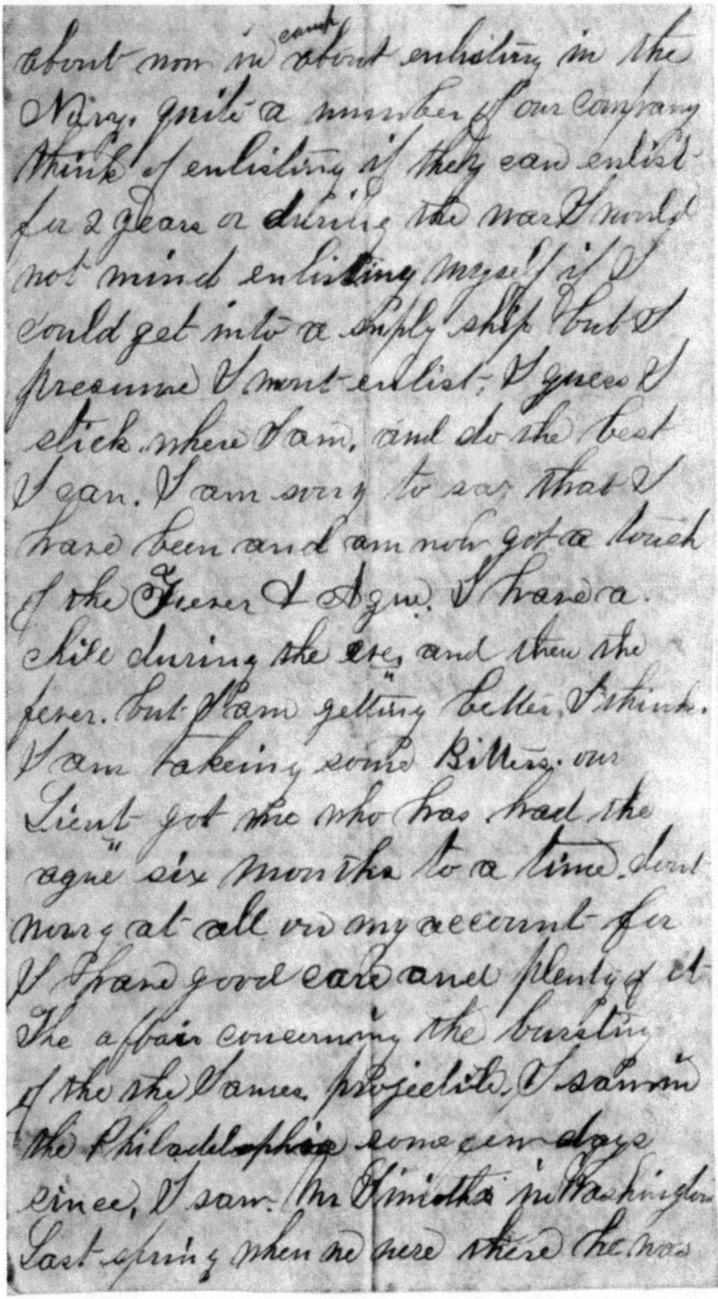
about now in camp about enlisting in the
Navy. quite a number of our Company
think of enlisting if they can enlist
for 2 years or during the war I would
not mind enlisting myself if I
could get into a supply ship but I
presume I wont enlist, I guess I
stick where I am, and do the best
I can. I am sorry to say that I
have been and am now got a touch
of the Fever & Ague. I have a
chile during the eve, and then the
fever. but I am getting better I think.
I am takeing some Bitters. our
Lieut got one who has had the
ague six months to a time. dont
worry at all on my account for
I have good care and plenty of it
The affair concerning the bursting
of the the Vances projectiles I saw in
the Philadelphia some few days
since, I saw Mr Smith in Washington
Last spring when we were there he was

them looking well. ~~Hallo~~ Silas Young
of Orient was in the same Company
he was the one that used to bring
up Miss Terry once in a while there
were also some other Orient Boys also
and some few from Southold. there
Company and Comp I of there Regt
have been down there all summer
the rest of there was lain still
all summer doing nothing but
when the rebles come into Maryland
they went down to help McClellan
Where is the 6th N.Y. or the 2 Ira Harris
they were on camp [illegible] with us. In
the reconnoisance that McClellan
made a few days since they were
spoken of as taking an active
part. Our Brigade is now out at
Centreville watching the movements
of the enemy. and the rebles wont go
Richmond without our men knowing
it I would like to be there with but
I cannot at present I dont suppose

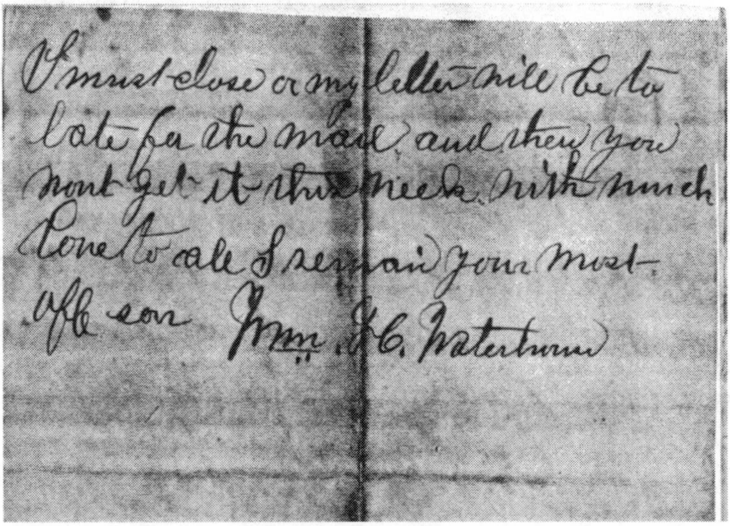
I must close or my letter will be to late for the mail and then you wont get it this week. With much Love to all I remain your most Aff son Wm. H. C. Waterman

The hospital area where I spent most of the month stood close enough to camp, so that we could be connected with any news or alerts, but far enough to keep our fevers away from others. The recovery was worse than the chills and fevers, but in early November, my good health returned.

The James Projectile I mentioned was named after Charles T. James, a US Senator in the 1850's. He was also a Major-General in the Rhode Island State Militia and became interested in the production of firearms and developed a rifled cannon and several artillery projectiles which proved successful, especially during the reduction of Fort Pulaski, Georgia, where the James rifles projectiles were reported to be extremely accurate. His first projectile was patented on February 26, 1856.

On October 16, 1862, at Sag Harbor, New York, Charles James was conducting a demonstration of his projectiles to a group of foreign military officers. A workman tried to remove a cap from one of the shells with pliers and the projectile exploded. The workman died instantly and James died from his wounds the next day, October 17, 1862.

All serviceable guns and cannons, either of bronze or iron, could have been rifled on the James system, for the use of James projectiles. The rifling was a gaining right-hand twist with shallow grooves and equal distance between the lands and grooves. The lands and grooves are flat and varied from seven in the 14-pounder (3.80-inch caliber) to eighteen for the 42-pounder gun (7-inch caliber). The rifling grooves in the bronze rifles were worn down quickly making the service life of the gun very short. The James projectile soon fell out of favor due to their constant stripping of the lead sabot and were replaced by the Hotchkiss projectile

October 25, 1862 Letter to Sister Cinty:

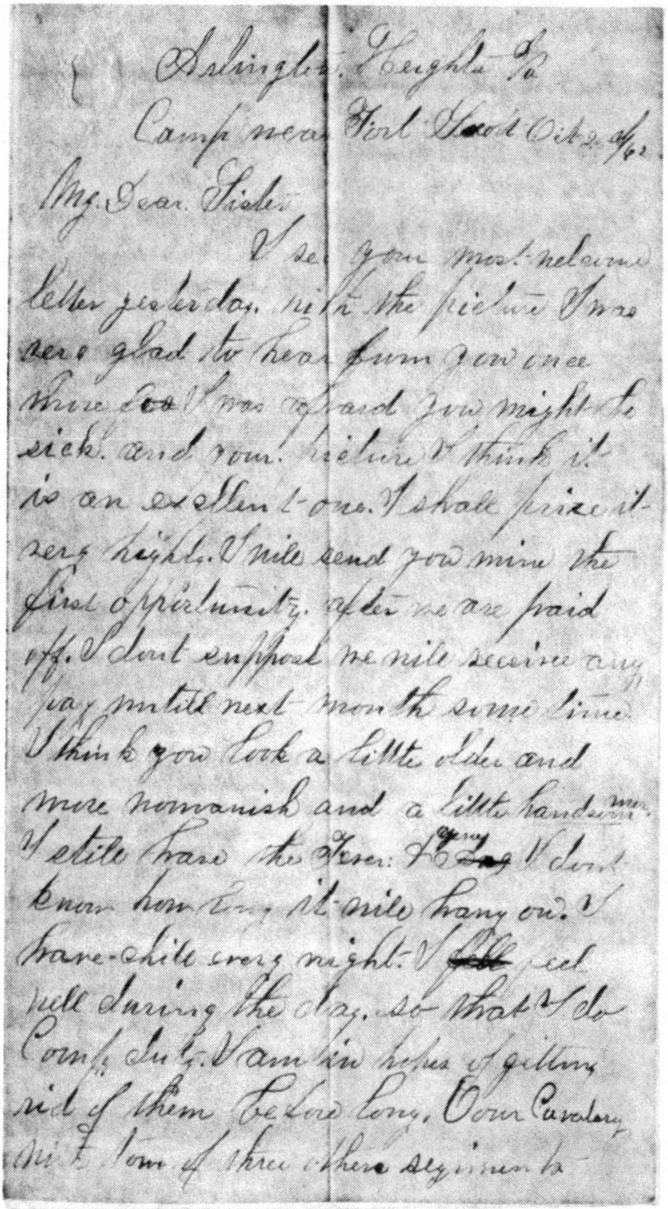

Arlington Heights Va
Camp near Fort Scott Oct 25/62

My Dear Sister

I rec your most welcome letter yesterday with the picture I was very glad to hear from you once more for I was afraid you might be sick. and your picture I think it is an excellent one. I shall prize it very highly. I will send you mine the first opportunity. after we are paid off. I dont suppose we will receive any pay until next month some time. I think you look a little older and more womanish and a little handsomer. I still have the fever & ague I dont know how long it will hang on. I have chills every night. I feel well during the day. so that I do Comp duty. I am in hopes of getting rid of them before long. Our Cavalry with some of three others regiments

were out beyond Centreville scouting
& doing picket duty if I were ~~will~~ well
I should be with them I never missed
any duty before I don't belive any
one can say that I have ever ~~shrunk~~
shrunk from duty. I wish this war
would be over by next spring and
we go home together perhaps I would
go back to Chicago with you
We have all got soldiering enough
and enough of the war and we all
wish it was over. I am in ~~hopes~~
hopes McClellan is about to make
a move, indications look a little like
it. I don't know what makes the
people your way think it will be
settled by the 8th of Jan. I am sure
but there is no knowing when it will
be closed up. I am thankful there
is an overruling power who has
control of all these things & who will
bring light out of darkness and
make things all right in his own time.

Transposition Page 3(as written) of Oct 25,1862 letter to Sister Cinty:

I am glad you have joined the Musical Union. I dont know but I shall forget how to sing before I get home again. I wish I was where I could some good singing once in a while. I have not heard any since I left home. Mother wrote me that Johnny was picking the apples and quinces how I would like to be home in time to get some of the sweetmeats they will be made into. she wrote that Pa had plenty of work I am glad of that. Who do you suppose that new somer in the family looks like. I think the Waterhouse family is getting to almost an incredulous size. but perhaps they will turn out big some of them (them) some future day God forbid they should ever be a curse to there parents but I must close my love to all remember me at the throne of grace. good by from your aff Bro.

Wm. H. Waterhouse

With all my sickness, I felt I had been in the war enough, but that only lasted until I was riding again.

Note: after 1st page of next letter, a transposition of that page and page two follows.

November 5 & 6, 1862 Letter to Sister Mela:

Camp near [illegible] Va. [illegible] Nov 5/62

My Dear Sister:

Having an opportunity to write you a few lines I thought I would improve it. Though I have not receive[d] any letter from you since I last wrote. It may be that the letters have been miscarried for I have not heard from home in some time. We still remain in camp on the Banks of the Potomac. And there is a possibility of our staying here this winter. Within the past three days no less than 20.000 troops moved out to Centreville. they were all encamped within the sound of a drum from where we are located. I should not be surprised if there was a battle to take place before. and it may be a pretty good sized one for there are

Camp near Fort Scott Nov 5th/62
My Dear Sister
(Amelia) *Having an opportunity to write you a few lines I thought I would improve it: though I have not received any letter from you since I last wrote. it may be that the letters have been miscarried. for I have not heard from home in some time. We till remain in camp on the Banks of the Potomac. and there is a possibility of our staying here this winter. within the past three days. no less than 20,000 troops moved out to Centreville. they were all encamped within the sound of a drum. from where we are located. I should not be surprised if there was a battle to take place before. and it may be a pretty good sized one to. there are certainly indications of one at all events. it seems as though as if the whole north was agoing into party politics stronger than ever. I wish there was a way to do away with all partys and be united. but dont suppose that time will come right away. a great many wish to know the opinion of the soldiers on the President's proclamation they all feel (that is within my knowledge) if it will help in putting down the war why put it in force and we will support it.*

Nov 6
Having been taken with a chill yesterday. I did not have an opportunity to finish it. I will now attempt to finish it the weather here now is quite winterish and being close to the Potomac we feel it more than we should if we were back in the country farther. the last letter I received from home brought one from Johnny written by himself.

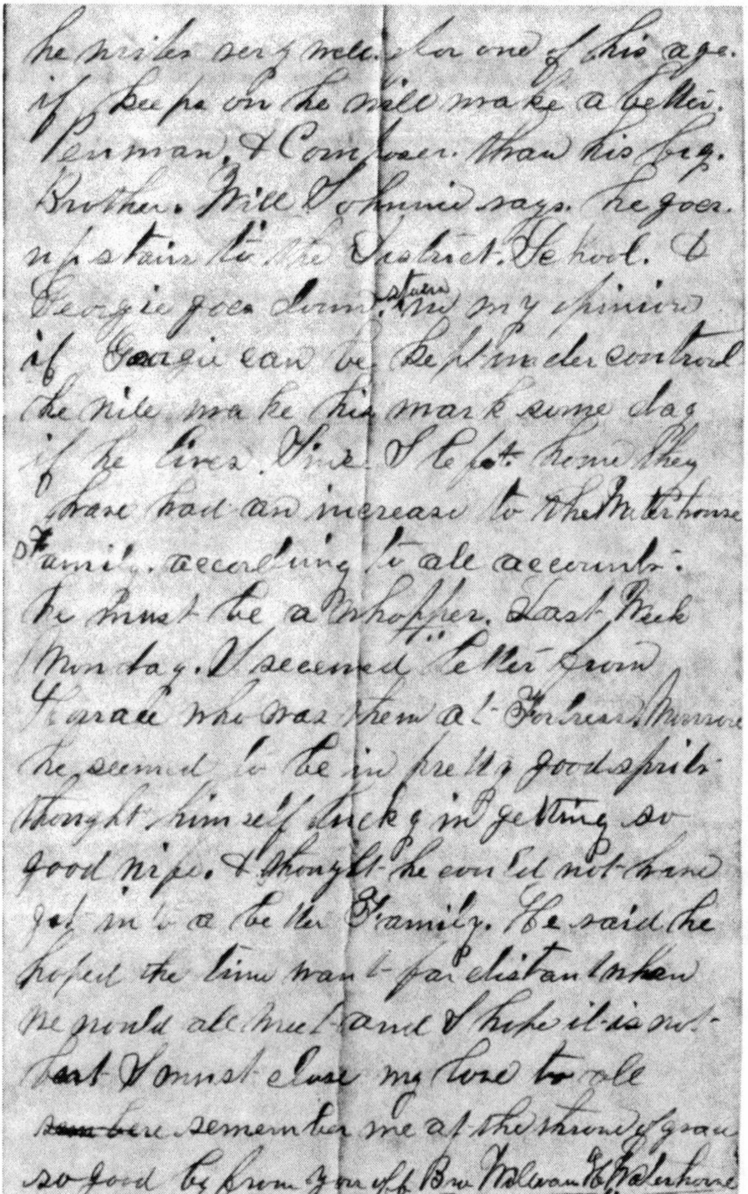

he writes very well for one of his age.
if he keeps on he will make a better
Penman & Composer than his big
Brother. Will Johnnie says he goes
up stairs to the District School. &
Georgie goes down stairs my opinion
if Georgie can be kept under control
he will make his mark some day
if he lives. Vine & Capt. Home they
have had an increase to the Waterhouse
Family according to all accounts.
he must be a whopper. Last Week
Monday I received letter from
Horace who was then at Fortress Monroe
he seemed to be in pretty good spirits
thought himself lucky in getting so
good wife & thought he could not have
got into a better Family. He said he
hoped the time wasn't far distant when
we would all meet and I hope it is not.
~~[illegible]~~ I must close my love to all
~~some here~~ remember me at the throne of grace
so good by from your off Bro Walcott H. Waterhouse

We soldiers were getting very confused and weary with so many replacements in our chain of command. It seemed that there was politics going on affecting military decisions and the strong leadership we needed on the battlefield. We felt things were not right and rumors flourished. In the near future, President Lincoln was expected to make a proclamation as to the object of the war. Many on both sides did not agree with his leanings. It was disturbing to us, the lowly fighting force, to be pursued by our political weaknesses as we tried to be strong against our true enemies.

November 23, 1862 Letter to Sister Cinty:

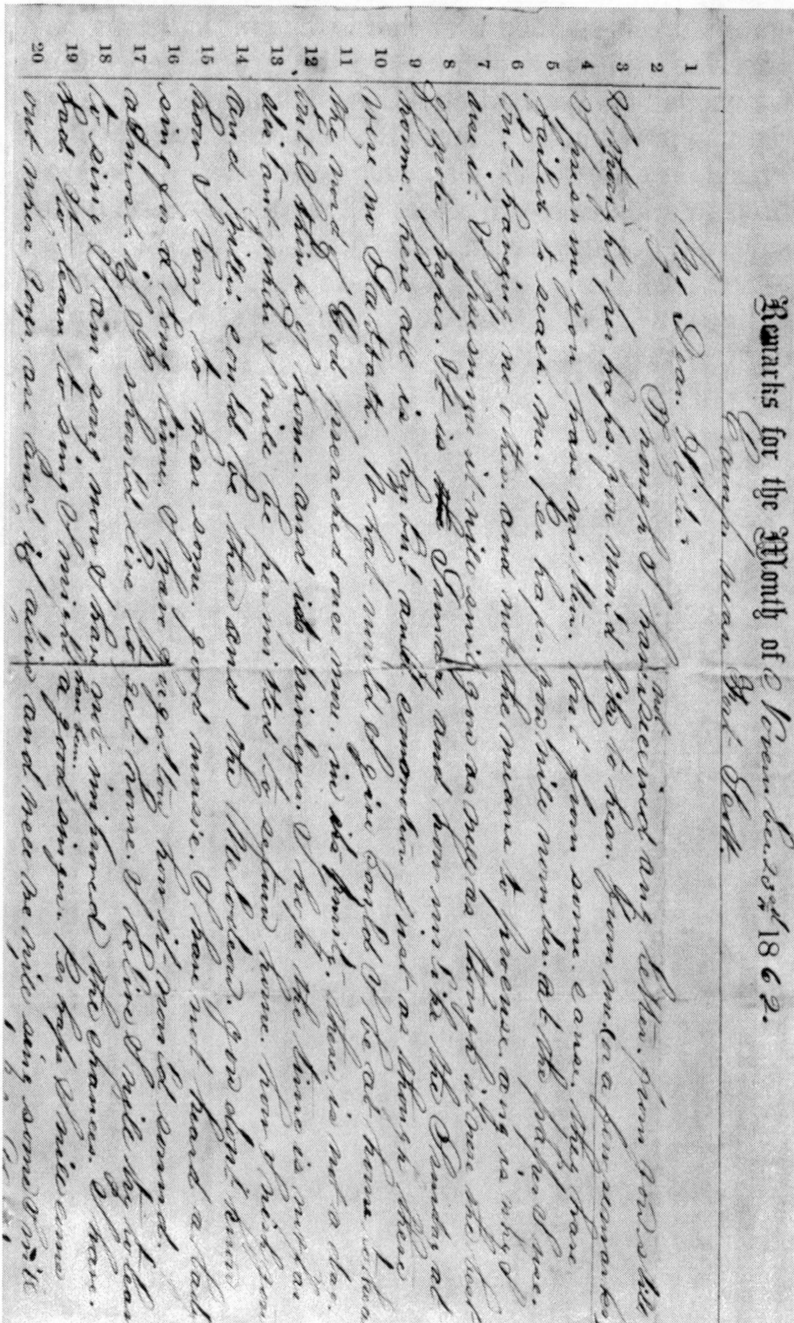

Remarks for the Month of November 23rd 1862.
Camp near Fort Scott.

My Dear Sister:
Though I have not received any letter from you still
I thought perhaps you would like to hear from me (or a few remarks)
I presume you have written but from some cause they have
failed to reach me. Perhaps you will wonder at the paper I use.
but having no other and not the means to procure any is why I
use it. I presume it will suit you as well as though it were the best
of note paper. It is ~~the~~ Sunday and how unlike the Sunday at
home. here all is hurry and commotion just as though there
were no Sabbath. What would I give could I be at home to hear
the word of God preached once more in its purity. there is not a day
but I think of home and its privileges. I hope the time is not far
distant when I will be permitted to return home. how I wish you
and Willie could be there and the Melodeon. you don't know
how I long to hear some good music. I have not heard a lady
sing for a long time. I have forgotten how it would sound
almost. if I should live to get home I believe I will try to learn
to sing. I am sorry now I have not improved the chances. I have
had to learn to sing I might have been a good singer. Perhaps I will come
out where you are and if alive and well we will sing some I will

a cookie. I suppose this week you will go out to Aunt Hattie's and spend thanksgiving. I hope you will have a pleasant time ask Aunt Hattie if she remembers the thanksgiving we spent down to Greenport a few years since in the White washed cottage I think if memory serves me right we had fine time that day. evening how I would like to see that same party together again but I dont suppose that can ever be. I'm happy to say that I think I am entirely over the Fever & Ague and such an appetite as I have I can devour almost every thing I can get to eat. I dont know but I have told you but Mother is a going to send me a box of Provision and clothing so that we can feast for a spell The Ladies seem to take quite an interest in my welfare at home I dont know how I will ever repay them for their deeds of kindness. a great many of the boys have been making bone rings so I thought I would make one & I will send it to you and if you think it worth wearing wear it for my sake. it is what our men do down in Richmond when prisoners the women used to give a dollar a piece for them. but I must close your aff Bro remember me to the three of grape so good by from

Wm H Waterhouse

The rumors ran rampart: we were going to move to Centerville; there would be another Bull Run; or we should all enlist in the Navy. These came from idle minds. When a lull came in the fighting, not only rumors festered, but memories of home and loved ones stood heavy on the heart. Holidays started coming into view and recollections of good, warm family times loomed in the head; sometimes squeezing the breath out of the body, with longing. And so it was with the close of November, 1862. I was promoted to Quarter Master Sergeant on November 3, but still had the Fever, so had to wait awhile to realize the promotion.

At this time the Army of the Potomac had undergone another large change in command. The President and General-in-Chief Halleck were not happy with McClellan's lack of attacking Lee's army during October. He was removed on November 7, 1862, replaced by General Ambrose Burnside, who from the first said he was not ready to take command of such a large army even though he had great success in North Carolina. A new commander always took time to bring his strategies into place, thus November proved to be a quiet month for me also.

9

FORT SCOTT TO CHANTILLY & FREDERICKSBURG, VIRGINIA DECEMBER,1862 into JANUARY,1863 30 MILES FROM WASHINGTON & 6 MILES FROM FAIRFAX

December, duty called and kept us on a twenty-four hour alert, horses saddled at all times, and running an extensive picket line, meeting the outreach picket line's messenger every two hours. Because of our loss of persons from the regiment, each turn came around often. It was nice to use the cozy, living space we had made out of pines for us and our horses when we could rest. At least we were warm with the fireplaces we made.

I was able to accept my promotion to Quarter Master Sergeant on December 1, 1862. I know this was an honor, but it was awfully hard to have to stay behind to guard all the supplies when my regiment was called to battle. I wanted to go also and it hurt when they came back with all their adventure stories. Looking back, it probably saved my life, because we lost a lot of men in our company during the time I was Quarter Master Sergeant.

History tells us: Burnside's main strategy was to abandon the Shenandoah Valley and turn his whole direction to invade and conquer Fredericksburg, opening up a direct route to take Richmond. He believed that to hold Richmond, the Confederates could not stay together. On November 17th, the movement arrived to cross the Rappahannock River, but all the bridges to Fredericksburg had been destroyed.

On November 21st, Sumner sent over a message to the corporate authorities of the town, demanding its surrender, under pain of bombardment in case of refusal. The civic authorities were told by the military commander that 'while the town would not be occupied for military purposes, its occupation by the enemy would be resisted.' Directions were given for the removal of the people and almost the entire population left their homes. No bombardment then took place; but a fortnight later, when the movement across the river was made, Fredericksburg, which was then being used by the Confederates for 'military purposes,' and almost the entire population having been removed in consequence, was bombarded. This was fiercely denounced as a violation of the laws of war, without the slightest provocation by the city's citizens.

To get across at two different areas, Burnside ordered pontoons to be sent from Washington to form new bridges. Although politics delayed the order by a week, allowing the Confederates to ready their defenses, the attempt to cross with these pontoons was attempted on December 11th. It failed all day, due to the Confederate line along the river with short range ability killed or wounded every Federal attempting to place a part of the bridge. Burnside ordered a heavy cannon shelling of the city, which did an enormous amount of fire damage, making it impossible for the rebels to even use their rifles. Later in the afternoon two brave regiments from Massachusetts and one from Michigan were successful in crossing in pontoon boats and were able to cross over and enter the city.

Through December 12, the Union army of 100,000 crossed the river, 55,000 with Franklin and 45,000 with Sumner, and both armies settled into their places for the next day's battle. December 13th, the Confederate right was protected by a canal where all the bridges had been destroyed and also had a millpond, making it unassailable. An attack on this right could only be made against the steep front of Marye's Hill, rising in the rear of Fredericksburg and presenting a front of a mile, then sloping off sharply to a ravine crossed by a small stream and behind a plain heavily wooded.

80,00 Confederates fought the Union force in many deadly battles on December 13, each side winning and losing ground in turn. Franklin was to attack on the plain and Sumner in the ravine. Franklin misunderstood Burnside's order and instead of attacking with full force, only used a quarter of his strength. That day on the plain, the Federals had 3700 killed or wounded. The Confederate toll was 3200.

Same day Sumner attacked area of Marye's Hill which fell off abruptly toward Fredericksburg to a stone wall which formed a terrace on the side of the hill and a twenty-five foot wide road that ran along the foot of the hill. On the city side it faced a four foot stone wall that could not be seen above the surface of the ground. It was invisible from the direction which Sumner's army arrived. As soon as the Union columns moved in masses out of the ravine, they came into the sights of the Confederate artillery posted upon the crests. Of the 10,000 in French and Hancock's regiments there were 4,000 either killed or wounded. Burnside sent Humphrey's unit the same way. At first they made progress as the Confederates in front with no bullets left changed places with those fully loaded causing Humphrey a loss of half of his 4,000, downed within fifteen minutes.

That night Burnside consulted with his officers. New plans to assault the stone wall again were made for the following day. General Sumner spoke, "General, I hope you will desist from this attack. I do not know any general officer that approves of it, and I think it will prove disastrous to the army." Burnside again asked his generals and all agreed with Sumner, including Franklin. By nightfall, he had announced they wouldretreat back across the river, but leave enough of an army to hold Fredericksburg. However, later Hooker and Butterfield convinced Burnside this could not be done due to distance from rest of army.

December 14th the two great armies lay in expectation, the Confederates having excellent position to wait for the Union army to move into their gun-sites and fire for a sure kill. On the 15th a truce was called for both sides to remove their dead and wounded. During that night, using a cold rain storm as cover, the complete Union army retreated across the Rappahannock. The morning of the 16th, the Confederates saw their enemy again divided from them by the river. Burnside left a part of his dead by the stone wall, some ammunition and 9000 muskets which had fallen from his 1500 dead and 9,000 wounded. The Confederates had 600 killed and 4,000 wounded.

December 18, 1862 Letter to Sister Cinty::

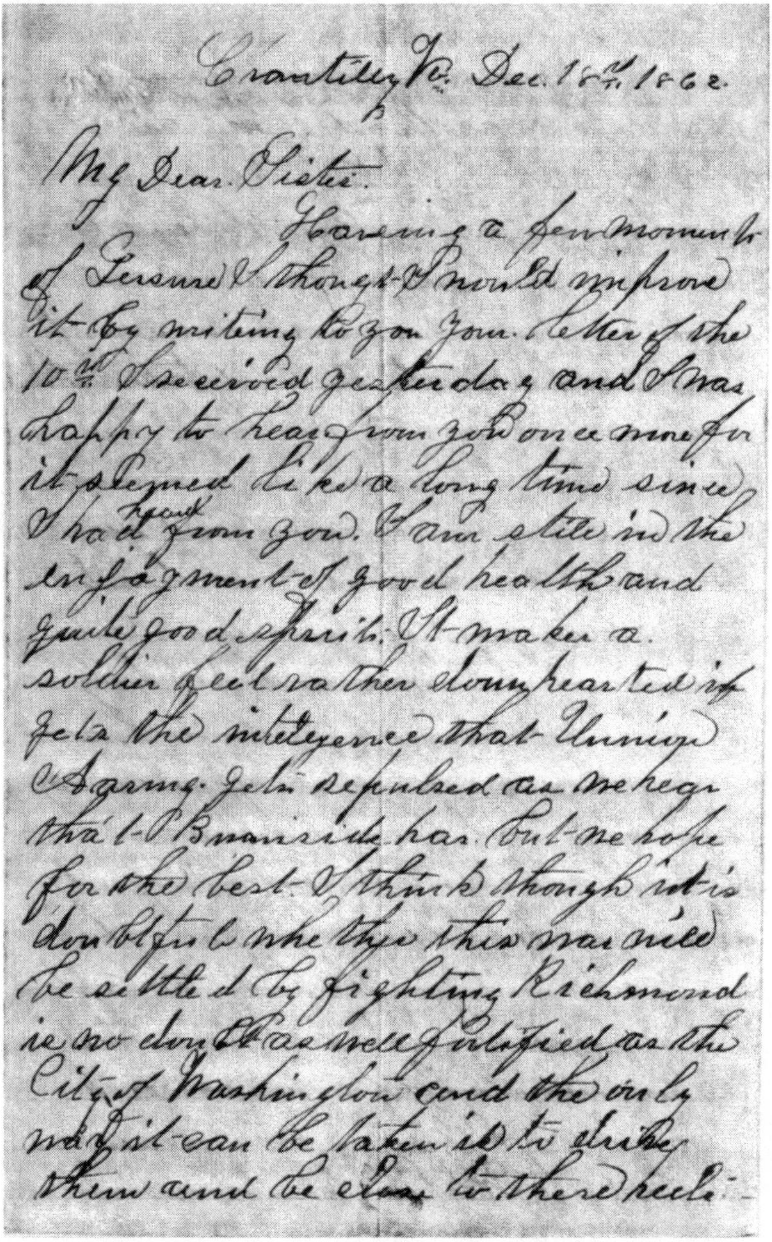

Chantilly Va. Dec. 18th 1862.

My Dear Sister.

Having a few moments of leisure I thought I would improve it by writing to you. Your letter of the 10th I received yesterday and I was happy to hear from you once more for it seemed like a long time since I had heard from you. I am still in the enjoyment of good health and quite good spirits. It makes a soldier feel rather downhearted if gets the intelegence that Union Army gets repulsed as we hear that Burnside has. But we hope for the best. I think though it is doubtful whether this war will be settled by fighting. Richmond is no doubt as well fortified as the City of Washington and the only way it can be taken is to strike them and be close to there heels.

and then a great many lives
would be sacrificed if both can
compromise by making them come
back to their allegiance I think it
would be best way. Since I last
wrote you we have moved our camp
from the fortifications and taken the
field we are down to the front and
doing picket duty. since we have moved
out here. we have lost one of best men
we had in the Company he was detailed
as a scout at Headquarters. and
while one the performance of his duty
he was shot through the brain by some
rebel cavalry. who come upon him by
surprise he shot near a house and
the people who there buried him quite
decently. They told our Company that
went up and got the body. the Captain
of the rebel cavalry. felt real sorry that
the man was shot. for he was such
a smart looking young man. We sent
his body to Washington to have it

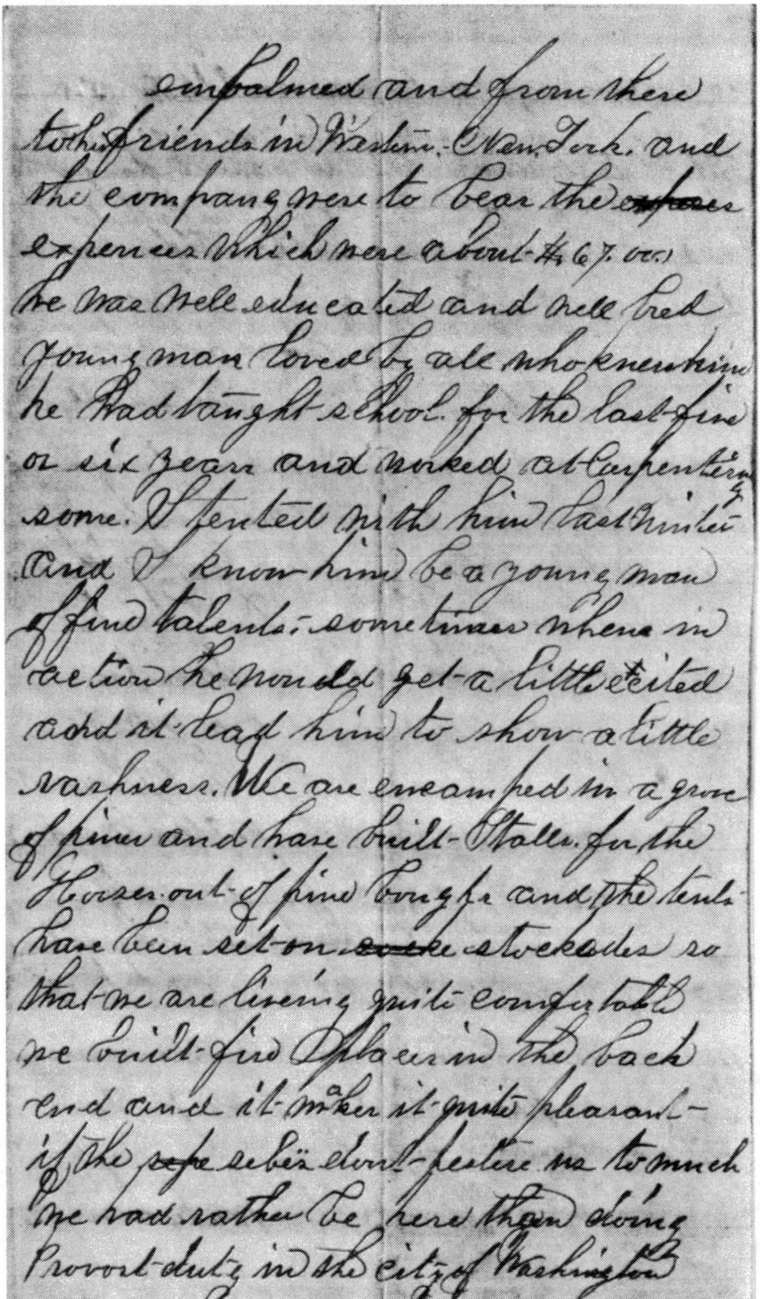

embalmed and from there
to his friends in Western New York. and
the company were to bear the ~~expences~~
expences which were about $67.00
he was well educated and well bred
young man loved by all who knew him
he had taught school for the last five
or six years and worked at carpentering
some. I tented with him last winter
and I know him be a young man
of fine talents. sometimes when in
action he would get a little excited
and it lead him to show a little
rashness. We are encamped in a grove
of pines and have built stalls for the
Horses out of pine boughs and the tents
have been set on ~~[illegible]~~ stockades so
that we are living quite comfortable
we built fire places in the back
end and it makes it quite pleasant
if the ~~[illegible]~~ rebels don't pester us to much
we had rather be here than doing
Provost duty in the city of Washington

we have to keep our horses saddled
all night to be ready for any emergency
but I don't think there is much danger
of an attack so long as we keep our pickets
out. I think I would a sparerib for my
dinner. we get fresh hog here but we can't
roast it very well the boys go a foraging
and sometimes bring in a mutton
and often some poultry. sometimes
a bit of honey. so that we live pretty
well where there is plenty of stuff
in the land. I presume Charlie
is getting to be quite a dandy.
I think he never will get over stage
if he lives many years. But I must
close. Give my love to Willie and
take a good share for yourself.
I still wish to be ~~[illegible]~~ remembered
in your prayers that we may at last
meet where there is no sin no sorrow
but all is peace and love so good by
from your most aff. Bro

Wm. H. Waterhouse.

December 23, 1862 Letter to Uncle Levi in Illinois:

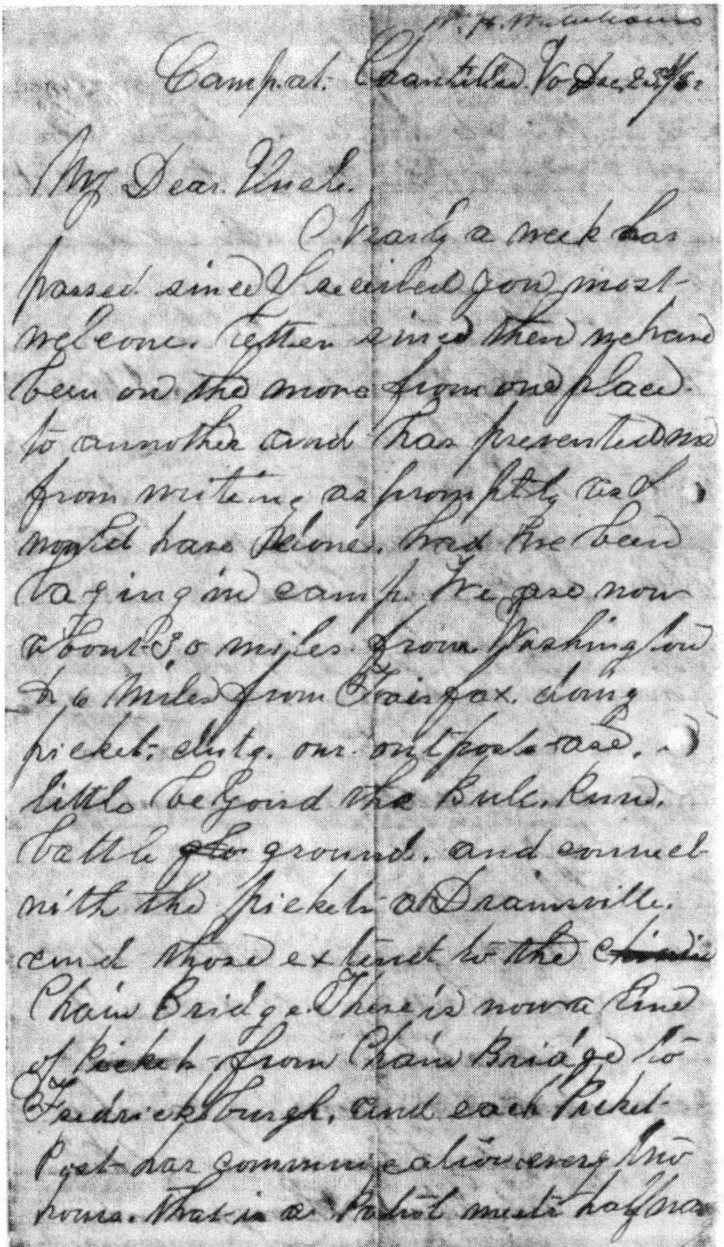
[illegible]

Camp at Chantilla Va Dec 23/62

My Dear Uncle.

Nearly a week has passed since I received your most welcome letter since then we have been on the move from one place to annother and has prevented me from writing as promptly as I would have done had we been laying in camp. We are now about 30 miles from Washington & 6 Miles from Fairfax, doing picket duty. our outposts are a little beyond the Bull Run battle ground. and connect with the pickets at Dranesville. and those extend to the Chain Bridge. There is now a line of Pickets from Chain Bridge to Fredricksburgh, and each Picket Post has communication every two hours. That is a Patrol must half

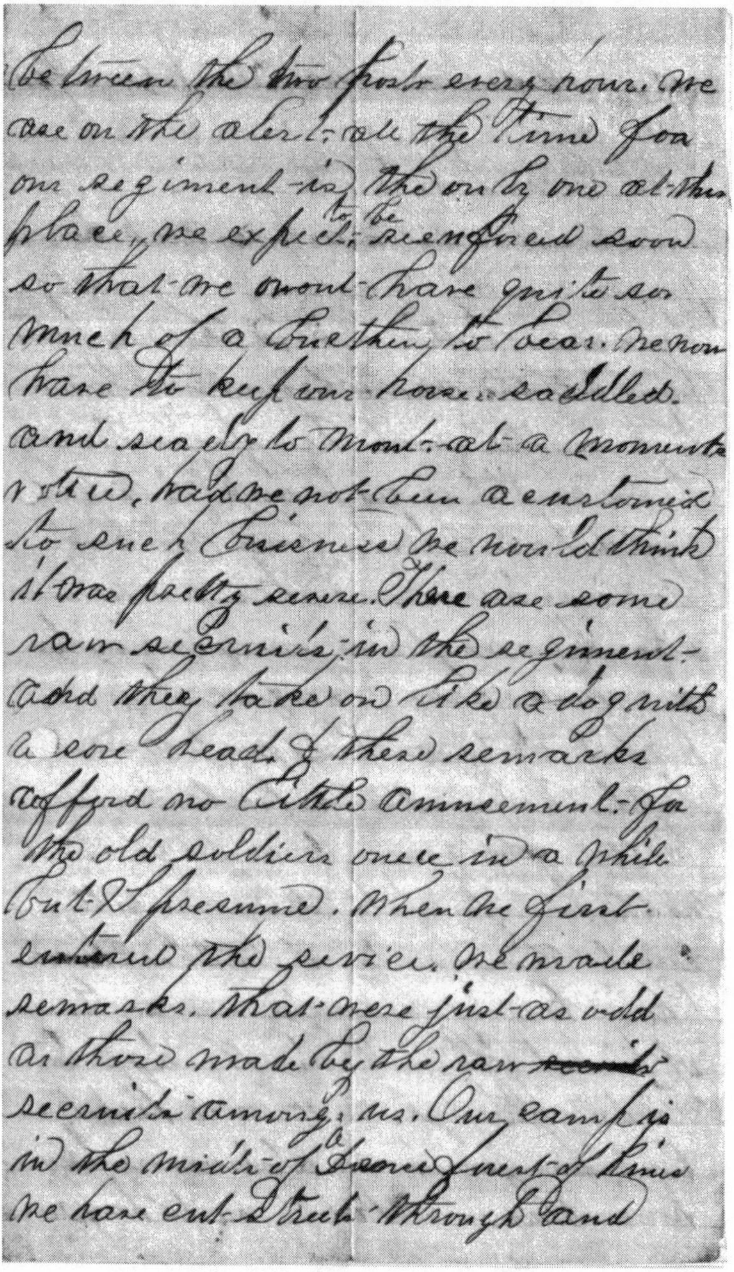
between the two posts every hour. We
are on the alert all the time for
our regiment is the only one at this
place, we expect to be reinforced soon
so that we won't have quite so
much of a burthen to bear. We now
have to keep our horses saddled
and ready to mount at a moments
notice, had we not been accustomed
to such business we would think
it was pretty severe. There are some
raw recruits in the regiment
and they take on like a dog with
a sore head. & their remarks
afford no little amusement for
the old soldiers once in a while
but I presume when we first
entered the service we made
remarks that were just as odd
as those made by the raw ~~recruits~~
recruits among us. Our camp is
in the midst of a once forest of pines
we have cut streets through and

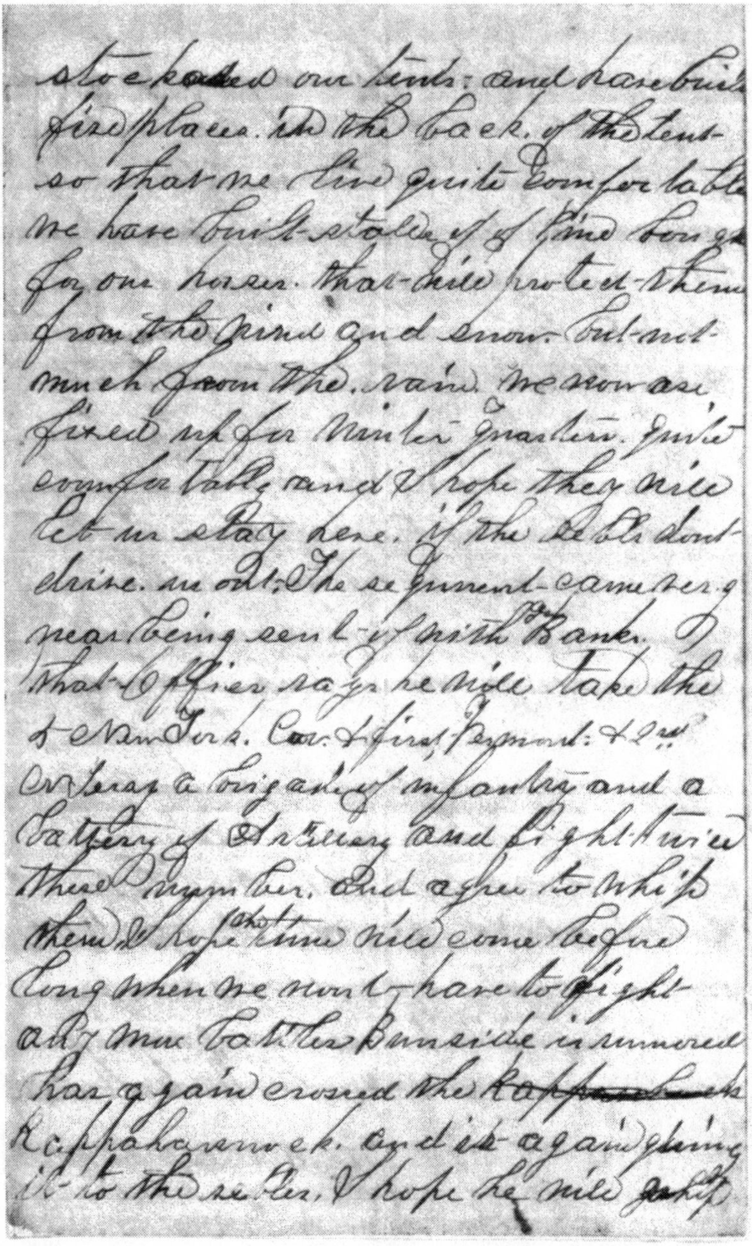
stockaded our tents: and have built
fireplaces in the back of the tent
so that we live quite comfortable
we have built stables of pine boughs
for our horses that will protect them
from the wind and snow but not
much from the rain we now are
fixed up for winter quarters quite
comfortable and I hope they will
let us stay here if the Rebels don't
drive us out. The regiment came very
near being cut off with Banks. If
that Officer says he will take the
5 New York Cav. & first Vermont & 2nd
[illegible] a brigade of infantry and a
battery of Artillery and fight twice
there number and agree to whip
them I hope the time will come before
long when we won't have to fight
any more battles Burnside is rumored
has again crossed the ~~Rappahannock~~
Rappahannock and is again giving
it to the rebels. I hope he will [illegible]

them out this time. Richmond I presume
is as well fortified as Washington
if not better. We lost one of our best
men a few days since. he was shot
while on a scout by a squad of rebel
cavalry. he was a well educated
young man and was loved by all.
we went up and recovered the body.
and sent it home. it makes us feel
sad when we think of our lost
comrads and how well it becomes
us to be prepared to meet death.
for we are exposed daily to danger
seen and unseen. Christmas has
almost come again I wonder where
I will be the next Christmas.
but I must close. give my love
to Aunt Hattie & kiss the little
ones for me. so good by from your
most aff Nephew.

Wm. H. Waterhouse

December 24, 1862 Letter to Sister Cinty:

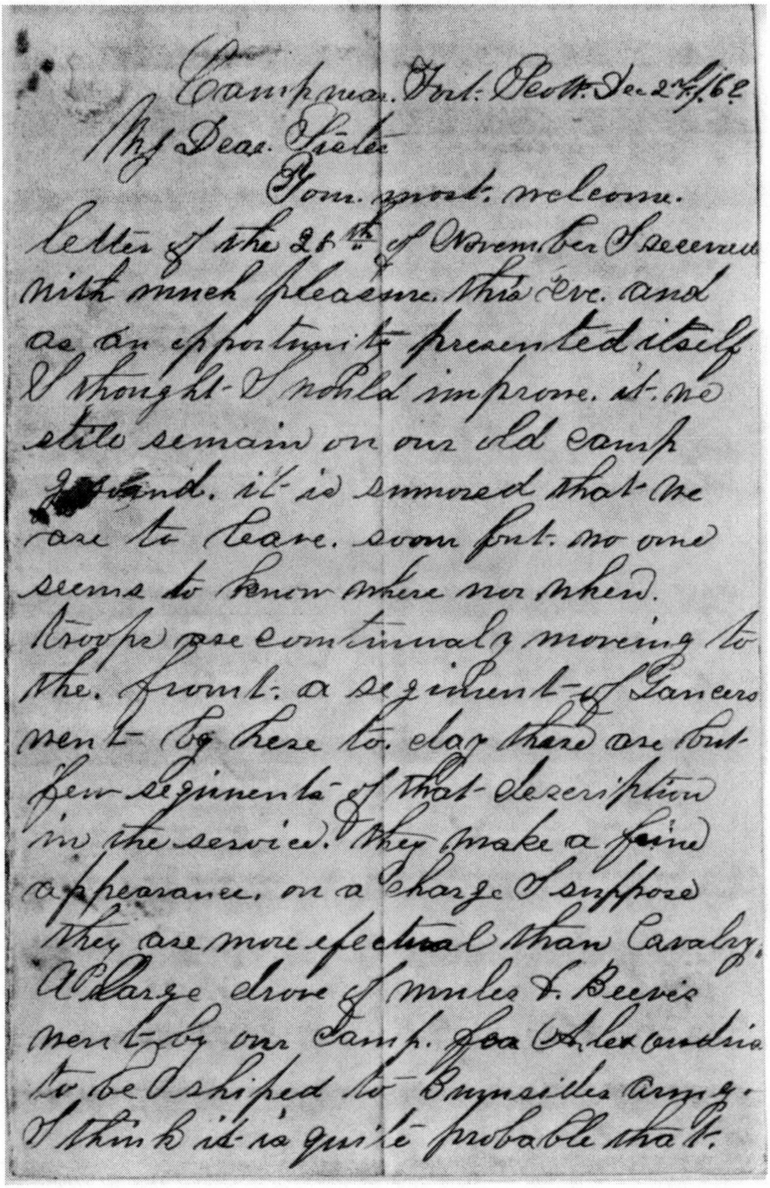

Camp near Fort Scott Dec 24/62

My Dear Sister

Your most welcome letter of the 26th of November I received with much pleasure this eve. and as an opportunity presented itself I thought I would improve it. we still remain on our old camp ground. it is rumored that we are to leave soon but no one seems to know where nor when. troops are continualy moving to the front. a regiment of Lancers went by here to day there are but few regiments of that description in the service. they make a fine appearance on a charge I suppose they are more efectual than Cavalry. A large drove of mules & Beeves went by our Camp for Alexandria to be shiped to Burnsides army. I think it is quite probable that

there will be a change of some
sort in regard to South before the
Spring opens. I think the North
will offer terms of peace. I was
reading the President's 2nd Annual
Message to day and I say he is
sound on the Goose I think he is
in favor of Compromise if an honorable
one can be made. He is strongly
opposed to a Seperation. and he shows
the difficulties there would be to
make a seperation. in my opinion
his Message is right to the point.
I am now I think entirely free
from the ague I feel perfectly well as
well now as ever in my life, so that
I think I could stand another
campaign, though I should regret
to do so. I had a letter from Lud
Smith. he sick of the war says he is
highly disgusted and thinks there
is a deal of Humbug in it. I will send
his letter to you for I think you.

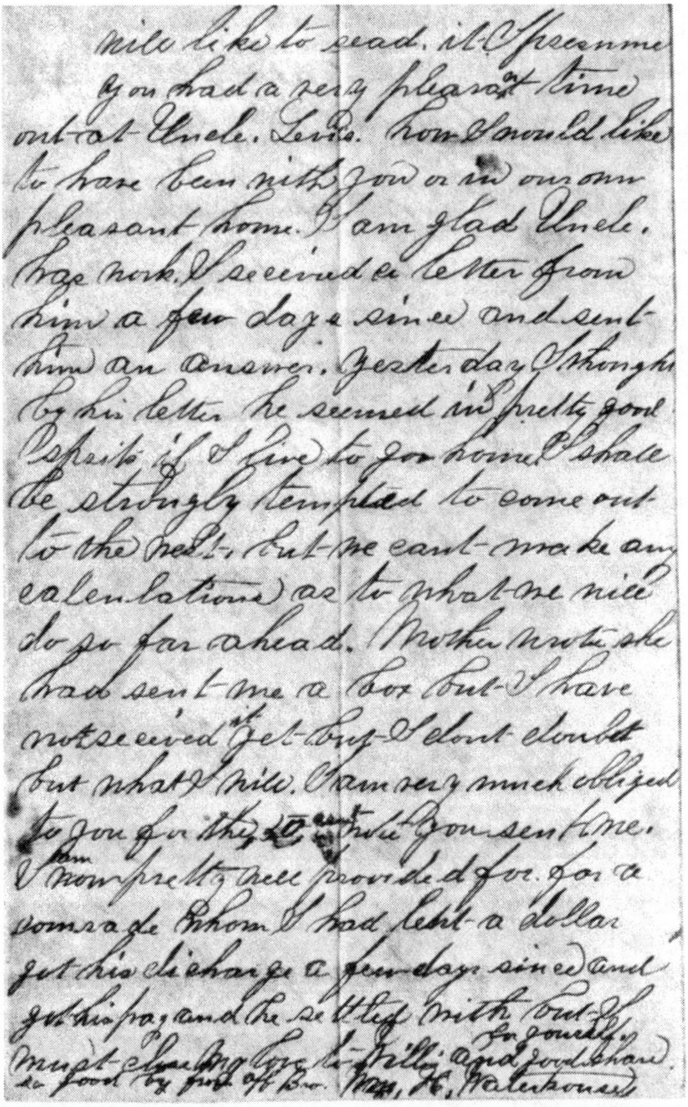
mile like to read it. I presume
you had a very pleasant time
out at Uncle Levis. how I would like
to have been with you or in our own
pleasant home. I am glad Uncle
[illegible] wrote. I received a letter from
him a few days since and sent
him an answer. Yesterday I thought
by his letter he seemed in pretty good
spirits if I live to go home I shall
be strongly tempted to come out
to the west. but we cant make any
calculations as to what we will
do so far ahead. Mother wrote she
had sent me a box but I have
not received it yet but I dont doubt
but what I will. I am very much obliged
to you for the 50 cents you sent me.
I am now pretty well provided for. for a
comrade whom I had lent a dollar
got his discharge a few days since and
got his pay and he settled with but I
must close by love to Willie and good share for yourself
so good by from your Bro. Wm. H. Waterhouse

Mixed emotions ended the year. Being over my illness and the regiment moving back to the front lines where we did active picket duty made life content again. Then we heard of Burnside's defeat and our own company suffered the useless loss of our best man, my first roommate, who had so much to live for and give to the nation. These bumped me right into another sad

Christmas away from the family.

General Burnside was determined to attack and again made new plans on December 26 to strike south of Fredericksburg, but received a letter from the President saying to hold these plans. In January, to make some reason for this Fredericksburg maneuver, Burnside thought of another plan to try to make some reason for this Fredericksburg maneuver: instead of a straight retreat, he wanted to take some units of cavalry, infantry, and artillery, pass around Richmond to the south, and 'blow up the locks on the James River Canal, the iron bridge of Nottoway, on the Richmond and Weldon Railroad,' thereby seriously interrupting the Confederate communications and sources of supply.

Franklin and Sumner dispatched a letter to the President painting this idea as a definite disaster due to the mileage involved in enemy territory. The President gave the order prohibiting any movement of which he was not previously informed. Burnside resolved to make another move at his own responsibility. He made a feint to retreat, but planned to double back, cross the river into Fredericksburg and attack. The weather had been mild, thus the roads through forests could be made and the artillery moved.

Finally, on January 20th, the retreat began, but the weather changed into a strong sleet and ice storm, raging all night and the next day. All day the 21st, the army struggled in its march through the mud. Not a gun or a wagon could be moved without doubling or trebling the teams. Sometimes a hundred men had to pull on one rope to move a pontoon boat. The roads were strewed with shipwrecked wagons, horses and mules dead and dying, pontoons and guns immovable in the mud. Confederates fixed their defense. The plan was deemed impossible. Burnside recalled the troops to their former positions and the three day mud campaign came to an end.

After retreating, Burnside took two requests to the

President. One, he wished for the dismissal of Hooker, Brooks, Newton and Cochrane and relieving from duty Franklin, Smith, Taylor, Sturgis and Ferrero. He felt he could no longer lead the Army if they stayed. He took this request in one hand and his resignation in the other to the President, declaring it had to be one or the other.

The President deliberated for a day, took Burnside out of command but would not accept his resignation. On January 26, 1863, Hooker was named in charge of the Army of the Potomac, Burnside was 'at his own request' relieved of command, given thirty days to handle personal affairs and then take command of the Department of the Ohio where he started. Sumner 'at his own request' was relieved from the Potomac and sent to Department of Missouri (unfortunately on the way there he died after having served forty-four years in active service). Franklin was also relieved, but not 'at own request.'

Due to the hard campaign with bitter loss, the Union army's morale was seriously impaired. The tone of the army was indicated by resignations among officers, desertions from privates, and the chatter of despair from all tents.

10

GERMANTOWN, VIRGINIA & CAMP NEARBY END OF JANUARY, FEBRUARY & EARLY MARCH, 1863

History shows us: due to the change in political attitude toward the war in Ohio, New York, Pennsylvania, Indiana and Illinois after Lincoln's Proclamation in January, the populous had elected fresh leaders wanting an end to the war. There was a chance for the South to be persuaded that any great success gained over the Union army would elicit such a feeling throughout the North compelling the government to desist from the pursuit of the war. In the last six months, the Confederates had defeated Burnside at Fredericksburg, foiled Hooker at Chancellorsville, Vicksburg and Charleston had held out against Federal assaults, none of the Union operations on the Lower Mississippi and Gulf had succeeded, the capture of Galveston had given all of Texas into the hand of the Confederates and the Alabama and the Florida had swept American commerce from the high seas. Except for the few miles occupied by the main armies, the Union forces actually held no portion of the Confederate territory of which they had taken possession.

The new year brought many new recruits not used to the demands of war, which unsettled some of us 'old' members, but they learned quickly not to scare us with wild imagination reporting.

Transposition of Page 1 &2 of January 15, 1863 lettter to Sister Mela; page 3 of letter follows this page: as written.

Camp near Germantown, Virginia

January 15th, 1863

My Dear Sister

It is a long time since I have heard from you. Thinking your letters or mine might have been miscarried I thought write again. Since I heard from you we have again been going through the realities of war. again & again have we struck and restruck our tents pitched & repitched them also. and some of our comrads has met an untimely end by the destructive missles of the foe. Stuart also has made us leave our camp in double quick time or else we would have been captured by this rebel chief but the forces have been increased to a Brigade of Cavalry & a regiment of Infantry so that we can keep quite a large force of the enemy at bay. one of the regiments is a new one they get scared at imaginations and arouse the whole Brigade. some of their men came running saying he saw the rebles Their men started the greatest yelling & screeching I ever saw or heard. They calling each other cowards. Every one turned out and mounted his horse while the glorious old 5th noted for her bravery and coolness in the time of action lay still scarcely a word was said but after they found the pennsylvanians were scared and that was all they all went to bed again and in five minutes were fast asleep again but I am afraid our regiment will never be what it was for the Officers are all resigning Major Pratt it is

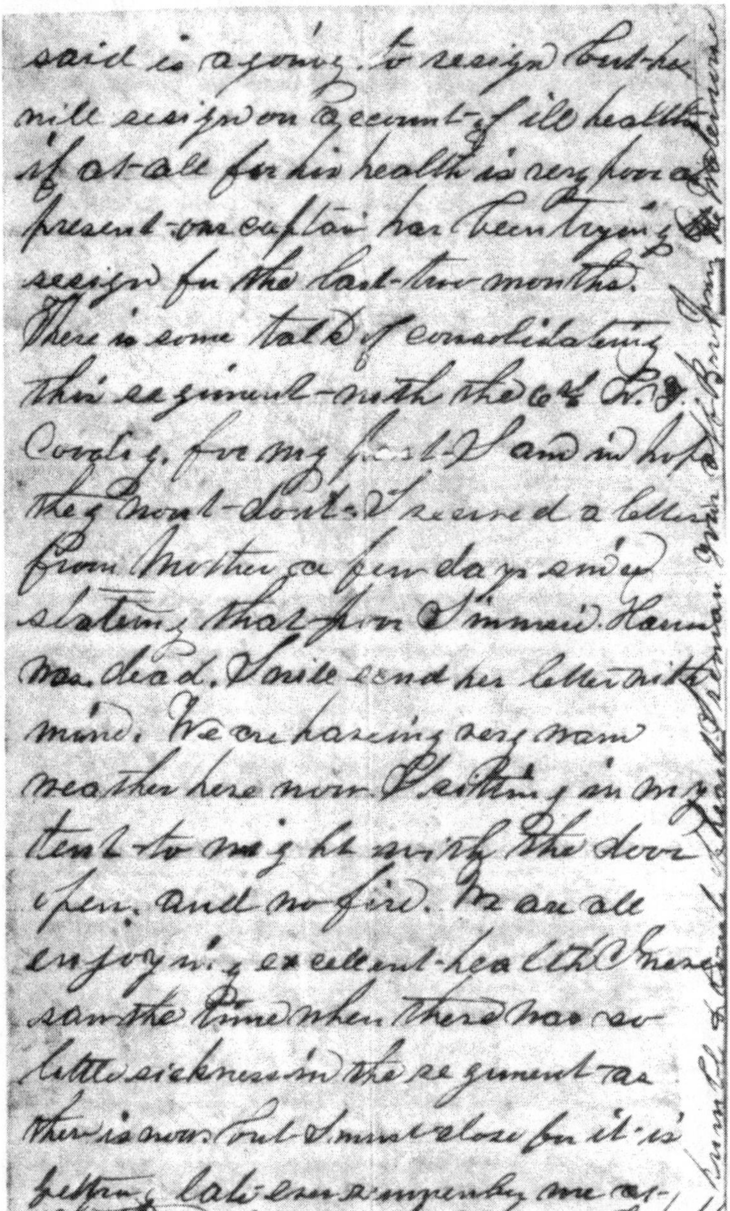

said is agoing to resign but he will resign on account of ill health if at all for his health is very poor at present. One captain has been trying to resign for the last two months. There is some talk of consolidating this regiment with the 6th N.Y. Cavalry, for my part I am in hope they won't don't. I received a letter from Mother a few days since stating that Miss Simmons Hann was dead. I will send her letter with mine. We are having very warm weather here now. I am sitting in my tent to night with the door open, and no fire. We are all enjoying excellent health. I never saw the time when there was so little sickness in the regiment as there is now. But I must close for it is getting late. Remember me at the throne of grace that I may be kept

Transposition of this entire letter follows this page: January 29, 1863 Letter to Sister Cinty:

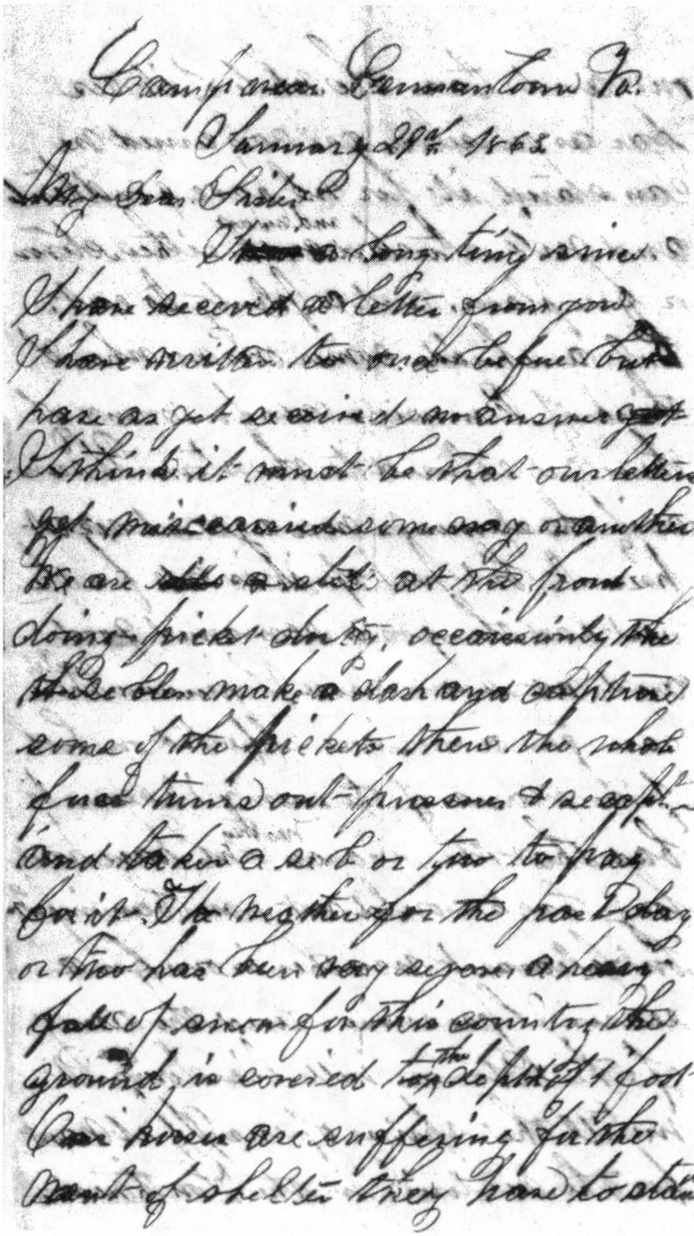

Camp near Germantown Va.
January 28th 1863
My dear Sister
[illegible] long time since
I have received a letter from you
I have written to you before but
have as yet received no answer yet
I think it cannot be that our letters
get miscarried some way or another
We are [illegible] at the front
doing picket duty, occasionally the
Rebels make a dash and capture
some of the pickets then the whole
force turns out prisoners & recapture
and takes a [illegible] or two to pay
for it. The weather for the past day
or two has been very severe a heavy
fall of snow for this country the
ground is covered to the depth of 1 foot
Our horses are suffering for the
want of shelter they have to stan

Transposition of January 29, 1863 letter to Sister

Camp near Germantown, Va
January 29th, 1863
My Dear Sister (Cindy)

It is a long time since I have received a letter from you I have written to once before but have as yet received no answer yet(scratched) I think it must be that our letters got miscarried some way or another. We are ---still at the front doing picket duty. occassionally the --rebles make a dash and capture some of the pickets then the whole force turns out. Pursues & recaptured and takes a reb or two to pay for it. The weather for the past day or two has been very severe. A heavy fall of snow for this country the ground is covered to the depth of 1 foot Our horses are suffering for the want of shelters they have to stand out and take the whole of it as for as ourselves are concerned we can stand it for we have good tents and well stocked and we have either stoves or fireplaces, and a plenty to eat. but a shudder comes over me when I think of Burnside's men for many of them are exposed to the storm it seems as if the elements were against us at present. but perhaps it is for the best had the roads remained good and no storm arose I presume there would have been a crossing effected on both of the flanks of the enemy. it seems to bad that the pleasant weather we have had long back could not have been improved but pleasant weather is over for a season I presume and the Army of the Potomac will lie dormant until the spring opens. If it wasnt for the victories in the Southwest we soldiers would feel pretty much discouraged I hope Rosecrans will be able to follow up his success and be able to drive the rebles out of Miss. I am in hopes also of hearing some good news from our army in North Carolina. An army of 80,000 wont be likely to lay still in that section of the country doing nothing. I think I read something in regard to the Battery that has got up in Chicago under the auspices of the Board of Trade if I am not mistaken the paper stated that they done good executions. I long to see the time when the rebellion shall be put down and we be permitted to go to our homes once more but I expect that time is some way into the future. I received a letter from home day before yesterday stating that John Reeves and Lib Horton were married. I did think John would never get married for he like myself cared but little for the society of the fair sex. Dan and Eliza seem to be prospering Finely have got a boy a month old bully for them perhaps Dan gained something by not going to the war but I would not shirked the service the way he did. Mother says they have got one of those Organ Hammond in the choir. how I wish we could be there and listen to it well mabe we will sometime it is a long time since I have heard any good music if I ever live to get home I will know less about music than I ever did and you know I never knew but a precious little but I must close love to all your most aff Bro

Wm H Waterhouse

I was impressed with the victory of Major General Rosecrans had in Stones River, Tennessee when his Army of the Cumberland fought General Bragg's Confederate Army of Tennessee starting on December 31, 1862. The Union army was driven back to the Nashville Pike, but then reinforcements of the Chicago Mercantile Independent Battery Light Artillery arrived.

Mercantile Independent Battery Light Artillery arrived and with great valor helped the Federals establish a new strong line. On January 1, 1863, Bragg had crossed Stones River and taken a position on the bluff east of the river. The Confederates drove most of the Federals back across McFadden's Ford, but with the assistance of the artillery, the Federals repulsed the attack, compelling the rebels to retire to their original position. Bragg left the field on the January 4-5, retreating to Shelbyville and Tullahoma, Tennessee. Rosecrans did not pursue, but as the Confederates retired, he claimed the victory. Stones River boosted Union morale. The Confederates had been thrown back in the east, west, and in the Trans-Mississippi

News of the naming of General Joseph Hooker in charge of the Army of the Potomac filtered down to us only in February, but he had immediately seen the desperate mental and physical condition of the whole army and vowed to change it for the better quickly. When he took command, desertions numbered 200 daily. By ordering better supplies and uniforms, disallowing or limiting many furloughs and leaves, examining express trains for deserters, burning any civilian clothing, and building comfortable winter huts, desertions ceased, absentees returned, ratio of sickness sank from more than 10% to 5%.

I turned 21 on February 11, 1863.

February 13, 1863 Letter to Brother-in-Law Willis::

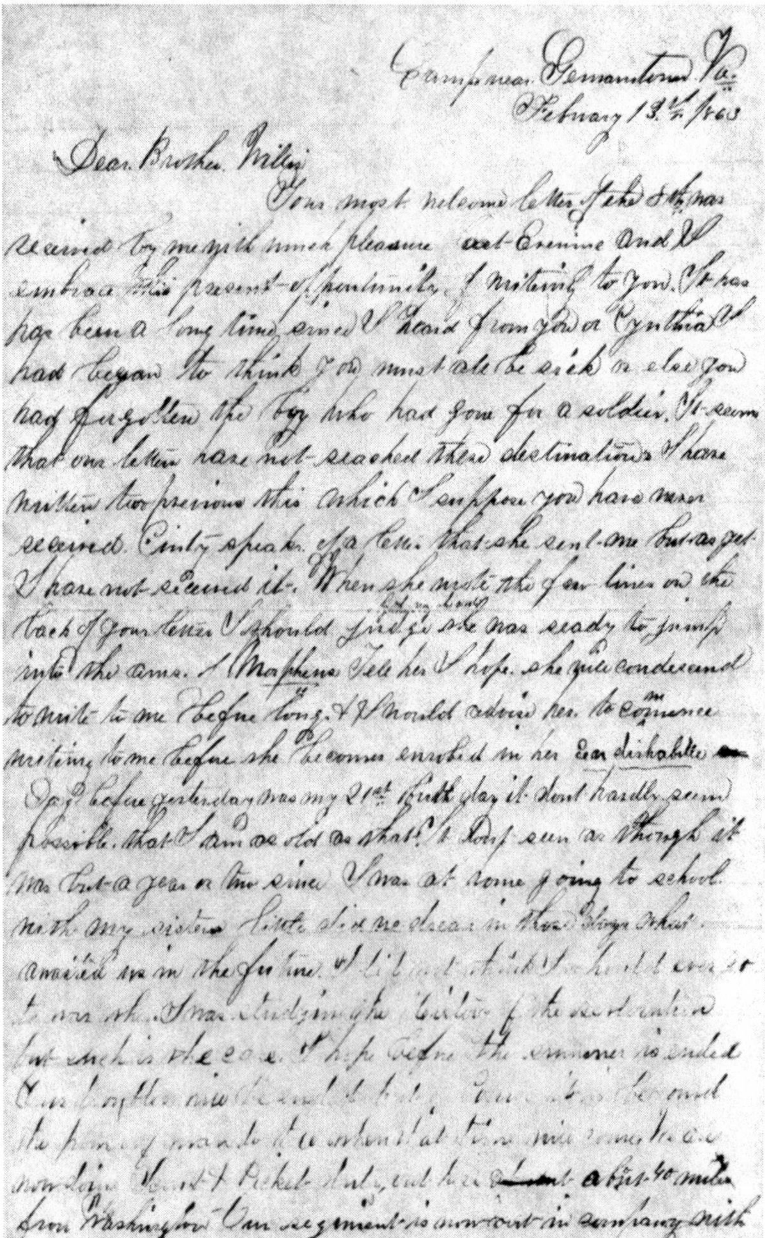

Camp near Germantown Va.
February 13th/1863

Dear Brother Willis
Your most welcome letter of the 8th was received by me with much pleasure last Evening and I embrace this present opportunity of writing to you. It has been a long time since I heard from you or Cynthia. I had began to think you must all be sick or else you had forgotten the boy who had gone for a soldier. It seems that our letters have not reached their destinations I have written two previous this which I suppose you have never received. Cinty speaks of a letter that she sent me but as yet I have not received it. When she wrote the few lines on the back of your letter I should judge by her looks she was ready to jump into the arms of Morpheus. Tell her I hope she will condescend to write to me before long. & I would advise her to commence writing to me before she becomes enrobed in her dear dishabille
Day before yesterday was my 21st Birth day it dont hardly seem possible that I am as old as that. It does seem as though it was but a year or two since I was at home going to school with my sisters. Little did we dream in those days what awaited us in the future. I did not think I should ever go to war when I was studying the history of the revolution but such is the case. I hope before the summer is ended [illegible] [illegible] We are now doing Scout & Picket duty, out here about 40 miles from Washington. Our regiment is now out in company with

the 1st. I'm on a scout. I shall have to leave my letter until
the evening. I will now finish my letter though it is after
tattoo sick call and nearly time for taps. Since I left starting
our regiment has returned. They left here proceeded on to
Centreville from there to Manassas Junction. from there
to Bristow Station from there to Warrenton Junction
and then took a turn through Warrenton and then
down to Stafford Court House. where Hookers grand
reserve Corps, is stationed. I suppose the above intelligence
but: if you could get one of Loyds Maps of Va. you
could easily find every one of the above named places
and also where we are doing picket duty our camp is
near Germantown. our outposts are about five (5) miles
from here a little beyond Chantilly occasionally
a few rebel scouts dash down on our picket posts, and
then a company or two is sent out and chase them
about twenty miles or so and so it goes. Within the
past week or two. no less than 8 sutlers have been brought
into camp who were caught trying to smuggle goods
through our lines over to the rebels where they would
fetch them a good round sum each wagon contained
about 18.00 dollars worth of goods. they were confiscated
among the Brigade though a very small portion has
fallen to us. the officers retaining most of the goods.
Yesterday we received pay for 4th months my clothing bill
for the past year amounted to $73.82. perhaps you think
that is pretty large well I do myself. but the way
our debt comes to be so large is on Banks retreat
down the Shenandoah we lost everything but one

order of Gen. Halck. the extra clothing was sent to
Alexandria which we have never heard from since
and which we have had to pay for. The Goverment allows us
$42. a year for clothing I overdrawed clothing amounting
to $31.32. which was deducted out of our last payment.
so you see we did not get a very large amount of Green
Backs. 4 months pay would have amounted to $56 dollars
but all that I got was $25.32. I think it a shame that
were obliged to pay for clothing that was sent away and
lost by neglect if Uncle Sam got this money that we
are paying for extra clothing we would not think so
much of it but it is my firm impression that it dont
go out of the Paymasters hands unless it is for his own
benefit. There is awful sight of swindling done by
contractors who are employed by the Goverment especially those
who are engaged in buying horses. the Goverment pays
the contractors $120 dollars for each horse. and they are
supposed to get horses that are worth that but I dont
suppose they ever pay over $100. dollars last fall we got
new horses and there is scarcely a horse in the whole
regiment that would get $50.00 at home. and some
are only three year old colts. but enough of this I received
a letter from home to day Mother writes that there seems to
be an awakening in the church. How I would like to enter
the old basement this evening and join in the worship
of God. I find myself answering the question when will I go home. the prospect looks
rather dark ahead but we must hope for the best & remember
me at the throne of grace good night Yours aff Bro. Wm. H. Waterhouse.

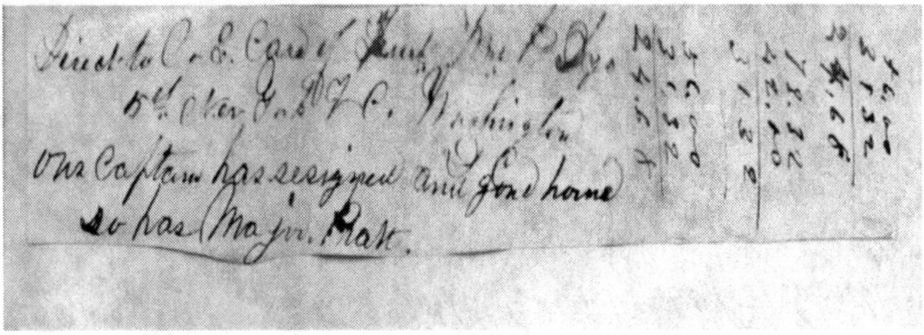
Our Captain has resigned and gone home
so has Major Platt.

Hooker divided his army into seven corps. All the cavalry that had been scattered was formed into one group with a strong leader, Stoneman. He made his picket lines almost impenetrable by doubling not only the duties, but the encampments of the cavalry. Knowing that idleness is an army's worst enemy, whenever the weather permitted, Hooker ordered field exercises. His secret plan, which could not be enacted until the spring thaw, was to destroy the Confederate Army of North Virginia, not to take Richmond. Lincoln had tried in vain to impress McClellan with this idea and Grant grasped it months later.

To accomplish this, Hooker planned to turn the Confederate right wing above Fredericksburg, Instead of crossing the Rappahannock to battle Lee's waiting troops directly on the other side, he decided to split his forces, and stealthily send a fortified part to a point father north, which would attack Lee by making a forceful sweep down the river using the sandwich effect, with the southern unit attacking below Lee's army, separating it from their supplies, but it had to be a surprise. They would have to cross miles beyond the confrontation point, the United States and Banks' Fords, and attack them from the rear. Once the column would be open, the heavy forces could follow down on the rebels in force. All through March, Hooker prepared for this without ever divulging the full movement to his generals or Washington.

This winter brought very cold weather with many severe snow storms and though we had built our tent compound into a well protected area with fireplaces for warmth, our horses had no cover and we lost quite a few in the freezing temperatures. Trying to buy new horses, we found many swindlers. These people trying to make quick money appeared frequently. Also we heard of traitors in the North to our cause, which made us furious. We were engaged in no major battles but many skirmishes with our picket duty between Chantilly and our camp.

Our clothing bill for the year came in and we were appalled. Because of Banks' retreat, when we lost all our clothing, we were charged for the replacement. We agreed that Banks should have been charged for that, since we did not order the retreat! We needed good news from some place and better weather.

January 21 should be February 21, 1863 Letter to Sister Mela: Transposition of entire letter follows this page:

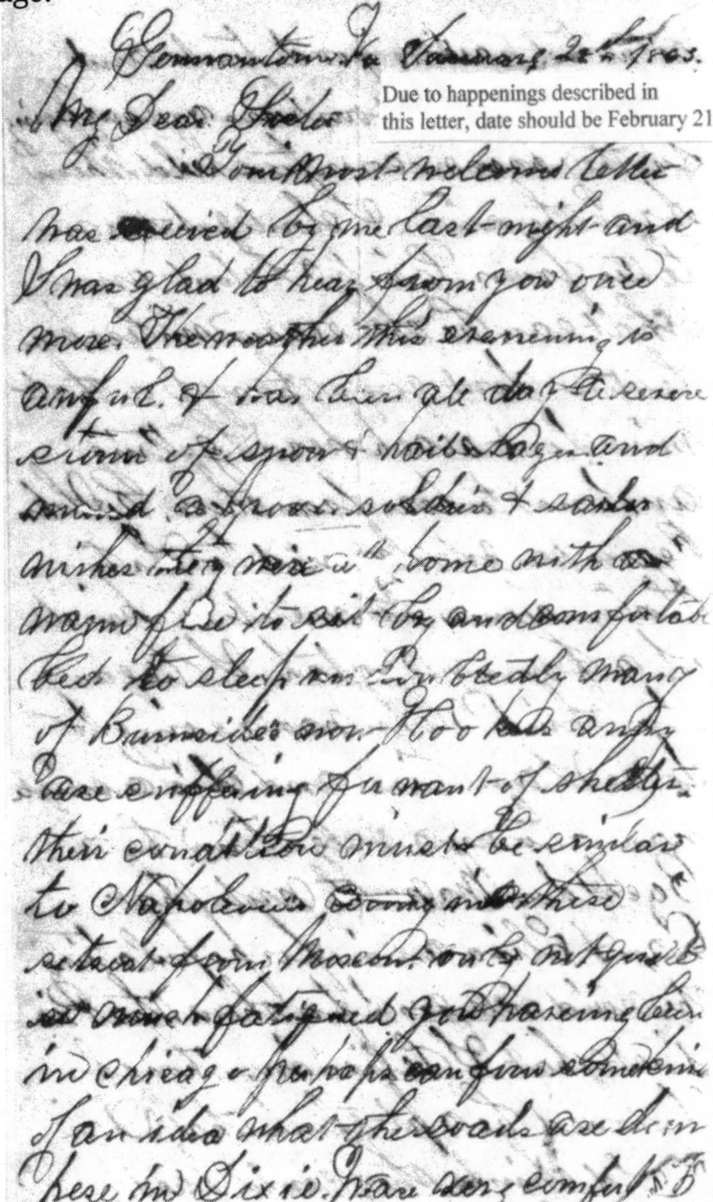

Germantown Va January 21st 1863.

Due to happenings described in this letter, date should be February 21

My Dear Sister

Your most welcome letter was received by me last night and I was glad to hear from you once more. The weather this evening is awful. It was been all day the severe storm of snow & hail again and around us poor soldiers & sailors wishes they were at home with a warm fire to sit by and comfortable bed to sleep in. Probably many of Burnside's now Hooker's army are suffering for want of shelter. Their condition must be similar to Napoleon's army in their retreat from Moscow only not quite as much fatigued. You having been in Chicago perhaps can form somewhat of an idea what the roads are down here in Dixie. I have very comfort

Transposition of all pages of January 21, 1863 letter to Sister Mela. (Should be February 21)

Germantown, Va. January 21st 1863

(but should be February 21 due to facts in letter):

My Dear Sister (Mela)

Your most welcome letter was received by me last night an I was glad to hear from you once more. The weather this evening is awful. It has been all day. A severe storm of snow and hail rages and many a poor soldier & sailor wishes they were at home with a warm fire to sat by and comfortable bed to sleep in. Undoubtedly many of Burnsides. now Hookers army are suffering for want of shelter. Their condition must be similar to Napoleon's army in there retreat from Moscow, only not quite so much fatigued you haveing been in Chicago perhaps can form some ;kind of an idea what the roads are down here in Dixie. We are very comfortably situated having good tents and well stocked but our horses are suffering for they have no cover to shield them from the storm. I don't get no letter from Cindy. I don't know what can be the reason unless her letters don't come through or that mine don't reach her. I getting anxious to hear from them. So John Reaves has got married to Ruby Horton seems to me it is kind of a funny match. I began to think John was going to do as I am live and die a single man or to use a vulgar term be a Bachelder. Ma wrote that Dan & Elisa are in for populating the world well good for them that is just what I belive in. though I should be apt think that Dan would think they could hardly afford it. I hope Uncle Sam wont draft him into service for it will undoubtedly cut there calculations most mightily if he was single I would just like to see him drafted for I think he rather shirked the service of Uncle Sam but I suppose somebody needs to stay at home and he was just the man If I am not most greatly mistaken there will have to be some drafting done if there is to be any more fighting done after first of May I wish there would be no more need of fighting after that time but I am fearful there will there is doubt but what the Army of the Potomac will have to cease operations until after the muddy season is over. McClellen's Division left Fairfax nearly two weeks ago some said to go to North Carolina and others to Fredericksburg I think from the appearances of things that we will hear of a large battle from that quarter before long. They done exceedingly well at the S C nation I should like to have attended first rate sorie but I expect I shall appear awkward when I get in the company of ladies it so long since I have spoken to one of the fair sex. A woman is a rare sight to the soldier & you know I want never noted for gallantry. I was glad to learn that Henry has succeeded so well if he will only sober down and save his wages. His Mother wont have to labor quite so hard to get along. do you whether Uncle John is in Washington or where he is Major Pratt asks me in regard to him and I don't know what to tell him. Major's resignation I believe was not accepted. I am sorry on his account for his health is very poor. He don't report for duty at all. I presume if he should go to Washington in person he would get clear from the service since he has been in the service he has grown old very fast, he is quite gray. Generally he is not liked by the officers & men of the regiment the former because he wont drink as much whiskey as they wish the latter because his discipline is so strict I don't think though he is second to any officer in the regiment to be sure he is a little passionate but that don't hurt his fighting nor military qualities but I must close my love to all tell Sosie she must not be jealous she must write when Lina does then I will answer it where is Johnny & Georgie I dont hear anything from them tell them they must help Pa & Ma all they can. I suppose they are getting to be quite large Boys. I should like to be home to ring that bull for Pa. I would bring all the noise there is in it out well good by remember me at the throne of grace and if we are not in the Providence of God permitted to meet on earth may we meet in Heaven where there are no wars nor tears nor parting. Your most affectionate Brother Wm H. Waterhouse

February 24, 1863 Letter to Sister Mela:

Camp near Germantown Va
Febuary 24th 1863.

My Dear Sister

I have received your most welcome letter in connection with Mothers and I was ~~glad to~~ happy to hear from you once more. I dont know what can be the reason your letters dont come through I am sure. I am still in the enjoyment of good health. And fine spirits considering the circumstances in which we are situated Sunday the 22nd we had a most severe storm of Snow the most by far I think that I have seen since I have been a soldier Sunday morning I arose and found my tent half buried in the snow so that I was obliged to stand inside and kick the tent to get the snow of before I could make my exit; the snow Sunday night lay on the ground to the depth of 12 inches. Our poor horses suffered far more than the men for our

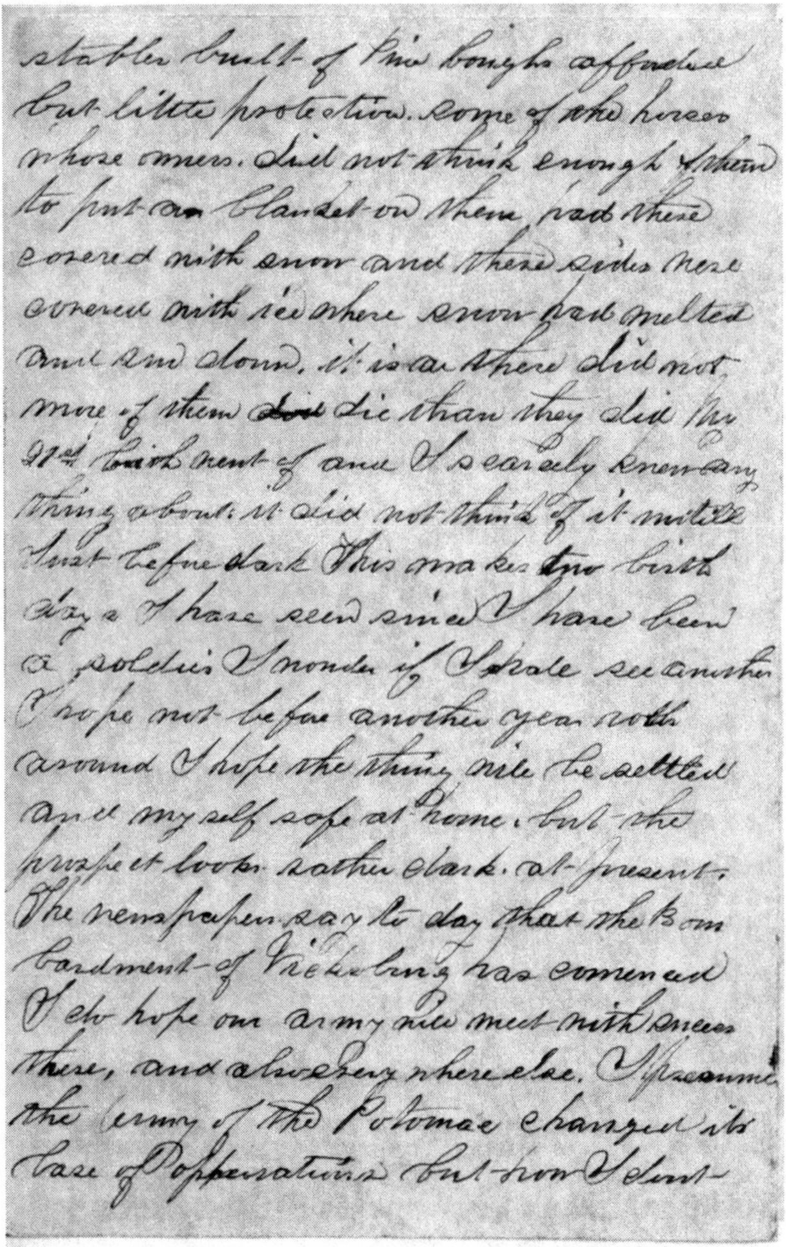

stables built of pine boughs afforded
but little protection. some of the horses
whose owners did not think enough of them
to put a blanket on them had there
covered with snow and there sides were
covered with ice where snow had melted
and run down. it is a there did not
more of them ~~die~~ die than they did the
22nd birth went of and I scarcely knew any
thing about it did not think of it untill
just before dark This makes two birth
days I have seen since I have been
a soldier I wonder if I shall see another
I hope not before another year rolls
around I hope the thing will be settled
and my self safe at home. but the
prospect looks rather dark. at present.
The newspapers say to day that the Bom
bardment of Vicksburg has commenced
I do hope our army will meet with success
there, and also every where else. I presume
the army of the Potomac changed its
base of opperations but how I dont

I dont know. Our regiment went down
to Falmouth within four miles of Fredericks
burg last week and they found the whole
army on the move but know one seemed
to know where nor for what purpose.
We have had what we call muddy roads
here but down there it is about 4 times
as bad. I see the letter Wilcox wrote me
and answered it have you received it
yet. I received a letter from Uncle
& Horace they in New York. I should
judge money was plenty in Greenport
for the Domminies have all received a
large donation & Henry Wells has made
the church a present of a Harmonium
costing $200. How are you hard times
I should like to be there to hear it
much now but you Charlie [illegible]
is a going into the Oil business I think
he had better stick to his carpentering for
he can do well at that but I must close
for this time love to all when you write to
Uncle Levi tell him I believe he owes me a letter. Direct
to Washington D.C. Co. E. 5th N.Y. Vol Cavalry.

I still remain your most aff Bro Wm. H. Watertown

March 2, 1863 Letter to Sister Cinty:

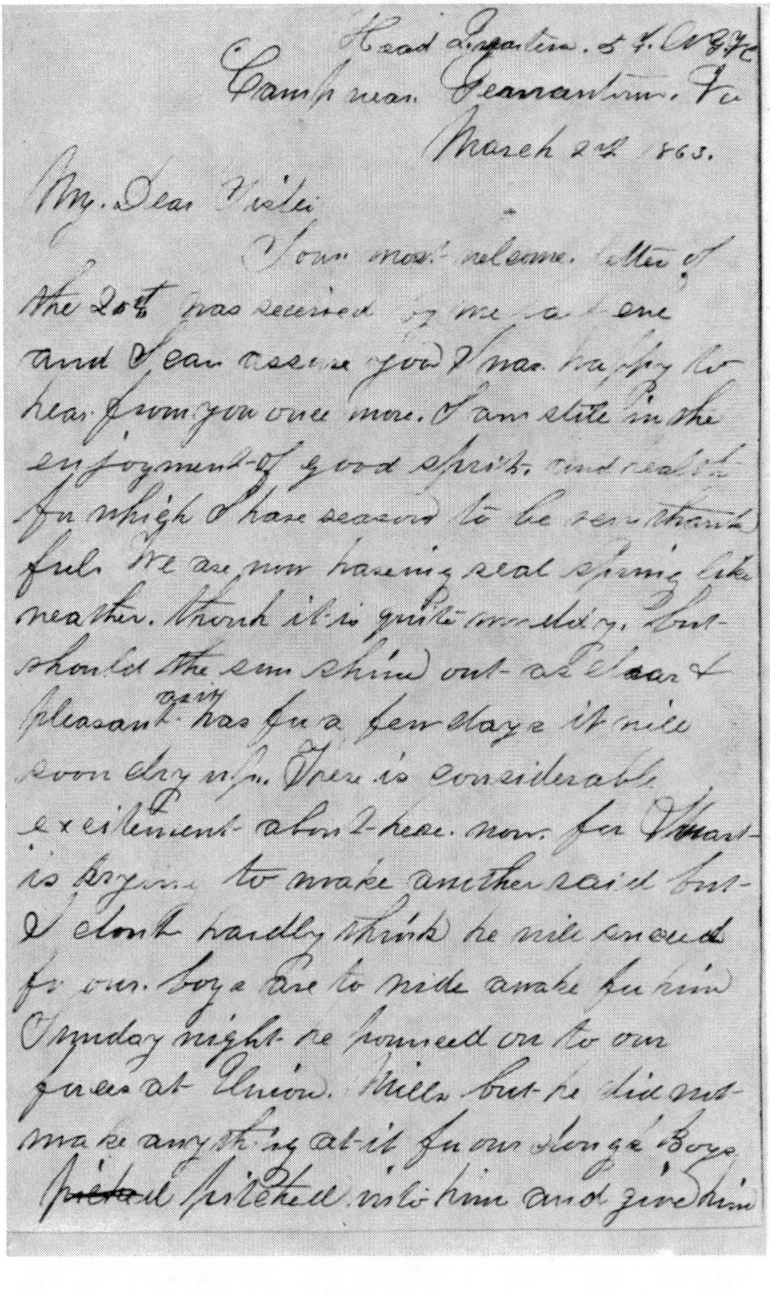

Head Quarters. 5 N.Y.V.C.
Camp near Germantown. Va
March 2d 1863.

My Dear Sister

Your most welcome letter of the 20th was received by me last eve and I can assure you I was happy to hear from you once more. I am still in the enjoyment of good spirits and health for which I have reason to be very thankful. We are now having real Spring like weather. though it is quite muddy. but should the sun shine out as clear & pleasant as it has for a few days it will soon dry up. There is considerable excitement about here now for Stuart is trying to make another raid but I don't hardly think he will succeed for our boys are to wide awake for him Sunday night he pounced on to our pickets at Union Mills but he did not make anything at it for our Yonge Boys ~~pitched~~ pitched into him and give him

tail Columbia and made him
skedaddle back double quick. The
rebel guerillas that are pestering (?) us
around here ~~[illegible]~~ pounched down
on the pickets and captured 2 of
the Penn & 3 of these men. had they
been our regiment I don't think they
would have been quite so successful.
for our boys fight like tigers. Our
Brigade in connection with a cavalry
force from Alexandria are out on
a scout they have now been gone five
days. we have not heard from them
since they went out. I wish I was
with them. but being Q. M. Sergeant
I have to stay by the stuff. There has
not been many scouts nor skirmishes
but what I have been in them. Tell
Willie I don't think he will be obliged
to go into the service nor do I think
he would be accepted as a volunteer
because I very (?) much doubt whether
he would stand a medical examination

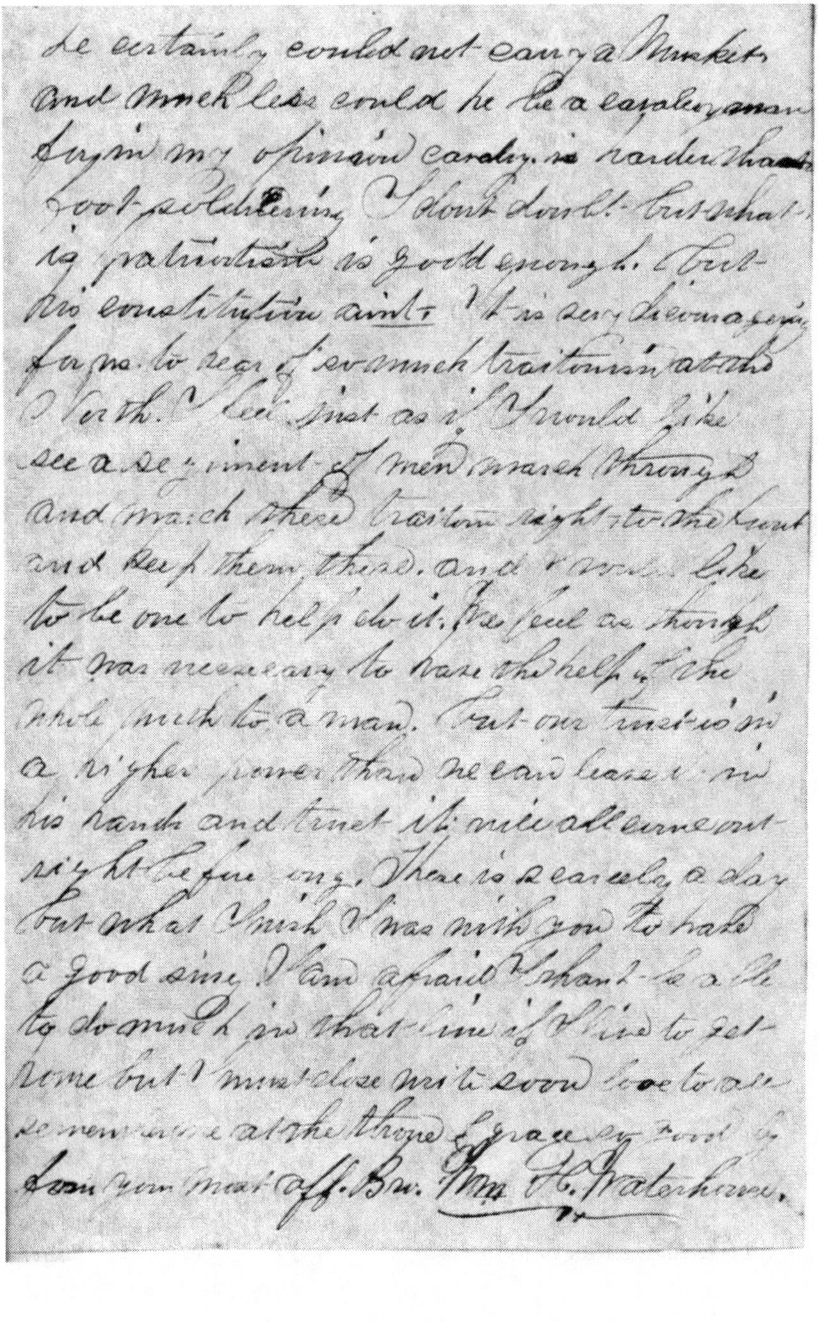
he certainly could not carry a Musket
and much less could he be a cavalryman
for in my opinion cavalry is harder than
foot soldiering I dont doubt but what
his patriotism is good enough but
his constitution aint. It is very discouraging
for me to hear of so much traitorism at the
North. I feel just as if I would like
see a regiment of men march through
and march these traitors right to the front
and keep them there. and I would like
to be one to help do it. We feel as though
it was necessary to have the help of the
whole North to a man. But our trust is in
a higher power than we can leave it in
his hands and trust it will all come out
right before long. There is scarcely a day
but what I wish I was with you to have
a good time. I am afraid I shant be able
to do much in that line if I live to get
home but I must close write soon love to all
remember me at the throne of grace. Good by
from your most Aff. Bro. Wm H. Waterhouse.

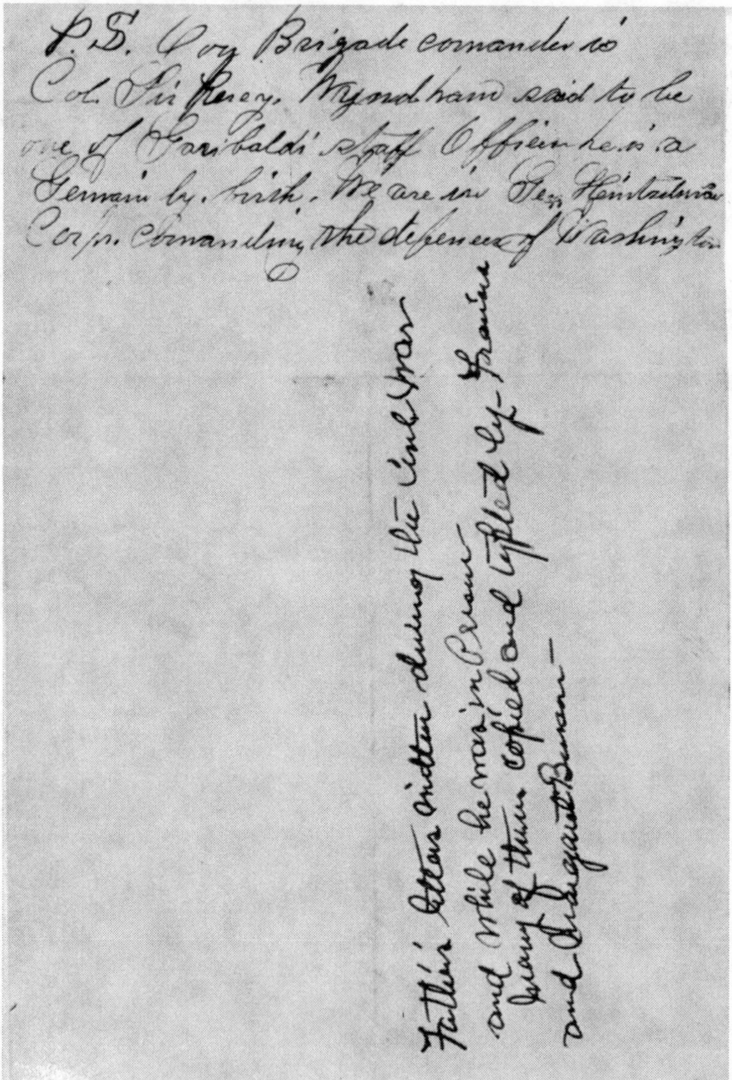

P.S. Our Brigade commander is Col. Sir Percy Wyndham said to be one of Garibaldi's Staff Officers he is a German by birth. We are in Gen. Heintzelman's Corps. Commanding the defences of Washington

Father's letters written during the Civil War and while he was in Prison many of them copied and typed by Frances and Margaret Bowen—

The note on this letter was put there by Stella when at one time she had safely put these letters into the attic of the home in Maitland, like a good librarian.

11

HEADQUARTERS 5th N.Y. VOLUNTARY CAVALRY CAMP AT FAIRFAX, VIRGINIA MID MARCH-MAY, 1863

During this spring, we spent a lot of time at our new encampment, which topped a hill above Fairfax; thus not as low and much healthier. When there, we guarded the stores, the city of Washington and surrounding areas and heard happy news of Union victories or sad news of their retreats. At times, we were called into the main battles.

Our biggest enemy was Rebel Mosby, who conducted severe raids against our pickets and even entered our campsites and nearby villages.

He was a direct result of how the Confederacy sometimes used unorthodox ways of fighting. On April 21, 1862, the Confederate Congress sanctioned "partisan rangers", which consisted of local bands, native to an area and therefore completely knowledgeable with every hill, stream, path, etc. These 'rangers' staged blatant hit-and-run attacks, usually at night and became the organized Union armies' biggest embarrassment.

One of the most infamous of these leaders, John Singleton Mosby, raised on rim of the Blue Ridge, graduated from University of Virginia, practiced law in southwest Virginia, had been the major scout for Stuart's cavalry through 1862. When Stuart left Fairfax County in 1863, Mosby and his nine men had been permitted to remain. Northern Virginia became known as 'Mosby's Confederacy.' Over the next few years, with less than fifty men at times, he carried out numerous raids, stealing guns, ammunition, mules and horses; destroyed railroads; robbed Union paymasters; fought and captured Union pickets.

Always having a bounty on his head and with fewer than 250 men, he immobilized 30,000 Union troops keeping them from active duty. When the Union army was encamped in a tight circle around Washington, they put remote picket points out to ward off the enemy and intercept any enemy pickets. It was these posts Mosby's men almost completely wiped out by waiting until the middle of the night, sneaking in and with revolvers taking the Union soldiers prisoners along with stealing all their mules, horses and supplies. They were allowed to keep any of their Union spoils from their many daily raids, thus these bands became very popular

March 22, 1863 Letter to Sister Cinty:

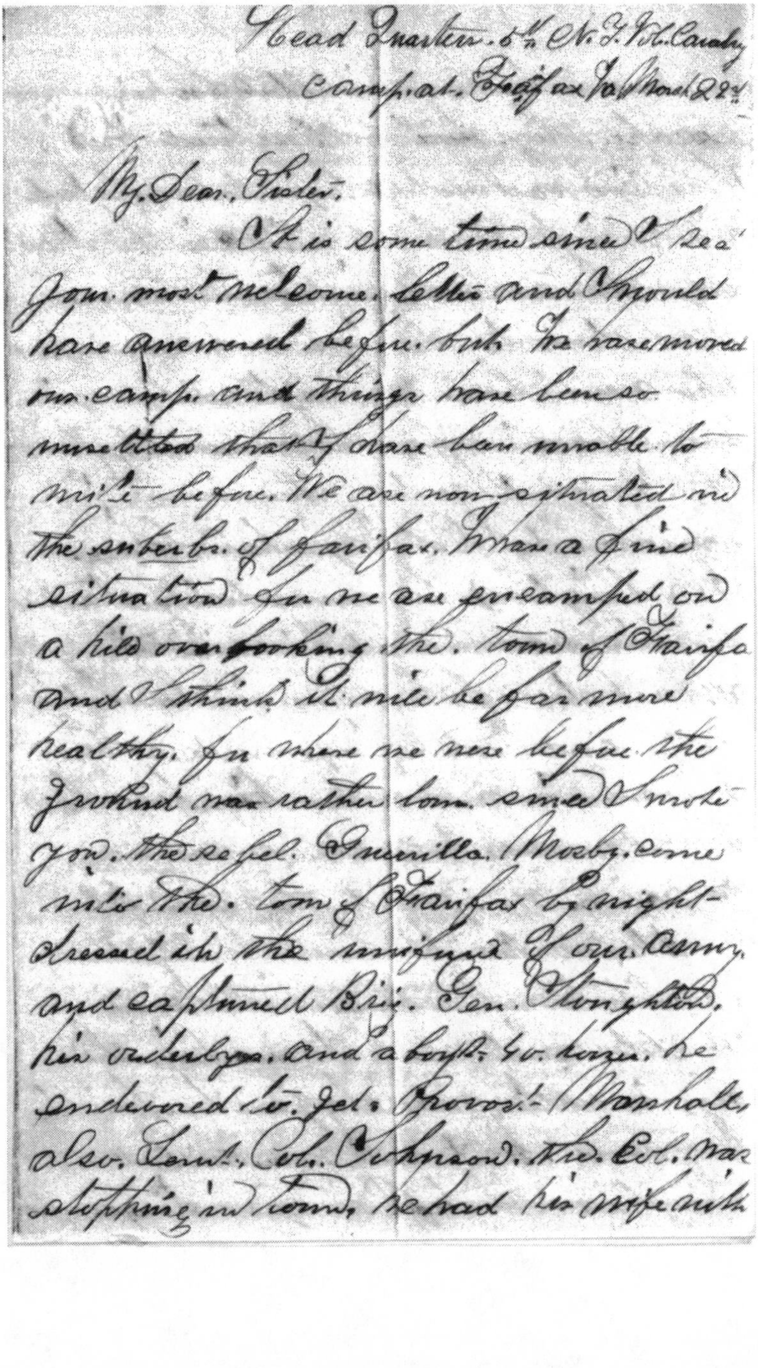

Head Quarter. 5th N.Y. Vol. Cavalry
Camp at Fairfax Va March 22nd

My Dear Sister
It is some time since I rec'd
your most welcome letter and I would
have answered before but we have moved
our camp and things have been so
unsettled that I have been unable to
write before. We are now situated in
the suburbs of Fairfax. It is a fine
situation for we are encamped on
a hill overlooking the town of Fairfax
and I think it will be far more
healthy for where we were before the
ground was rather low. since I wrote
you the rebel Guerilla Mosby came
into the town of Fairfax by night
dressed in the uniform of our army
and captured Brig. Gen. Stoughton
his orderlys and about 40 horses he
endeavored to get Provost Marshall
also Lieut. Col. Johnson the Col. was
stopping in town he had his wife with

him and tells her he is indebted for his
escape. they ~~were~~ had both retired but
Whelire had not yet partaken of sleep.
and his wife hearing a noise in the street
say. there are rebels in town. The Col.
went down to the door. and asked them
who went there. they replied by saying
we are looking for the commander of
the Brigade he told them he was in
command. (Col. Wayanhand being
Washington) they immediately started
for him. and he made his exit through
a back door of the house. in the shortest
notice and took refuge under a barn.
they come in and asked ~~him~~ her where
the Col was she told him. he had gone
to alarm the guard. they then told
her they wanted his arms. she told them
he had taken them ~~them~~ with him.
they told her it was a damn lie, the
only insulting word they gave her. finding
they could not do any more without
being taken. they left. it was a disgraceful

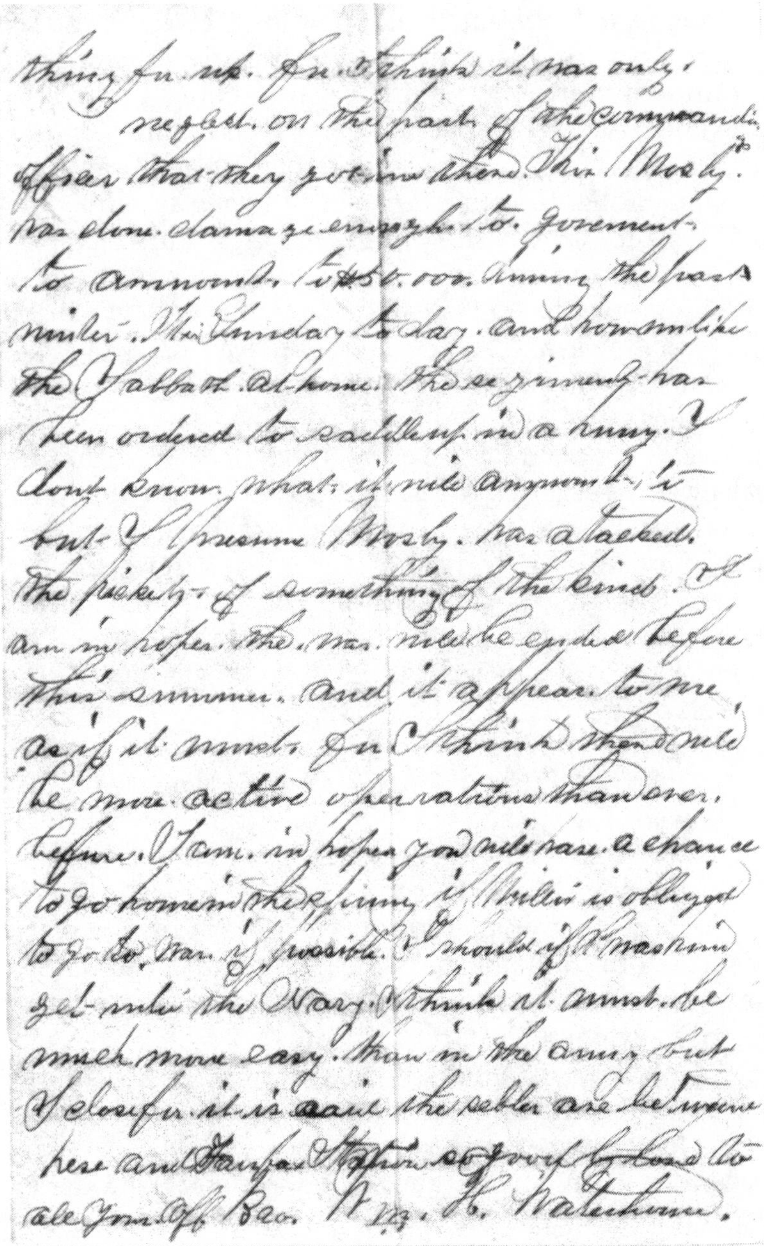

thing for us. I think it was only
neglect on the part of the commanding
officer that they got in there. This Mosby
has done damage enough to government
to amount to $50.000 during the past
winter. This Sunday today and how unlike
the Sabbath at home. The regiment has
been ordered to saddle up in a hurry. I
dont know what it will amount to
but I presume Mosby has attacked
the pickets or something of the kind. I
am in hopes the war will be ended before
this summer. And it appear to me
as if it must. I think there will
be more active operations than ever
before. I am in hopes you will have a chance
to go home in the spring if Walter is obliged
to go to war if possible. I should if I was him
get into the Navy. I think it must be
much more easy than in the army but
I close for it is said the rebles are between
here and Fairfax Station so good by love to
all from Your Bro. Wm. H. Waterman.

Charles A. Mills, author of *The Hidden History of Northern Virginia,* relates a tale of Mosby's most daring exploit: General Edwin Stoughton, son of prominent Vermont politician, was being named a brigadier general before his twenty-fifth birthday. Being a vain man with a weakness for rich living and beautiful women, Stoughton entertained a glittering assembly in his comfortable two-story house in Fairfax on a March, 1863, evening. Brother officers and visitors to nearby Washington enjoyed the evening dancing and drinking the ever-flowing champagne, making all oblivious to war and thinking the nearest rebels were at least twenty-five miles away.

At 2:00 am, the sentry thought it was Union cavalry men entering the town until he was looking into a big Colt six shooter. The aide was awakened to shouts that they were delivering a dispatch to the general. When he opened the door, Mosby, complete with plume in his hat, overwhelmed him, went upstairs, found the general in a drunken sleep, lifted the general's nightshirt and slapped him on the backside.

General: "What is this? Do you know who I am?"

Mosby: "I reckon I do, General. Did you ever hear of Mosby?"

General: "Yes, have you caught him?"

Mosby: "No, but I caught you."

Mosby's raiders rode out of Fairfax Court House with General Stoughton, two captains, thirty privates and fifty-eight horses and took all to Culpepper to turn them into General Stuart as prisoners.

Mosby continued his raids until very end of war when he disbanded his men, so that they could never officially surrender to Federal forces. In later years he became a distinguished railway lawyer and lived to be eighty-three years old.

~ ~ ~ ~ ~ ~

Winter wore away and spring opened new thoughts of the attack that Hooker had been planning. First Hooker ordered Stoneman to take all the cavalry except a single brigade and cross below Lee's forces to attack him and draw the attention there.

Hooker commanded, "Harass the enemy day and night, on the march and in the camp unceasingly. If you can not cut off from his column large slices, do not fail to take small ones. Let your watchword be 'Fight'! and let all your orders be 'Fight'! Keep yourself informed of your enemy's whereabouts and attack him wherever you find him. Take the initiative in the forward movement of this grand army; bear in mind that celerity, audacity and resolution are everything in war."

This would have cut Lee's communication with Richmond via Fredericksburg. It did not work out, because after two days riding to the crossing point, one division reached the other side before an intense storm swelled the river causing those already across to have to swim back to keep from being stranded. The storm continued and left the river impassable. It was March 23 at Little River Turnpike that we lost forty-two of our precious men.

After this page a transposition of entire letter April 4, 1863 follows

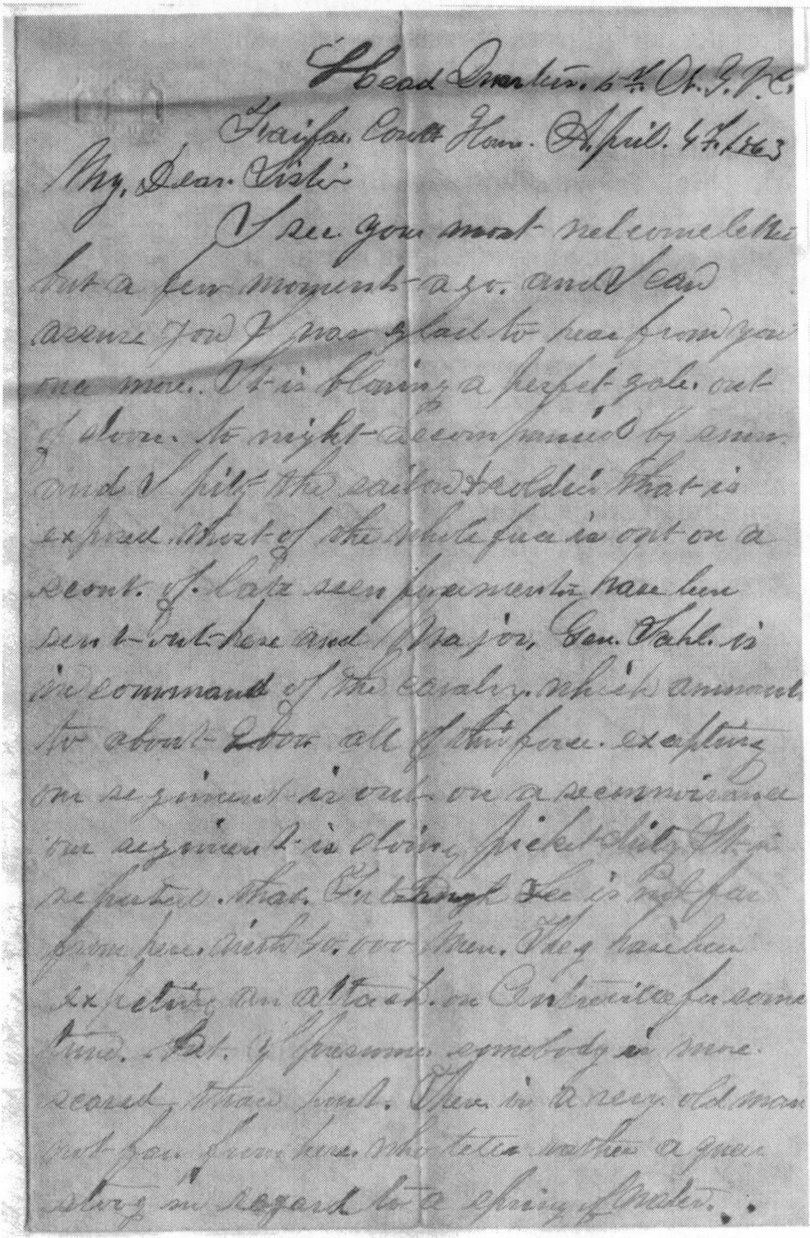
Head Quarters. 6th. O. V. C.
Fairfax. Court House. April. 4th. 1863
My. Dear. Sister
I rec. your most welcome letter but a few moments ago. and I can assure you I was glad to hear from you once more. It is blowing a perfect gale out of doors. to night accompanied by snow and I pity the sailor & soldier that is exposed. Most of the whole force is out on a scout. I have seen regiments have been sent out here and Major. Gen. Stahl. is in command of the cavalry. which amounts to about 2000 all of this force. excepting one regiment is out on a reconnoisance one regiment is doing picket duty. It is reported that Gen. ~~Longstreet~~ Lee is not far from here with 60.000 men. They have been expecting an attack on Centreville for some time. But I presume somebody is more scared than hurt. There is a very old man not far from here who tells rather a queer story in regard to a spring of water.

Transposition of entire April 4th (?) letter to Sister Cinty follows this page:
(Embossed in corner with bldg and O & Hq)

Head Quarters, 5th N.Y. V.C.
Fairfax Court House, April 4th, 1863
My Dear Sister

I rec your most welcome letter but a few moments go, and I can assure you I was glad to hear from once more. It is blowing a perfect gale, out of doors, tonight accompanied by snow and I pity the sailor & soldier that is exposed. most of the whole force is out on a scout of late reenforcements have been sent out here and Major Gen. Sahl is in command of the cavalry. which amounts to about 9000 all of this force excepting our regiment is out on a reconnoisance our regiment is doing picket duty It is reported that Grl Lee is not far from here with 40,000 men. They have been expecting an attack on Centreville for some time but I presume somebody is more scared than hurt. There is a very old man not far from here who tells rather a queer story in regard to a spring of water. he says just before the revolutionary war broke out, this all at once ceased to flow. 3 months before the war ended it commenced flowing again and just before the rebellion broke out, it stoped again. but a month or two ago, all at once it commenced to flow again and the old man says there will surely be peace by the 1st Of May. The old fellow reminded me of Uncl. Elam Conklin. Just before the war broke out, he would get up in Meeting and begin to tell there was going to be war for he had seen the signs in the Heavens & signs in the earth and sure enough the old fellows predictions proved true, but I think if we have peace by the 1st of May they will have to hurry up some. if we whip them in the Southwest, I think there might be a possibility of peace. I fear Rosecrans will be over powered if he has the men, though I dont think he will allow himself to be whiped by any inferior force. I think that is the only place very badly very badly deficient Vicksburg I dont doubt but what will eventually fall into our hands very much, as Fort Donaldson did last spring. They may have to little more fighting if the weather comes of(f) a little more favorable before long. the Army of the Potomac will make a move somewhere. I am in hopes before the coming summer closes this war will be at an end. I am sorry Charles has took into his to go in to the fish business over to New London. As good a carpenter he is I should he would do better to stick to his trade. I am afraid things wont run very well in the choir now if Dan Case takes the lead. I am sorry you did not send me a picture of Louie dont you think I deserve one. Ma I guess will send me hers. I have Horrace picture. I wish I could get Willis' also, but I must close for it is late so good night remember me at the Throne of grace that I may be kept in the strait and narrow path. love to all You aff Bro.

Wm. H. Waterhouse

Note: Major General Sahl should be Stahl.

April 19,1863 Letter to Sister Mela:

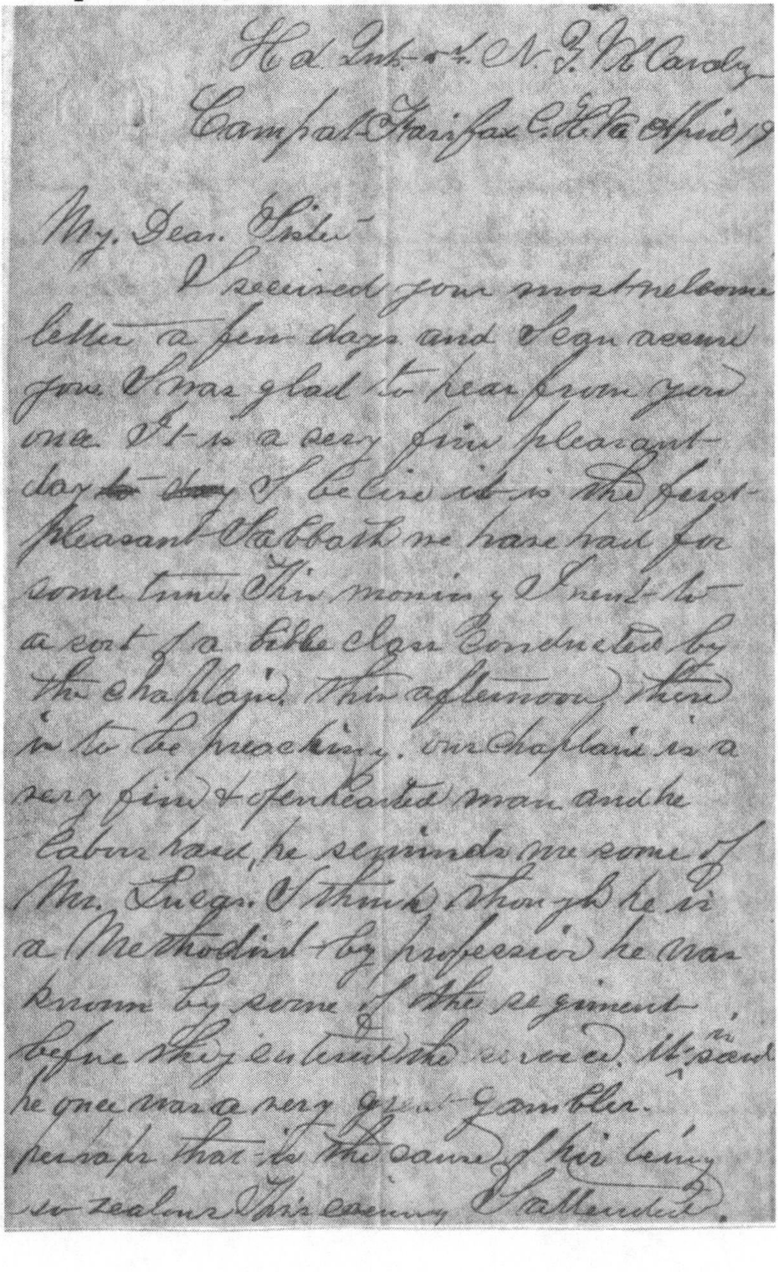

Hd. Qrs. 4th N.Y. V. Cavalry
Camp at Fairfax C.H. Va April 19

My. Dear. Sister
I received your most welcome letter a few days and I can assure you I was glad to hear from you once. It is a very fine pleasant day ~~to day~~ I believe it is the first pleasant Sabbath we have had for some time. This morning I went to a sort of a bible class conducted by the chaplain. This afternoon there is to be preaching. our chaplain is a very fine & openhearted man and he labors hard, he reminds me some of Mr. Lucas. I think though he is a Methodist by profession he was known by some of the regiment before they entered the service. It is said he once was a very great gambler. perhaps that is the cause of his being so zealous. This evening I attended.

the prayer meeting there was quite
a good number there I should
think about. So we had a very pleasant
season. as we were singing the familiar
Hymn say Brother will you meet...
The Chaplain remarked that it
often reminded him of acquaintances
he had formed and probably he would
never meet these persons on earth. and
so it was with all of us. but there
would be a time when we would meet
them in another world. and often
do we use the expression when writing
to our friends if we should never
meet here on earth may we be so happy
as to meet in heaven It is a
sweet thought and one that should
afford us much happiness it may
be I have my dear friends for the
last time but I have a hope of
meeting them in heaven. Mother
has sent me one of her photographs
they resembled her but dont look

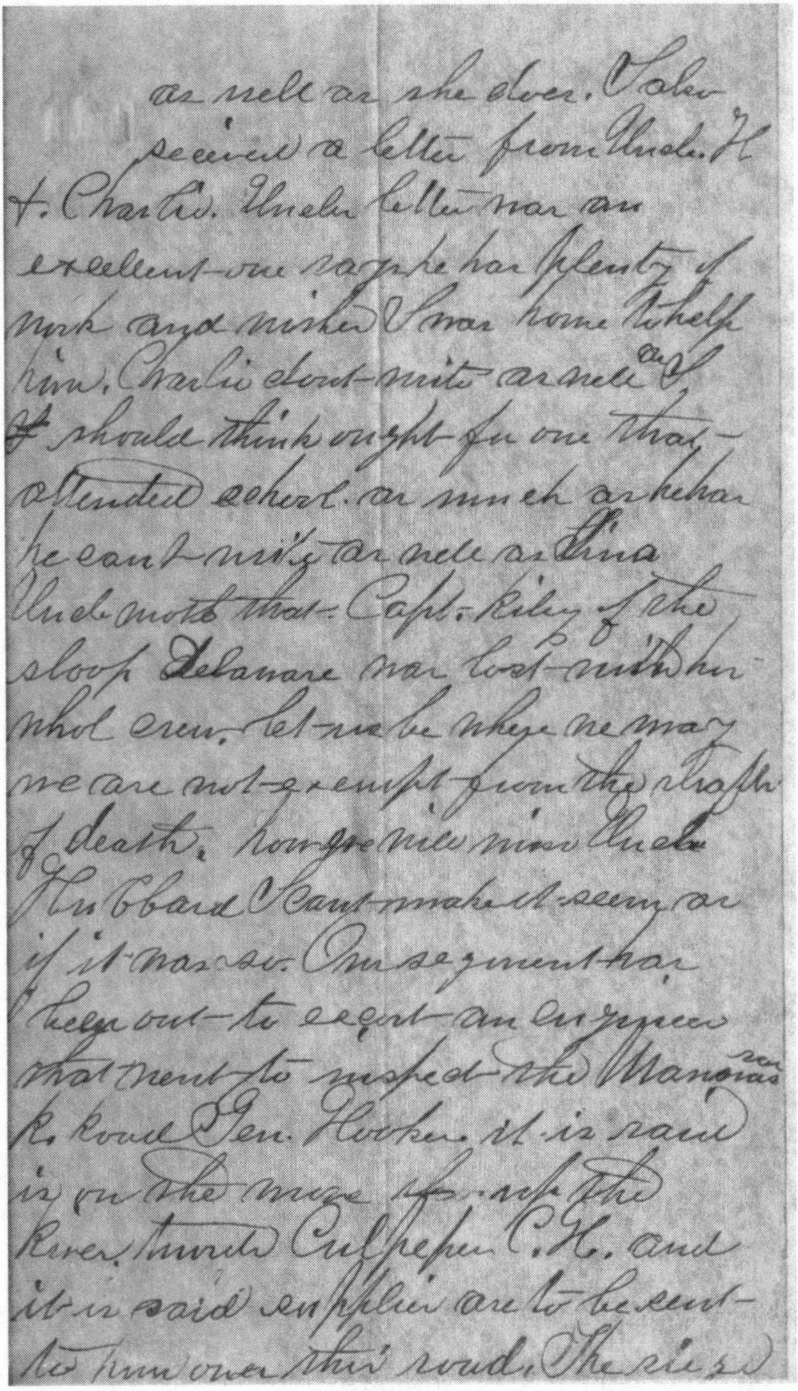
as well as she does. I also
received a letter from Uncle H
& Charlie. Uncles letter was an
excellent one says he has plenty of
work and wished I was home to help
him. Charlie dont write as well as I
should think ought for one that
attended school as much as he has
he cant write as well as Lina
Uncle wrote that Capt. Riley of the
sloop Delaware was lost with her
whol crew. let us be where we may
we are not exempt from the shafts
of death. how we will miss Uncle
Hubbard I cant make it seem as
if it was so. Our regiment has
been out to escort an engineer
that went to inspect the Manassas
R. Road Gen. Hooker it is said
is on the move up - up the
River toward Culpeper C.H. and
it is said supplies are to be sent
to him over this road. The [illegible]

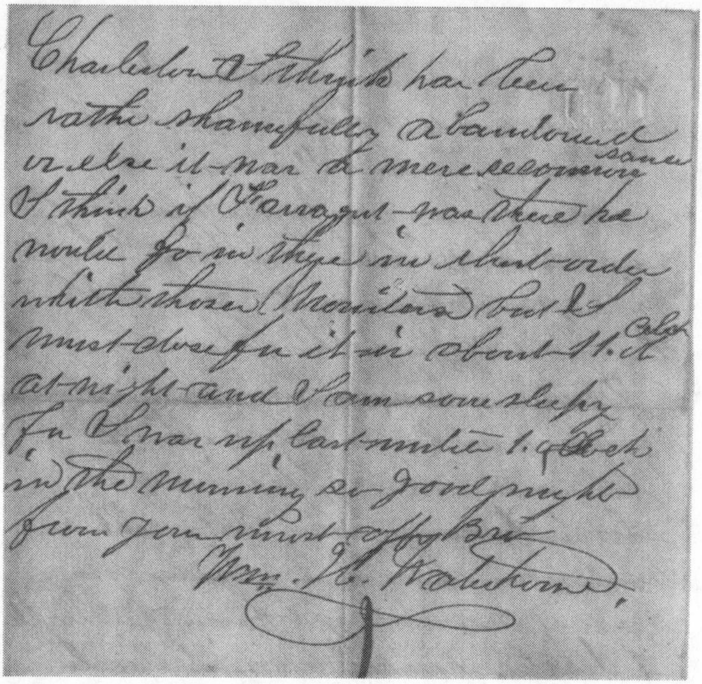

Charleston S.C. I think has been
rather shamefully abandoned
or else it was a mere reconnoissance
I think if Farragut was there he
would go in there in short order
with those Monitors but I
must close for it is about 11 O'clock
at night and I am some sleepy
for I was up last night 1 o'clock
in the morning so good night
from your most aff Bro
Wm. H. Waterhouse

I can honestly tell you that without my faith in God and the religion taught to me through my family and my church in Greenport, I could not have made it through my years of the fighting and the suffering I witnessed in the devastating war of the Rebellion. Prayer was my salvation. Hope was my strength. All these continued my life through, of which I am thankful.

~ ~ ~ ~

After a fortnight of better weather, Hooker materialized his master plan. It was April 26 when this order was given. The battles that followed for the next two days happened at Chancellorsville and its Wilderness, Groveton and Manassas. It is known as the 'Second Bull Run Battle' and second defeat at Bull Run for the Union. They lost General Taylor. Ewell and Taliaferro were severely wounded.

The Union's main turning column was to cross the Rappahannock on the 27th at Kelly's Ford, twenty-seven miles north of Fredericksburg, then cross and move down the southern side of the Rapidan. To move quickly, each man had a light pack with eight days rations. Each corps had a single battery, six ambulances and small ammunition on a mule. Another division was to follow behind, but halt at United States Ford for reinforcement later. The third regiment was to cross the Rappahannock below Fredericksburg and make a distracting demonstration. All of this worked in precision and the three reached their meeting point of Chancellorsville on April 30. The opponent never suspected, until the 28th, when messages from scouts told of the imposing force near the Wilderness.

On the 28th, Hooker issued premature bulletins of success. They had caught the rebels by surprise, but still did not realize the determination and cunning of both Jackson and Lee. Hooker had planned well, but made the deadly decision not to pursue the offense at Chancellorsville but to retreat to a safe defensive place, the Wilderness, which led to the massacre that followed. Had he marched one hour more, they would have been in open territory. Instead they were cooped up as if on an island. The Confederates were able to gather all their scattered forces together by the April 30 and were entrenched, set for the type battle they knew best.

Hooker started moving his force out on the three roads. As each one moved five miles out, they ran into the Confederates fire. The battles turned many times with enormous loss of lives. By the afternoon, Hooker had ordered all his generals to fall back to the position from where they had set out. Every general was against it, but followed orders, throwing themselves now in the defensive. Hooker's reasoning described the snarled Wilderness and its dangers.

Timing mistakes again made by the Union caused their failure and retreat. The Federal loss in Chancellorsville was more than 17,000 of whom 5000 were unwounded prisoners. They also lost 13 guns, 20,000 muskets and considerable ammunition. The Confederates lost 13,000 for whom 1581 killed, 8700 wounded and about 3000 prisoners. The biggest loss was the life of 'Stonewall' Jackson, wounded on May 2 and died May 10. "The Confederates might better have lost a battle than this one man," rightly said Harper History of the Great Rebellion. It was Jackson's both conception and execution that saved Lee from destruction at Chancellorsville in 1863 and many previous battles.

May 5,1863 Letter to Mother:

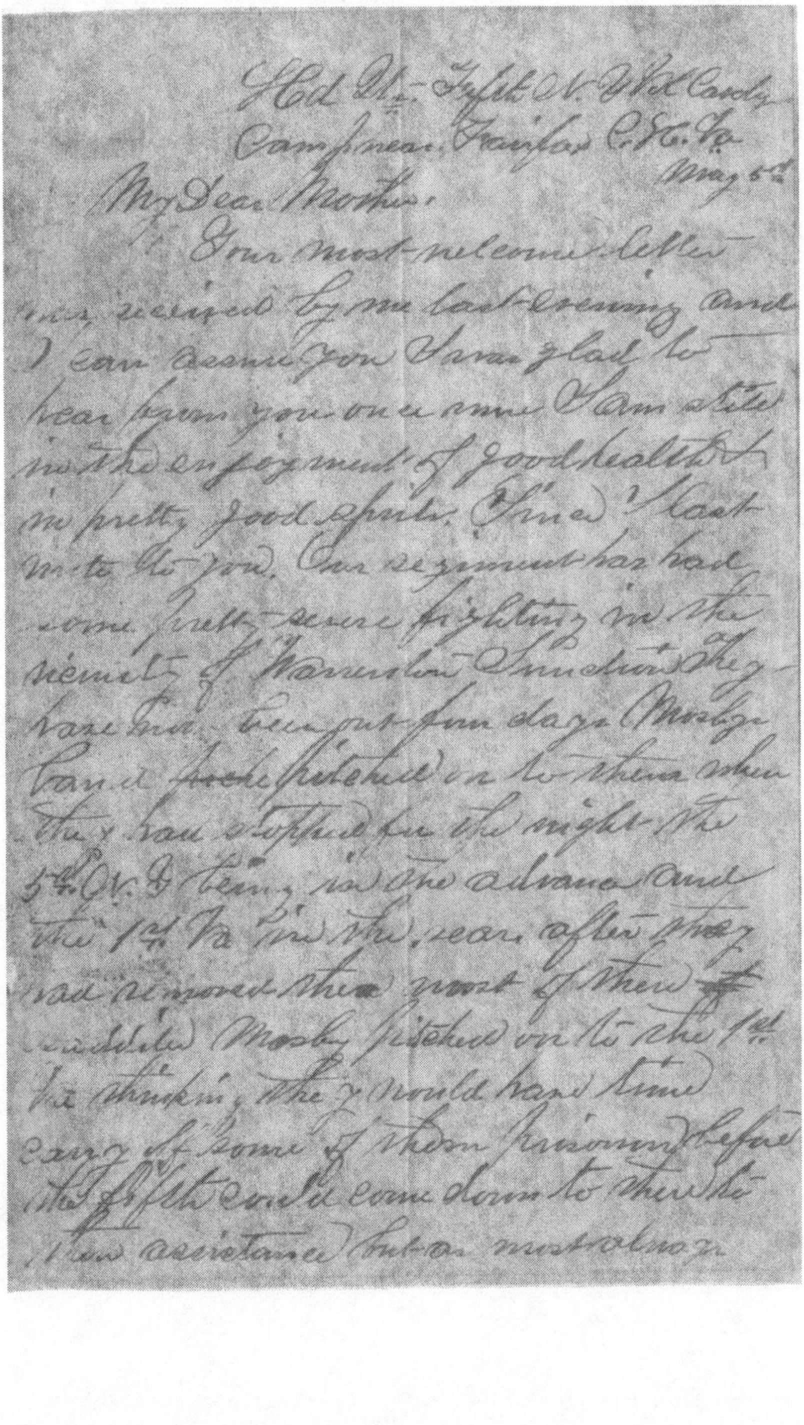

Hd Qrs. Fifth N. York Cavly
Camp near Fairfax C. H. Va.
May 5th

My Dear Mother.

Your most welcome letter
was received by me last evening and
I can assure you I was glad to
hear from you once more I am still
in the enjoyment of good health &
in pretty good spirits. Since I last
wrote to you Our regiment has had
some pretty severe fighting in the
vicinity of Warrenton Junction they
have been out four days Mosby's
band pitched on to them when
they had stopped for the night the
5th N.Y. being in the advance and
the 1st Va in the rear after they
had removed their most of their
saddles Mosby pitched on to the 1st
Va thinking they would have time
carry off some of them prisoners before
the Fifth could come down to their
assistance but in most always

in the road the old Fifth was on time
and it said they come down with
one of those unearthly yells they always
give and charged on Mosby like fury
our men emptied 11 saddles at the
first charge which sent them all
a flying we had 2 Lieuts wounded
lightly and one Capt (and the best
officer in the regiment) he command our
squadron he was wounded in the head
twice & once in the leg it is feared his
wounds are mortal, I ache to be with
them but I have to stay by the stuff
I should not be surprised though if
the camp moved out there. The news we
get from Gen. Hookers army is quite
cheering. it said that he has took
Fredricksburg & 9000 prisoners & dead
enough to fill the rifle pits the
news come in an extra of a Washington
paper. I presume is exaggerated some
I am in hopes though it is all true
we are having very warm weather

now and the trees begin
to show sign of life. I presume
it will become quite unhealthy as the
warm season advances there are so many
dead animals about here. I should like
much to be at home to get of the
boat into the grapes & take a sail
on two. there is plenty of nice shad
in the sutlers shops but they are most
to stale for me to eat. I think it would
be a good idea to put my money in
the if it is worth while to bother with
it. I will send $4.00 in this letter
use what ever you want for yourself
but I must close for I have got to go
and get some rations. Our Chaplain
has got up a class to study short-hand
writeing. I see a letter from Arald he
is down to Suffolk Va. I expect he
is seen enough of soldiering now my love
to all so good by from your loving
Aff son Wm. H. Waterhouse.
I wish you would send me a few P. O. Stamps

A dispatch from newspaper:

"Battle at Warrenton Junction.
EIGHTY MEN FIGHT DESPERATELY WITH THREE HUNDRED. THE FIFTH NEW YORK COME TO THEIR RESGUE. THE REBELS DEFEATED AND ROUTED.
FAIRFAX, C. H., May 3, 1863.

A fight occurred at Warrenton Junction this morning between a portion of Stahl's cavalry, under Col. De Forrest, and Mosby's guerrillas. Mosby with about 300 men attacked the 1st Virginia cavalry about daylight. The Rebels succeeded in surrounding our men, about eighty in number, who fought desperately.

The 5th New York came to the rescue, and the Rebels were utterly routed and scattered in all directions. Major Hammond, with a portion of the 6th N. Y., followed in pursuit, chasing the enemy beyond Warrenton.

Our loss is one killed; five officers and fourteen wounded. Maj. Steele of the 1st Va. is mortally wounded.

The Rebel loss is heavy, the dead being left upon the field. We have taken twenty-three prisoners, fifteen of whom are wounded. Among the prisoners is Dick Moras, the notorious bushwhacker, badly wounded. Templeton, Mosby's spy, was killed. Moseby is reported wounded. The wounded and prisoners have been sent in from Warrenton Junction.

Our men fought gallantly and the Rebels acknowledge that they got hold of the wrong party that time."

12

PENNSYLVANIA, MARYLAND AND VIRGINIA
REST OF 1863

During the first six months of 1863, the tide of success sat fully in favor of the Confederacy. It appeared that nothing but a successful invasion of the North was left to secure a final triumph, recognized by all the great powers of Europe. The entire disposable strength of the Confederacy was placed with Lee. This was divided into three corps under Longstreet, A. P. Hill and Ewell, with the cavalry under Stuart.

June 1, 1863 Letter to Brother-in-Law Willis:

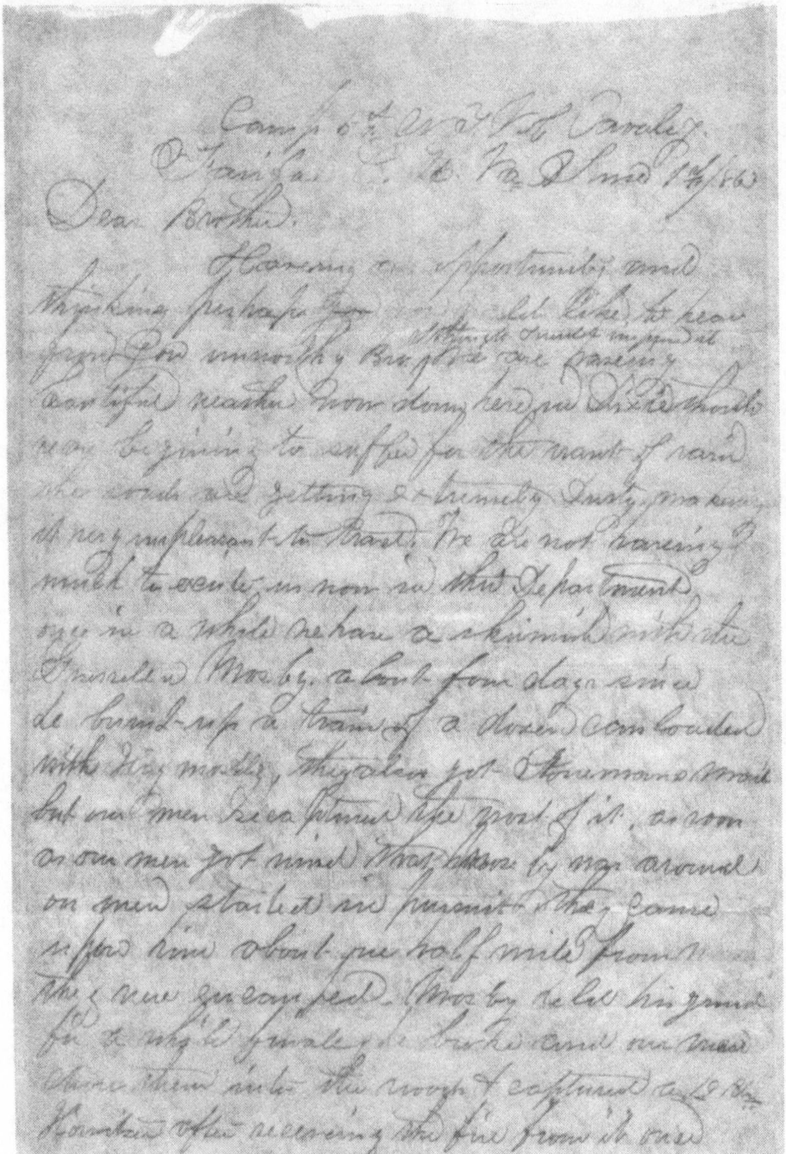

Camp 6th [illegible] Cavalry
Fairfax C. H. Va. June 1st/63
Dear Brother
Having an opportunity and
thinking perhaps you would like to hear
from your unworthy Bro. (although I must [illegible] it) we are having
beautiful weather now down here in Dixie though
now beginning to suffer for the want of rain
the roads are getting extremely dusty making
it very unpleasant to travel. We are not having
much to excite us now in this Department
once in a while we have a skirmish with the
Guerrilla Mosby. about four days since
he burnt up a train of a dozen cars loaded
with Hay mostly, they also got [illegible]
but our men recaptured the most of it, as soon
as our men got wind that Mosby was around
our men started in pursuit & they came
upon him about one half mile from where
they were encamped. Mosby rallied his guns
for a single [illegible] & broke and our men
drove them into the woods & captured a 12 lb
Howitzer after receiving the fire from it once

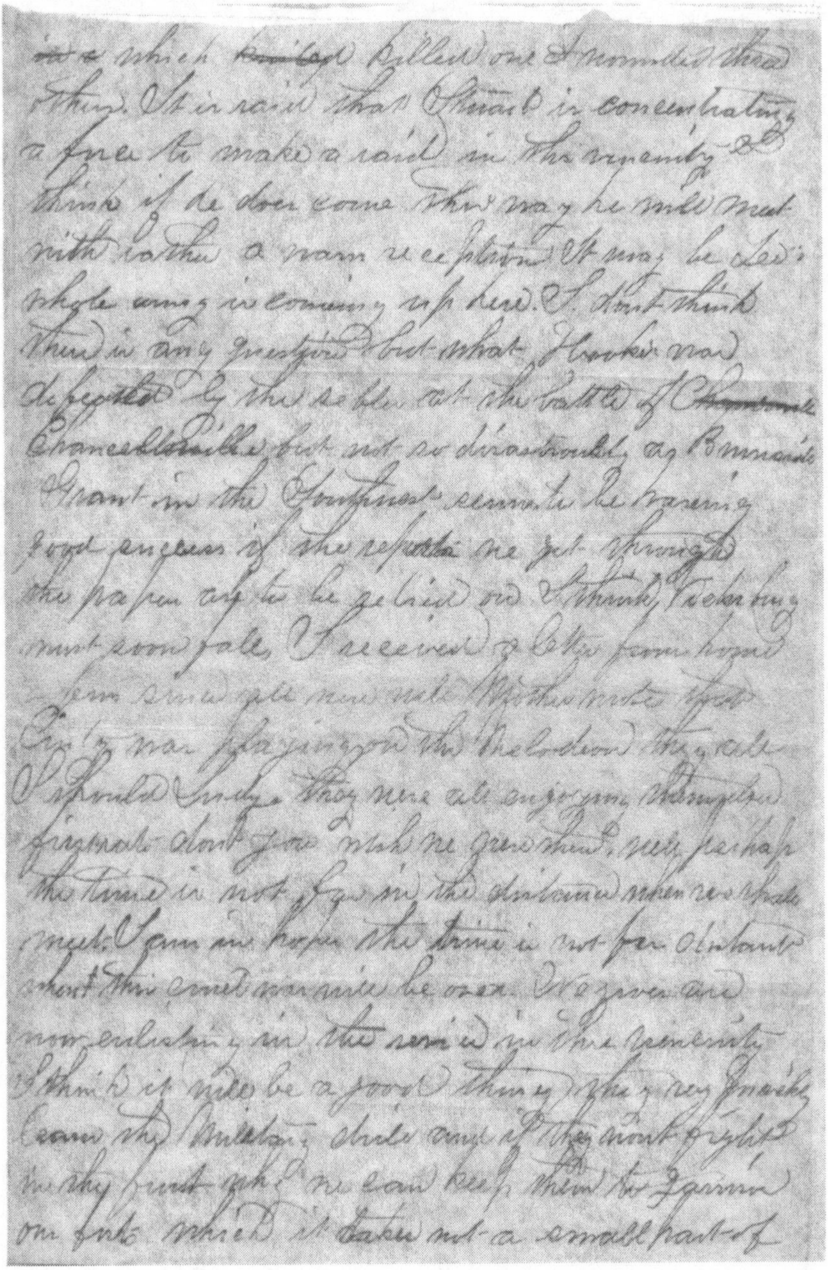
in a which ~~killed~~ killed one & wounded three others. It is said that Stuart is concentrating a force to make a raid in this vicinity I think if he does come this way he will meet with rather a warm reception. It may be Lee's whole army is coming up here. I don't think there is any question but what Hooker was defeated by the rebles at the battle of ~~Chancel~~ Chancellorsville but not so disastrously as Burnside. Grant in the Southwest seems to be having good success if the reports we get through the papers are to be believed and I think Vicksburg must soon fall. I received a letter from home a few days ago. Mother wrote that [illegible] was playing on the melodeon they all I should judge they were all enjoying themselves finely. don't you wish we were there. Well perhaps the time is not far in the distance when we shall meet. I am in hopes the time is not far distant when this cruel war will be over. Two years men now enlisting in the new regiments I think it will be a good thing if they only make [illegible] the Militia [illegible] if they won't fight in the field we can keep them to garrison our forts which it takes not a small part of

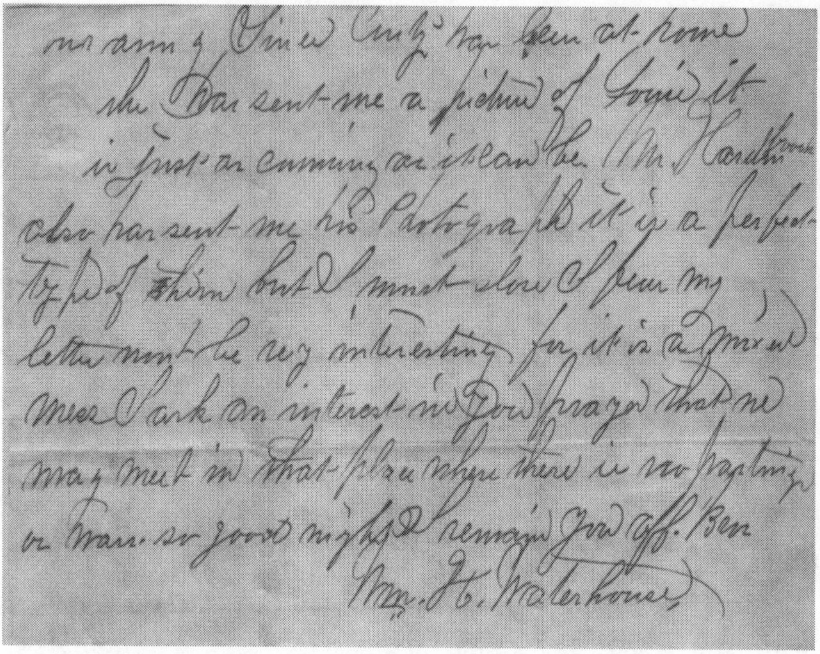
no army of Since Cutz has been at home
she has sent me a picture of Louie it
is just as cunning as it can be Mr Hawthorne
also has sent me his Photograph it is a perfect
type of them but I must close I fear my
letter wont be very interesting for it is a mixed
mess I ask an interest in your prayer that we
may meet in that place where there is no parting
or war. so good night I remain your Aff. Ben
Wm. H. Waterhouse

Lee decided to quickly fight the Army of the Potomac, not in North Virginia, but in Pennsylvania, pulling them away from Washington and supplies. Lee commenced his move in early June.

Two weeks before, the Confederate Stuart had moved his regiment into Culpepper. There were many skirmishes with the Union cavalry around the nearby Brandy Station, before Stuart routed Kilpatrick's division. Then Stuart moved north to join Lee's main force and Kilpatrick moved north to head the Union advancement.

Hooker heard of this northward march on June 12th and withdrew his army from opposite Fredericksburg, moving northward. Lee hoped Hooker would send an army to encounter Lee's movement, giving Lee the chance to attack Washington. But Hooker kept his main force there and waited. Lincoln wanted Hooker to attack, but Hooker held firm, sending out feelers of his cavalry, which came into frequent collision with Stuart's force. As Lee moved northward, his troops were spread out like a long thin worm, hoping to entice Hooker to leave Washington so the last force could double back to seize it, but Hooker mirrored this maneuver as both moved over the Potomac and Blue Ridge, Lee to west and Hooker to east.

General Hooker wanted to abandon Harper's Ferry and take in the 10,000 men there for the upcoming Pennsylvania battle against Lee's forces. Halleck, Lincoln's General-in-Chief and Hooker's ardent enemy, stepped in to refuse, causing Hooker to resign and now the Army of the Potomac again changed command. General Meade took control on June 27, 1863. Gettysburg was fought on June 30 – July 3.

Our Union cavalry went to join Kilpatrick. Each army sent out their cavalry pickets and were frequently in skirmishes, some formidable. We took a slight edge. Kilpatrick led successes at Brandy Station near Culpepper against Stuart's Cavalry and Stevensburg against Hampton's Legion; also we had a big scare at Buckland Mills against Stuart's Cavalry. Hagerstown, Maryland gave us our hardest fight and at Falling Water, Maryland, General Kilpatrick took us to victory over rebel Stuart. These were our heaviest war battles as we moved into Maryland and Pennsylvania toward Gettysburg. The Hannover battle devastated us losing over half our camp. Gettysburg lost us our Brigadier General Farnsworth on July 3rd after we fought with him in that horrific battle.

This is the report made in the "History of the 5th Cavalry of New York." It tells it better than I can: "The Fifth Cavalry, commanded by Col. John Hammond, of Crown Point, N. Y., had already signalized itself under its intrepid leader, General (then Major) Hammond, in the sanguinary struggles of the Army of the Potomac, with its desperate foe, the army of General Lee.

On the 30th of June, 1863, at Hanover, Pa., fourteen miles from Gettysburg, this regiment was the first to exchange shots and cross sabers on free soil with the daring and desperate invaders who fought under the justly celebrated leader of the Confederacy, Gen. J. E. B. Stuart.

That accurate military critic, the Comte de Paris, himself a participant in most of our great battles of the War of the Rebellion, speaks in his work upon our Civil War of this engagement as " the bloody battle of Hanover." The Fifth New York Cavalry, under Colonel Hammond, bore the brunt of the attack, and, after repelling the charge, charged the foe in turn and gloriously drove him from the field. The sad and long list of casualties in killed and wounded attest the desperate character of that conflict.

This was the real beginning of the famous battle of Gettysburg, fought July 1, 2, and 3, 1863. Then this command, with the brigade and division to which it was attached, under Kilpatrick and the lamented Farnsworth, hung upon and harassed the enemy in the vicinity of Gettysburg until, in the early morning of July 3d, the regiment took a position on our extreme left, the Fifth supporting Elder's U. S. Battery.

Lieutenant Elder was a glorious type of the born soldier, here commanding a battery of the regular army, who only wanted to know "if John Hammond, and his famous New York troopers were with him," to brave the most daring deeds. Here at the base of Big Round Top, just before Pickett made his famous charge, this cavalry went over ground today deemed impassable for horse, gallantly, desperately, charged the enemy's infantry and in a large degree diverted Lee's forces, so that the mad, grand, historic charge of Pickett proved a brilliant but disastrous failure, and "the blood-flecked tidal wave of fratricidal war" here receded and so continued, until it settled into the blessed calm of national peace."

With both sides marching side by side, each leader was looking for the perfect spot to have this ensuing battle of all times. Lee had planned to arrive first and set up for a battle he wanted. The choice was neither leader, but Alfred Pleasonton, now commanding our cavalry corps, who studied the topography of the land and chose the Gettysburg area. He sent Buford to encamp near there on June 30, waiting for Reynolds to join him.

Lee was moving his force slowly up from Chambersburg and Carlisle, not realizing that any Union resistance was waiting. His cavalry scout Stuart was still far away and not able to give him the report he needed. That was the first of many crucial military actions during the next three days to make this devastating battle one of history's most lethal.

Although mistakes were made on both sides, the Union corps claimed the victory sending Lee in retreat back to Virginia. One big mistake was allowing this to happen. Meade had misjudged his opponent and by not attacking the retreating rebels at Williamsport on the Potomac where they seemed to be stuck due to a storm's high water knocking out a bridge, he waited until the next day. When dawn broke on July 8, the rebel army was gone, having created a new bridge and crossed the river during the night back into Virginia.

It was on July 6, our regiment took our greatest loss of ninety-one at Hagerstown trying to stop Lee's retreat. We skirmished with them five more days of July as they moved south toward Richmond.

In a year and a week, from beginning of Seven Days before Richmond to the close of Gettysburg, the two Armies of the Civil War had fought in six desperate struggles, each lasting for days – the Confederates winning four and the Union winning two. There had been many minor engagements. Each had lost at least 110,000. This did not count the scores of thousands dying from diseases in camps and long marches. Gettysburg's three days alone counted for almost 59,000 killed or wounded.

Return to Virginia brought us quiet time before being put on the line of the Rappahannock for picket duty in the Army of the Potomac.

This dispatch to the Mirror newspaper best describes the 5th New York's day by day part of the Gettysburg Battle*:*

"FROM THE 5TH N. Y. CAVALRY. UPPERVILLE, VA., July 22d, 1863.
EDITOR MIRROR:—Six long weeks have passed since I presented my last letter to the Mirror; weeks frought with interest to our beloved country. Once more success has crowned our efforts. Truly they have been weeks of toil and hardship to the soldier, but he has been compensated for all this by the success of our arms. The fall of Vicksburg and Port Hudson, and the defeat of Lee's army cheers us on; and we cherish the hope of soon seeing our Union restored to the foremost position among the nations of the earth.

I will endeavor to give you a brief account of the part performed by our Cavalry division the past four weeks. We broke camp at Fairfax Court House, Sunday, June 21st, and made a reconnaissance to Warrenton. Here Comp. F with two companies from the 1st Virginia and 1st Vermont were sent down to the fords on the Rappahannock. We got back to Fairfax about 3 P. M. on the 24th just in time to hear Boots and Saddles sounding and in a short time the whole Division was on its way to the Potomac,—excepting our three corps which were allowed to pass another night in the old camp. At daybreak we moved out and at 4 P. M. crossed at the ford near Edward's Ferry, and that night camped near Poolesville, Md.—We guarded the wagon train from that place to Frederick City where we joined the division.

Moving towards Hanover, Penn., we passed

through several towns where we were warmly greeted by the loyal people,—especially the ladies, who waved the starry flags and sang patriotic songs besides distributing refreshments through the ranks. We found it quite different to the treatment we receive from the fair sex in Virginia.

At Hanover, the whole town turned out to welcome us. It was about 9 o'clock A. M. when we entered the place. Our brigade was drawn up in column of fours in the main street, and we were enjoying ourselves finely, when the report of a cannon and the bursting of a shell in our rear caused a great commotion. The rebels had attacked our rear. It was so unexpected as to almost create a panic. But our regiment, after forming line in an open lot, charged through the town driving the rebels back to their battery, capturing a lt. Col. and fifty other prisoners, with the battle flag of the 2nd North Carolina Cavalry.

Our loss was twelve killed and about forty wounded. Capt. Eldridge of the 4th regular Artillery soon got his four pieces into operation and chose our regiment to support, which we did till the rebels withdrew leaving many of their dead on the field.—A detachment from our regiment under Major Hammond followed them four miles, skirmishing with their rear guard. Next day (the 1st of July) we reconnoitered to within twenty miles of Harrisburg.

On the 2d we marched towards Gettysburg, where heavy cannonading was heard, and we could see the smoke of battle. Our division was ordered to the right wing of the army, and just at sundown encountered the enemy's cavalry, their battery opening on our advance. The 18th Penn. Cavalry made a charge driving the rebels out of Huntertown.
Our battery took position on an eminence, and did excellent work dismounting one of the guns in the rebel battery. Our advance was called in, and the 6th Mich. cavalry, armed with the Spencer Rifle, (seven-shooters) were posted so as to command the ground in front. Soon, as was expected the rebel cavalry came up on a

charge, but being met with a shower of canister shot and rifle balls, they went back faster than they came. Darkness now settled down upon us and thus ended the fight for that day.

During the night we moved along our lines and next morning found ourselves on the extreme left flank of our line of battle. At daylight the ball opened all along the lines. At 10 o'clock Capt. Eldridge had his guns at work. The rebels replied throwing shell into our ranks with great accuracy of range. Our regiment seemed to be favored with more than their proper share of bursting shells. Several exploded in our ranks; three horses were killed, but only two men were struck, one being killed instantly. We were obliged to change our position to get out of range.

About 5 P. M. a charge was ordered, and Gen. Farnsworth led the 1st Virginia cavalry; but on account of the nature of the ground it resulted disastrously. The column was repulsed by the storm of bullets and iron hail, but a squadron of the 1st Vermont was more successful in charging on the right, and brought in about thirty prisoners—all infantry of Longstreet's Corps. We found out what we were contending with. Fearing that Gen. Kilpatrick would turn his right, Lee had sent up a division of Infantry to support his cavalry force. By thus harassing his flanks we drew forces from the center and did not allow him to concentrate all his strength on one point, as is the favorite plan in his tactics.

We slept near the battle field, and next morning, the 4th of July, we drew three days rations, and started on a raid to intercept a wagon train. The whole of us felt in excellent spirits when we heard what had been done the day previous, and that Lee's army was in full retreat to towards the Potomac. Even a heavy thunder shower that came up soon after we got on the road did not dampen the ardor of any in the division. We marched steadily all day, passing through Emmetsburg, Md., then we took a road leading through a Gap in the Blue Ridge. It was in this pass Gen. Kilpatrick proposed to celebrate Anniversary of our Independence.

Our advance had a slight skirmish with a body of cavalry but drove them out of Gap, and dark came up with the train. There was another skirmish in which the artillery participated, but escort in charge of the train made slight resistance, scattering in all directions through the woods. Our cavalry charged down the road for miles halting the teams whilst dismounted men skirmished in the woods on either side. At daybreak we ascertained that 200 wagons, of all descriptions, with 1,870 prisoners, two pieces of cannon, caissons, &c., were the fruit of our night's work.

Next day we rested at Smithsburg, where we were attacked, or at least shelled, by a rebel battery. But our guns soon silenced theirs, and before sundown we took up our line of march for Boonsboro, Md. Marched nearly all night. On Monday the 6th of July, moved on to Hagerstown, where we found quite a force of the enemy. Their battery opened on us on entering the town, but did no damage. Our artillery soon replied, and the Carbineer were dismounted to skirmish with the rebel Sharpshooters. They were infantry armed with Minnie rifles and it seemed impossible to dislodge them or drive them from the town. The 18th Penn. cavalry charged through the town and took several prisoners from their line of skirmishers. They had, on first entering the town, captured Col. Davis who was commanding a brigade of cavalry, and was opposed to our division in the fight at Huntertown, night of the 1st of July. He acknowledged they were badly handled at that point.

We held one side of the town till nearly sundown, when Gen, K. withdrew the greater portion of his command to reinforce Buford who had engaged Ibadan's forces and was shelling a large train of wagons near Williamsport. Our brigade with two pieces of artillery were left to keep the forces at H. in check; and at the same time fall back to the main body.

" Johnny Reb." took advantage of this state of affairs, and followed us up closely. Our regiment supported the battery, and their cavalry charged with the intention of capturing the cannon. The cannon was loaded with double charges of canister and the rebel cavalry were repulsed with heavy loss. They fought with desperation, one of their number succeeded in reaching the gun, to get knocked from his horse by the swab in the hands of our cannonries. All this time their infantry were coming up in overwhelming numbers, on a double quick. For a short time the prospect was gloomy in the extreme. Their Infantry were posted behind trees and stone walls, the skirmishers being up with their cavalry.

However, we succeeded in joining Buford about dusk. Our loss for the small number engaged was quite heavy.—Capt. Lucas and six men from company F, are among the missing. Their names are, Thomas Donlon, George Wells, Nicholas Lzahter,—all Wyoming County boys. Brooks, Devanoe, and Lewis,—from New York city. Tuesday, the 7th, we rested at Boonsboro; the first day in seven without firing a shot. About noon next day we were attacked by Stewart's Cavalry and a force of mounted infantry. Our artillery took position on a ridge half a mile from town, and for two hours the cannonading was brisk. All our Carbineer fought dismounted as skirmishers, and before sundown, your humble servant, with other skirmishers had the satisfaction of chasing them off the field. Some, in their haste, left their guns behind.

On the 11th we skirmished with Stewart's cavalry, near Hagerstown. On the 12th drove them out of the town, inside their rifle pits, on the Williamsport road. The 12th and 13th passed with no fighting except in the skirmish line. The morning of the 14th found the Rebel army on the other side of the Potomac, except a rear guard at Falling Waters, consisting of three brigades of infantry of A. P. Hill's Corps. Our brigade picked up many straggling grey-backs, minus shoes as well as respect for the confederate humbug for which they had fought.

At Falling Waters the 2nd brigade of our division charged on their breastworks, and drove the rebels with the loss of 103 killed and 900 prisoners. We passed the latter on the road to Harper's Ferry, and one of them remarked to me "you are beginning to do something for your country." In fact our Infantry acknowledge that Cavalry is now worth something. In the past three weeks our division has captured more than its number of rebel prisoners. The sarcastic remark attributed to Gen. Hooker, "Who ever saw a dead cavalry man," is heard no more. At Falling Waters twenty-eight brave men fell on our side. But it was a glorious death to die.

As ever, yours for the Union, J. W. J."

5th Cavalry New York records show their at Hagerstown: 3 killed. 9 wounded and 79 captured on July 6.

Transposition of entire Aug 22 letter follows this page.

Aug 22, 1863 Letter to Sister Cinty:

Camp on Eaton Hedge (Farm?) near the Rapahannock
Aug 22nd, 1863
My Dear Sister (Cindy)

A long time has elapsed since I have recd a letter from you or you from me. during that time our army has been into two different States. our stay in PA was short but while we were there we were seeing hard service most of the time. And we could fight with a will there for we received the smiles of the Ladies and the men gave us all the assistance in there power. At Hanover Pa we lost more from our Camp in Killed wounded & Missing than at any one time during the war. We had a severe fight at Hagerstown M.D. one of the hardest we ever had. At Falling Water Kilpatrick took command of our division soon after we entered M.D. & Capt Farnsworth who was in the 12th Ill Cavalry was promoted to Brigadier Gen of our Brigade. he was Killed on the 3rd of July at Gettysburg in the 2nd days fight. All that day we fought on the left wing of our army Gen. Farnsworth was a very fine man he was highly respected by all of his men and he was one of Gen. Kilpatricks firmest friends on the eve of 1st days fight we were on the right wing of our army and we whipped Stuart as finely as could be. Since we have come back into Va we have had no fighting to do of any account though we were at the heels of Lee's army all the time. We are now on the line of the Rappahannock and form the left wing of the army. Our Regt are doing picket duty at United States Ford. the enemies pickets lay on the other side and occasionally we join them in a bath in the river and our boys got a Richmond Examiner in exchange for York State paper. There were no particular news in it most of it being extracts from Northern paper. I saw E. G. Davis a few days since he been promoted to 2nd Lieutenant. I cant say I really like Ed. I think he is a little inclined to Copperheading he said he wished he had a Republican Watchman to show me. he said received them weekly but tore them up as soon as he had read them and that he writes for that sheet. The 127th is now in the Army of the Potomac I believe in the 2nd Army Corps. I have not seen them Ed said he saw them. the Greenport are all looking well. Ed says that Chat Arnile is the most homesick fellow he ever saw. Skinner stands it like a hero. Geo. R. Reaves formerly a Music teacher is now a private in that regiment I think he must be a patriotic fellow. I received a letter from Fredd he has been sick in a Hospital at Fortress Monroe he is not quite recovered yet. Think he will stay there some time. The citizens in this vicinity are in a starveing condition The government is furnishing with rations those who will take the oath allegiance but I must close now must excuse this poorly written letter I am afraid it wont prove very interesting so good by love to all Your aff Bro

Wm. H. Waterhouse *Write soon*

The "Greenpoint" I refer to in this letter was the brave, noble and compassionate Greenpoint Volunteer Ambulance Corps of New York who ardently tried to find and care for the wounded and often dying fellow fighters strewn on the battle fields.

During the treacherous month of August, 1863,

I wrote a poem to my mother. I was sure I wouldn't live.

A clearer version:

"On the field of battle Mother
All the night alone I lay
Angels watching o'er me Mother
Till the dawning of the day
In my thinking of you Mother
And the loving ones at home
Till to our dear cottage Mother
Boy again I seemed to come
He to whom you taught me Mother
On my infant knee to pray
Kept my heart from fainting Mother
When the vision passed away
Would I could repay you Mother
For your faithful love and care
May God uphold and bless you
In the better place again be there
I must soon be going Mother
Going to my home of rest
Kiss me as of old my Mother
Press me nearer to your breast
In the grey of morning Mother
Comrades bore me to the town
From my bosom tender fingers
Washed the blood that trickled down ..."

All along I tried to read as many newspapers as I could find to keep up with the results and movements of both sides. This proved to be difficult, yet necessary to know what to expect.

On July 31, The Confederate Army of Northern Virginia numbered only 41,000. Autumn gave time for the Confederate army to replenish itself by almost fifty percent. Jefferson Davis's appeal and promise of amnesty and pardon to all who should "with the least possible delay return to their posts of duty within twenty days. At 56,000 it still remained small compared to the Union force in Virginia, even sending a division to South

Carolina and another to New York to quell the riots of the 'draft' there.

Meade realized this and wanted to advance on Lee's army, but unwisely asked permission from Washington. It was forbidden; he could only "take up a threatening attitude upon the Rappahannock." The Confederate army lay beyond the river, as did their source of supply and communication; as did Richmond or any of the rebel connections, thus giving Lee time to spend the fall positioning his army, waiting for the winter months to gain numbers and strength.

Meade spent the same time trying to corner Lee, but in a region he knew nothing about, never attacking at the exact right time, sometimes due to receiving negative commands from Washington and sometimes hesitating on a decision which needed to be made swiftly. During this time things had gone badly at the West with Rosecrans. Meade was ordered to spare one quarter of his army to Hooker to restore balance in Tennessee.

Southern Stuart was active during this time and had many clashes with our northern cavalry and forces. Most of our activity was in Warrenton, Kelly's Ford, Brandy Station again, Rappahannock Station and the Rapidan river. We fought hard battles at Brandy Station on September 13 and 14th; again on October 11th with a total of fifty-three losses. October 19 and 20 in Buckland Mills carved away half that many again.

Transposition of entire letter follows this page
October 10, 1863 Letter to Sister Mela:

Transposition of October 10, 1863 entire letter to Sister Mela

Camp near Stevensburg, Va, October 10th 1863
(Embossed in upper left hand corner of lined stationery an oval with word DOVE in center)
My Dear Sister (Mela)

I received your most welcome letter a few day since and I was glad to hear from you once more. Since I last wrote you we have had some fighting to do. When the Army of the Potomac fell back from Culpeper, we covered the rear & Flank and we had more or less fighting the whole time at Brandy Station near Culpeper Kilpatricks division were surrounded by Stuarts Cavalry & some of A. P. Hills Infantry Corps and I can assure you we had some fighting to do before we got out. At Brandy Station the ground is level for miles around and occasionally a slight elevation which afforded a good position for Artillery Kilpatrick formed his division in a solid square and prepared for action he first charged the column of the enemy that cut of(f) our line of retreat we soon got them out our way then we went to fighting those in our rear and on flanks. There was some of finest movements I ever saw made in my life regiment after regiment would charge and every time one of our regiments charged the rebles would get out of the way in a hurry. at one time a brigade of rebles charged our battery and about 50 of our regiment repulsed them I never saw the rebles fight so poorly as they did that day with the advantage they and then they outnumbered us by one third About week after that we got into a worse scrape at Buckland Mills We fought Stuarts Cavalry drove him and he led us on and the rebles Infantry closed in on our rear and we had no show for a fight at all for a way to get out was through woods fields and over fences & everything else, and every man had to get out the best we could most of us got out but all pretty well scattered had two of our company taken prisoners. We are now once more on the south side of the Rappahannock When our army fell back to Centreville and Bull Run the Rebles tore up the railroad and we followed Lee again We could not advance any faster then the railroad was built the cars now run to Warrenton Junction on the 7th the Army again crossed the Rappahannock at Bealton Station the 6th Corps fought the enemy with success they took 300 prisoners & 4 pieces of artillery at Kellys Ford the 2nd Corps charged the enemy rifle pickets and took 800 prisoners. the next we crossed at Barnett ford farther down the river on left Flank but we found none of the enemy untill we came near Stevensburg then we met what was called Hamptons Legion they are mostly South Carolina Troops our Brigade drove them back to Culpeper and by that time it was dusk since then we have not advanced any since on this flank our troops are now in Culpeper it (is) said that Lee has fallen back over the Rapidan I dont think Gen Meade will advance much farther. I presume he trying keep Lee from going to fight Burnside. The rebles were not expecting us over the Rapahannock for they had commenced to build themselves Winter Quarters One of our men captured a rebls horse with saddile & all his nicknacks inside of a bible he found a letter that was written by a rebel to his Friends in Ga. It stated that while they were following up the Yanks they had lived for 6 days on roasted white oak acorns but I must close for the Mail is going now. I received the paper you sent me the fair must have been a fun thing Much love to all I remain you aff Bro Wm. H. Waterhouse

Thanksgiving was a time Meade felt he could proceed with great success to attack Lee's force which was divided into smaller units not close enough to come together quickly. He proposed to march rapidly on Fredericksburg and transfer his base of operations from Orange to Fredericksburg Railroad. Arguing this would be a complete surprise to the enemy because he could do this before Lee had time to get there and prepare, he then could threaten Richmond.

Again Halleck refused his consent to change the base, but said he found nothing wrong with the attack. What was Halleck thinking? With the bad weather months arriving and at this time Meade's numbers were down and Lee's were up from the month of nothing happening.

Rappahannock Station: the first encounter of surprise by the Federal army took 1600 prisoners one afternoon. Birley and Sedgwick in command wanted to continue at daybreak, but Meade dispatched an order to stop them. He then brought up his whole army to the station which took a few days. During this hesitation, Lee again crossed the Rapidan. Meade pushed his advance posts to Culpepper and beyond, but then lay inactive for almost three weeks. No historian can even guess why. His golden opportunity of falling with his whole force upon a portion of the Confederate army disappeared. With Lee now behind the Rapidan, it was too dangerous to follow until the railroad could be thoroughly repaired.

Lee again relaxed and spread his troops for the winter. In late November, Meade decided to suddenly cross the Rapidan, thinking he could crush Ewell before Hill could arrive to assist, thereby gaining Orange Court and Gordonsville. November 24 was set for the move, but again a fierce storm delayed the attack two days, giving Lee time to entrench in good position and bring up the bulk of his army. (As I said in my letters, bad weather was sure to happen when the Federal army decided to march.) It was planned for all units to arrive at Mine Run on 27th.

Warren arrived on time; French arrived three hours later lost on his route. Meade would not send one corps alone. Then someone measured the width of the river wrong and they were one pontoon boat short to make the bridge. Sedgwick opened fire and was ready to advance when Warren sent a message to hold because he saw the firepower ahead of him. Meade looked at both assault fronts and realized Lee's strength. Meade still wanted to attack but Warren and French found we were outnumbered on our attack route. Now winter weather approached and knowing any sudden storm would cut off our supply line, Meade had to withdraw his army to its former position and conclude that nothing more could be done until spring. This enterprise would almost certainly have been successful, but instead both armies retired to await spring.

As the year ended, our regiment was offered reenlistment in the Veteran Volunteer Cavalry, which I did on December 26, 1863, with promise of a furlough in the near future.

December 4, 1863 Letter to Sister Cinty:

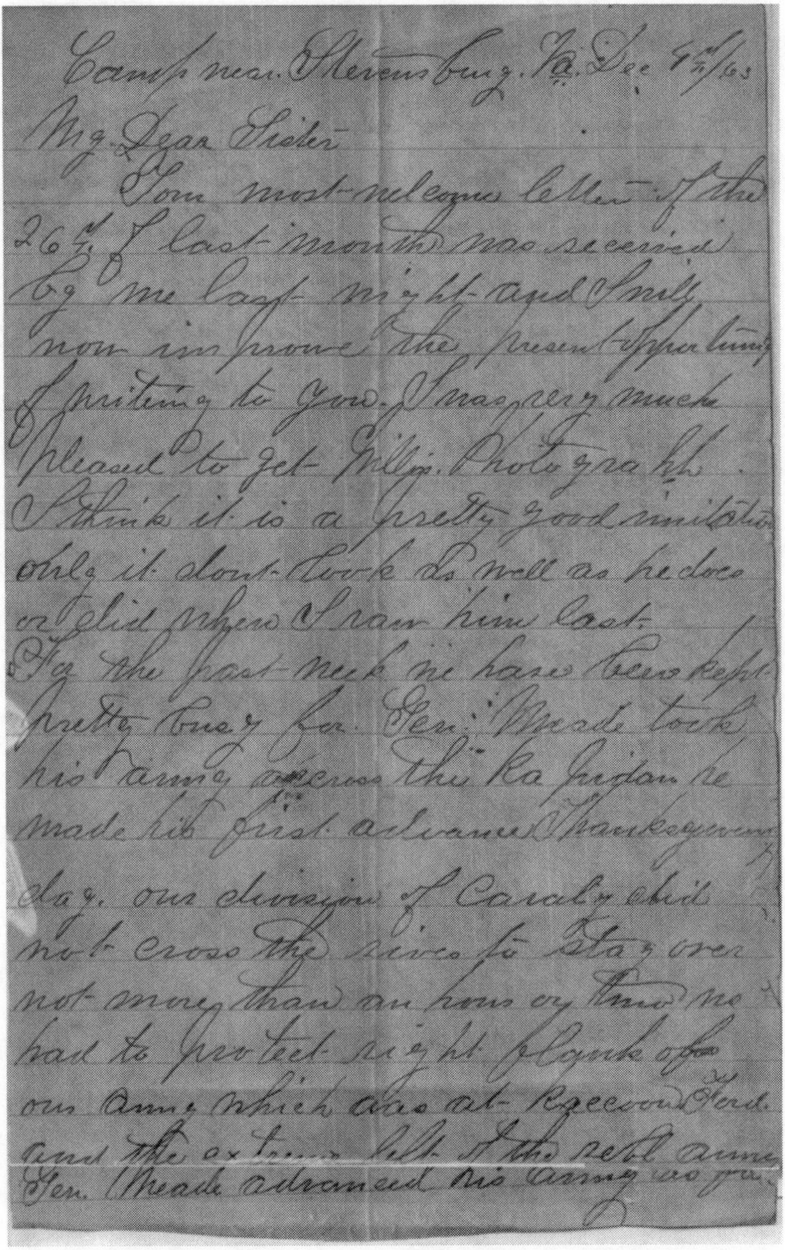

Camp near Stevensburg Va. Dec 4th/63
My Dear Sister
Your most welcome letter of the
26th of last month was received
by me last night and I will
now improve the present opportunity
of writing to you. I was very much
pleased to get Willy's Photograph.
I think it is a pretty good imitation
only it dont look as well as he does
or did when I saw him last.
For the past week we have been kept
pretty busy for Gen. Meade took
his army across the Rapidan he
made his first advance Thanksgiving
day. our division of Cavalry did
not cross the river to stay over
not more than an hour or two we
had to protect right flank of
our Army which was at Raccoon Ford.
and the extreme left of the rebel army
Gen. Meade advanced his army as far

as far Chancelorville on the Fredrick
burg & Richmond R.R. Lee declined
to give battle so our army had
nothing to do but heavy marching
& skirmishing I suppose the move
was made more to prevent Lee from
sending detachments from his army
to reinforce Bragg. The news we
get from Grant's Army is truly
encouraging I hope they will meet
with no reverses but success continue
to follow them. I presume you have
seen Julius Young of Orient
that young fellow that used to
bring up Frank Terry to church
sometimes he is in the 6th N.Y. Cavaly
I saw him this morning said he
the regiment was going to reenlist
and thought they would start for
home in about a week. there are
quite a number of Southold boys
in the same regiment they are all
agoing to reenlist I presume the

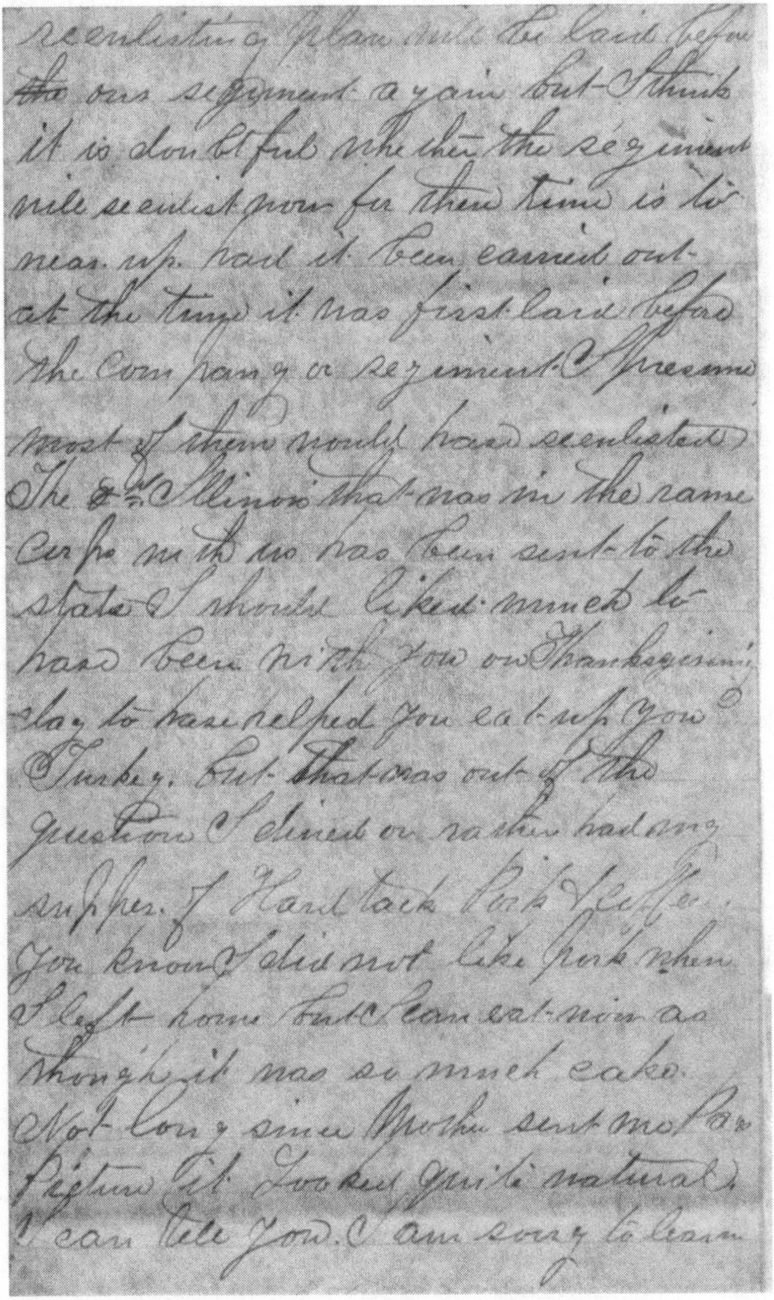
reenlisting plan will be laid before
~~the~~ ours regiment again but I think
it is doubtful whether the regiment
will reenlist now for there time is to
near up. had it been carried out
at the time it was first laid before
the Company or regiment I presume
most of them would have reenlisted
The 8th Illinois that was in the same
Corps with us has been sent to the
state I should liked much to
have been with you on Thanksgiving
day to have helped you eat up your
Turkey. but that was out of the
question I dined or rather had my
supper of Hard tack Pork & Coffee.
You know I did not like pork when
I left home but I can eat now as
though it was so much cake.
Not long since Mother sent me her
picture it looks quite natural
I can tell you. I am sorry to learn

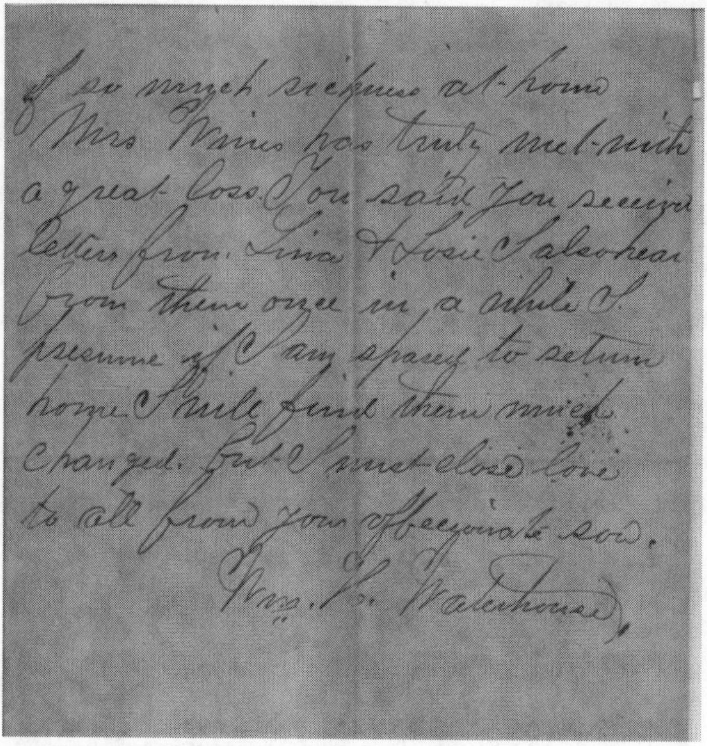

of so much sickness at home
Mrs Waines has truly met with
a great loss. You said you receive
letters from Lina & Josie I also hear
from them once in a while I
presume if I am spared to return
home I will find them much
changed. but I must close love
to all from your affecionate son.
Wm. J. Waterhouse

13

ARMY OF THE POTOMAC
JANUARY - JUNE, 1864

During January and into February, winter quarters for us was Stevensburg, Virginia. We were able to have fine stockades and wood to burn for warmth against the snowy, cold weather.

When I re-enlisted, I was given some of my new bounty and an advancement of a month's pay. While in Stevensburg, Virginia, I used some of my cash to have a silver cavalry pin made with my name, rank and regiment engraved on it. I wore it always with pride and for good luck. During the winter I was very healthy and weighed 169 pounds.

January 9, 1864 Letter to Sister Cinty:

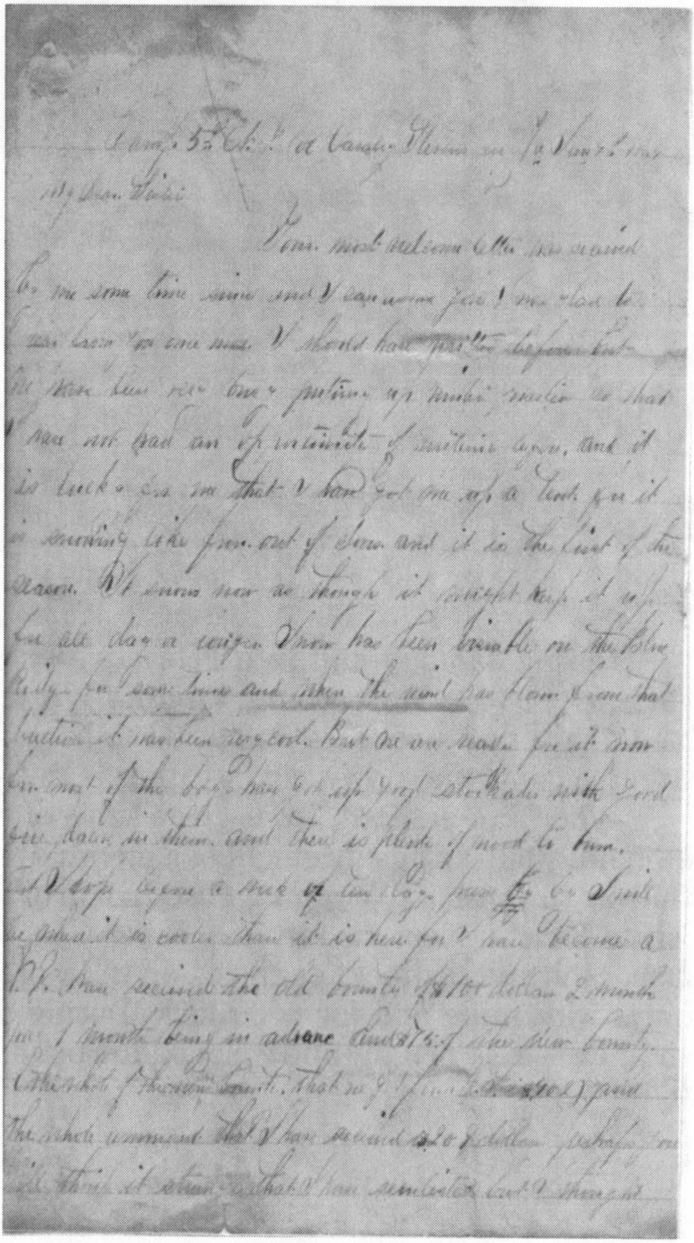

Transposition of entire letter follows this page:

Camp 5th N. Y. Vol Cavalry Stevensburg, Va. Jan 9th 1864
My Dear Sister (Cinty)

Your most welcome letter was received by me some time since and I can assure you I was glad to hear from you once more. I should have written before but we have been very busy puting up winter quarters so that I have not had an opportunity of writing before, and it is lucky for me that I have got me up a tent, for it is snowing like fure out of doors, and it is the first of the season. It snows now as though it might keep it up for all day or longer. Snow has been visiable on the Blue Ridge for some time and when the wind has blown from that direction it has been very cool. But we are ready for it now for most of the boys have got up good stockades with good fire places in them and there is plenty of wood to burn, but I hope before a week or ten days pass by I will be where it is cooler than it is here for I have become a F.V. Have received the old bounty of $100 dollars 2 months pay 1 month being in advance and $75. of the new bounty (the whole of the new bounty, that we get from U.S. is $902) and the whole amount that I have received is $209 dollars perhaps you think it strange that I have reenlisted but I thought that as I had been in so long I would see the thing through I dont think the war will last any longer than 18 months and the new term of service dates from 31st of last month. so that we serve 10 months of the old term on the new. Most of the 6th N. Y. Vol. Cavalry have reenlisted and been sent home. in that regiment there are quite a number from Orient & Southold. We get 35 days furlough The regiment that Chas. Willis has enlisted is the 2nd N.Y. Vol Cavalry. (I fear that I shall get my letter awfully mixed for the boys are reading some of there old love letters) That regiment is in our brigade They are going to reenlist that is the most of them. I wish he had come into our regiment. I am glad that you got up a box to send him if you had let me know about it sooner I would like to have contributed something towards it. I would like to have been to your concert on New Years Eve. I hope to hear some good singing while at home. I wish you and Willis could be there. I hope Willis will not be drafted I dont think he would bear an examination. he would not if they are as particular as they were in examining me but they could not find a blemish about me. Since I have been in the army I *have enjoyed excellent health. I have gained 25lbs. since I left home I now weigh 169lbs pretty solid fellow for a horse to carry around, but I have got a horse that has stood it better any with one exception. I received a picture of Father and it is excellent, but I have seen none from Sosey. I would like to see Uncle Levi very much. I dont suppose he is subject to a draft. give him my best love, also Aunt Hattie and all the young Waterhouses I received a letter from Mela not long since. Said she had a fine time on Christmas and that they were holding singing schools every week, but she said that most of them went for the fun rather than learn music I was surprised to hear that Mary Elnor Boot & Addie Brown were married. When I left home they had scarcely laid by there short dresses I reckon they will all get married of(f) before I go home for good. But I must close for this time dont write to mother about my coming home they dont expect it now. Well with a wish the New Year may happy one to you I will close Love to all I remain you most aff Brother Wm. H. Waterhouse*

February 7, 1864 Transposition of Letter to Brother-in-law Willis follows exactly as he wrote it:

Page One: "Camp 5th N.Y. Vol Cavalry, Feb 7, 1864

Last evening I received a dispatch from you dated Feb. 4th requesting me to visit you in Chicago either to or from my regiment. I am not prepared to say whether I can visit you or not. I could not very well do so on my way home for I will have to work to secure my State bounty, and if possible a county bounty. Nothing could please me better than to make a visit to Chicago but fear I shall not be able. When I wrote to Cinty it was supposed we would have our Furlough in a very few days, but we were obliged to wait untill some of the other furloughed regiments returned, which was supposed would be about...

Page Two: ...the 15th of this month I am in hopes we will than receive our furloughs but I dont know whether we will or not, for greatly to the surprise, of all yesterday morning about 4 o'clock orders were received for the regiment to be ready to march at 7. A.M. Whole Corps of Cavalry moved down to Elys. Ford on the Rapidan to cross I presume for the purpose of making a raid though it is yet unknown. three Corps of Infantry moved up to Raccoon Ford to draw the attention of of Lees Army I suppose while the Cavalry makes a move in there rear though I dont know what there real designs are. Whether it will interfere with our furloughs I dont know but I am in hopes not. The weather for a past few days has been very unpleasant xxx before that for nearly two weeks we had as fine weather as ever I saw It seems as though it would have been better...

Page Three: ...had Generals moved then rather than to have waited untill we again saw unsettled weather, but it is a noted fact that the Heavens weep when the Army of the Potomac moves. I received a letter from home a few days since Mela wrote that Cinty was learning the art of skateing she is *the last one I would have supposed would sought amusement in skateing for if my memory serves me right she when young was very timid on ice. She wrote also that they were to have a supper held in the Greenport House for the benefit of sick and wounded soldiers. I am in hopes to attend, Well I must close - my love to Cinty and a good share for yourself. I still remain your most aff. Bro.*

Wm H Waterhouse"

Ford on the Rapidan.

I never received the furlough because February 6, 1864, all Corps of Cavalry were moved down to Ely's Ford on the Rapidan.

History tells us that Washington again was disgruntled with their General of the Army of the Potomac. The Congressional Committee had met and asked that Meade be replaced. After a month of deliberation, it was offered to Ulysses Grant to be in charge of all the armies of the Union. He agreed only if President Lincoln relinquished being Commander-in-Chief of the army and Halleck was removed from service as General-in-Chief. Halleck was put in a position under the President, the Secretary of War and the Lieutenant General. Grant's headquarters would be Washington, from where all operations of the Union armies would be directed. Even the Secretary of War no longer had a say in the operations in the field. This bill was passed March 2, 1864.

Grant immediately began his plans for a complete and quick end to the war. He chose Sherman to lead the army of the Southeast and concentrate on attacking General Johnston of the Confederate Army. Grant would be in charge of the Army of the Potomac with many changes. He broke five corps of the army into three: known as the Second, Fifth and Sixth, naming Hancock as commander of the Second, Warren, the Fifth and Sedgwick the Sixth.

Under himself, to carry out his command, he needed a brave, smart and patriot officer. He named Meade knowing that Meade's failures were only because he didn't have confidence to execute what he knew to be correct. Grant knew that Meade would carry out every order given to him and would not have to make any major decision alone.

Another change resulted from Grant's understanding that the cavalry had not been used to its potential. The commanding generals failed to appreciate this division and use it correctly. They had been deployed as scouts and guards for trains. The new leader of the cavalry was Philip Sheridan, who believed our cavalry should fight the enemy's cavalry and that it would be a power to be reckoned with having strength of horse and man together.

We, members of the 5th cavalry of New York, fought our war in northern Virginia, except for our time to and from Gettysburg. During our four years as members of the Army of the Potomac, we fought, won, refought, and lost back and forth many areas such as Orange Court House, Manassas, Bull Run, Winchester, up and down the Rapidan and the Rappahannock valleys. Sometimes our battles or skirmishes in the same place were separated by a day, sometimes a week, a month, a year or years, but back we came to the same place to fight again. This whole strategic area meant success to both sides. Union's core in Washington and the center of the Confederacy in Richmond were the souls of each side.

Spring of 1864 found the combined Union armies to be over 662,000. Grant's plan was direct, to attack the enemy's strength in Virginia and Sherman to do the same in Georgia. He set the early part of May to start these operations. By the 4th of May, we were on the move to Ely's Ford and Germania Ford on the Rapidan River. The vendettas of the fords were swept back by Sheridan's cavalry and 4000 wagons and two columns of soldiers crossed the river and by that evening the entire Army of the Potomac was encamped in the Wilderness, the infamous area where Chancellorsville had been fought.

One area we dreaded most was this mire known as the Wilderness. Hooker lost drastically there in '62, Meade in '63 and then '64 proved the same for Grant. West of Chancellorsville there was a mile circuit of cleared fields then a twelve mile belt of iron ore mines. The poor soil kept away farmers, but Nature created a dense forest of trees, brambles, and many strong vines to make it almost impassible, even for a hunter much less a full army with wagons and artillery. Adding the marshy swamp-lands caused by the collision of the many little rivers, it became an area everyone dreaded; however, some Union generals saw it as an area to entrap the enemy.

They forgot the rebel forces knew every inch of the area, which fit their guerilla warfare perfectly. May 3rd, 1864 Grant moved all his divisions into the surrounding areas, feeling Lee would pull back toward Richmond in fear of his huge force on the march. But Lee found out the Union army was headed for the Rapidan and the Wilderness and decided upon a completely different movement – with his 60,000 men, he was going to move in on the Union army of more than twice his numbers. Grant made his headquarters in the very center, at the Wilderness Tavern. Grant was moving slowly across the Wilderness unaware that Lee's forces were near and moving toward him with a plan.

The Wilderness roads, two northwest to southeast that mainly ran parallel but joined together at times. The first from Germania Ford and the other from Ely's Ford came together at Spotsylvania Courthouse, eight miles southeast of Chancellorsville. These Grant was using to move his two columns through the Wilderness. The other two, west to east, one from Orange Court House, ran parallel for about three miles and met together near Chancellorsville, striking at a right angle with those Grant was using. In those thickets and swamps it was difficult to penetrate even a few feet, artillery could not be used, neutralizing Grant's numbers. Grant thought he might find an outpost or picket line, but never conceived the rebels were on their way south coming in force.

We scouted on May 4th, Wednesday, but found nothing. On the 5th, our General Warren as a precaution sent Griffin's division on one of the east-west roads. They encountered Johnson's group, the first phase of Ewell's and pushed them back. Meade said, "They have left a division here to fool us while they concentrate and prepare a position toward the North Anna, and what I want is to prevent these fellows from getting back to Mine Run."

Suddenly the Johnson's group was reinforced from Ewell and pushed Griffin all the way back where he started. Wadsworth, trying to help Griffin missed his way in the forest and exposed his flank to heavy firing, then recoiled in confusion.

We were returning from scouting to tell Crawford's advance group of the heavy force coming upon them. Crawford withdrew his division; however, one brigade became isolated and lost in prisoners nearly the whole of two regiments. The rest of the day until past midnight the shots of both sides could be heard as the different advancements of both sides were made.

Grant decided during the night to stay and fight rather than trying to leave the Wilderness and regroup. His plan he executed all night was to make a wall of regiments: Sedgwick on the right, then Warren, then Burnside, then Hancock. The plan was a simultaneous attack of anything that appeared along their whole five mile line of regiments. Lee planned for Longstreet and Hill to attack the Union's left. Ewell was to make a demonstration on the right. If it succeeded, Hancock would be pushed to center and the whole Union army massed together in impenetrable forces, where it could not act as an army. Grant had picked 5:00 am for his attack, but Ewell started fifteen minutes before.

On both sides many plans fell awry. Wadsworth was killed, Longstreet thought to be killed lived to fight later until the end of the war. No plans for either side happened correctly. The day was not a battle, but a series of fierce skirmishes between parts of each army, both ignorant of what the other was trying to do and the other's strength at any given moment.

The loss on both sides was extremely heavy, the Union fully 20,000 of whom 5,000 were prisoners. The Confederates loss was hardly 10,000, very few captured. It was a drawn battle. Both leaders failed in their purpose for the day, but Lee again had stopped Grant. The woods where the morning battle had taken place caught on fire and burned all day. The 5th New York lost sixty-three wonderful men, eighteen killed, twenty-one wounded and twenty-four captured, during these days in the dreaded Wilderness.

Grant decided to leave the Wilderness and take the fight to Spotsylvania Court House. During the weekend of May 7 and 8, our cavalry unit was again in the midst of heavy fighting, as we had been sent ahead to scout out the enemy in the area of this Court House. This battle continued during May up to North Anna where our regiment lost two more killed, thirteen wounded and ten taken prisoners. A bad month for our group.

Our regiment at Parker's Store lost more non commissioned officers than any other, having three Sergeants killed, three wounded and one taken prisoner.

May 20, 1864 Letter to Mother:

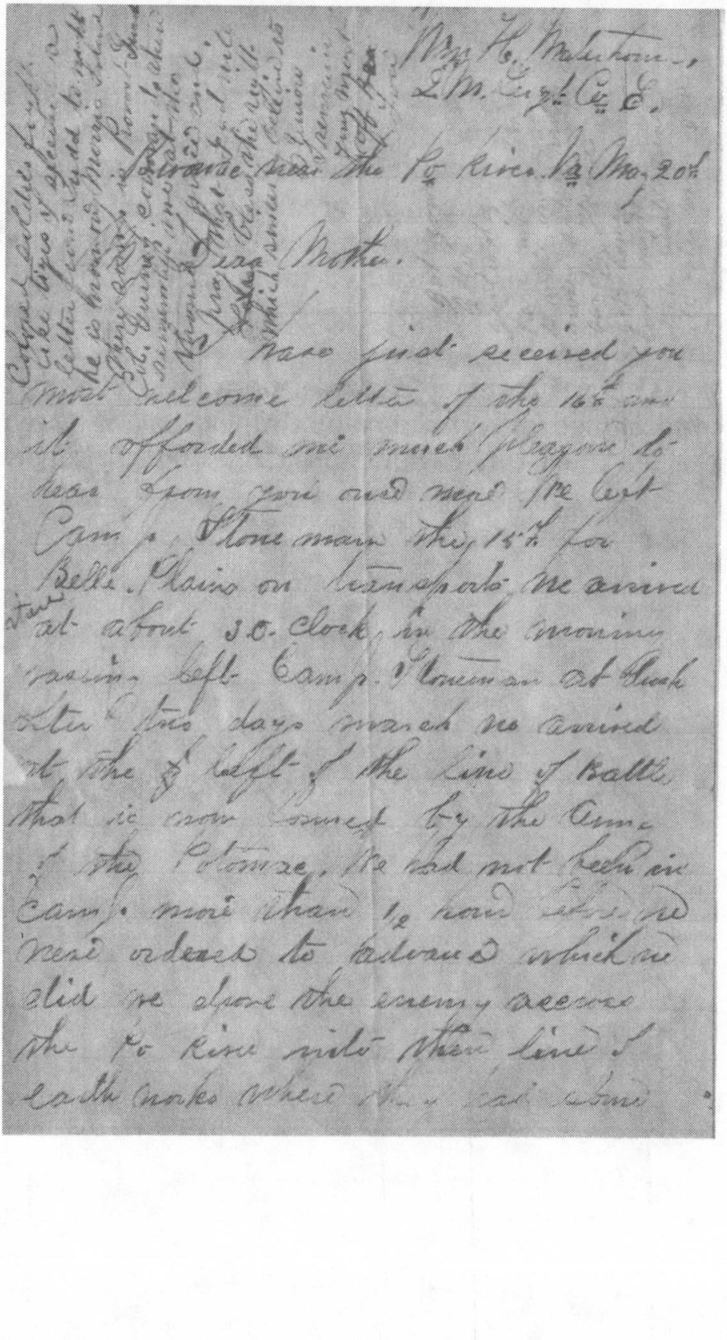

Wm. H. Mutchmore,
2 M. Engr. Co. C.

Bivouac near the Po River Va. May 20th

Dear Mother.

I have just received your most welcome letter of the 16th and it afforded me much pleasure to hear from you and [illegible] we left Camp Stoneman the 15th for Belle Plains on transports we arrived at about 3 O Clock in the morning [illegible] left Camp Stoneman at [illegible] after two days march we arrived at the left of the line of Battle that is now formed by the Army of the Potomac. We had not been in Camp more than 1/2 hour before we were ordered to advance which we did we drove the enemy across the Po River into their line of earth works where they had come

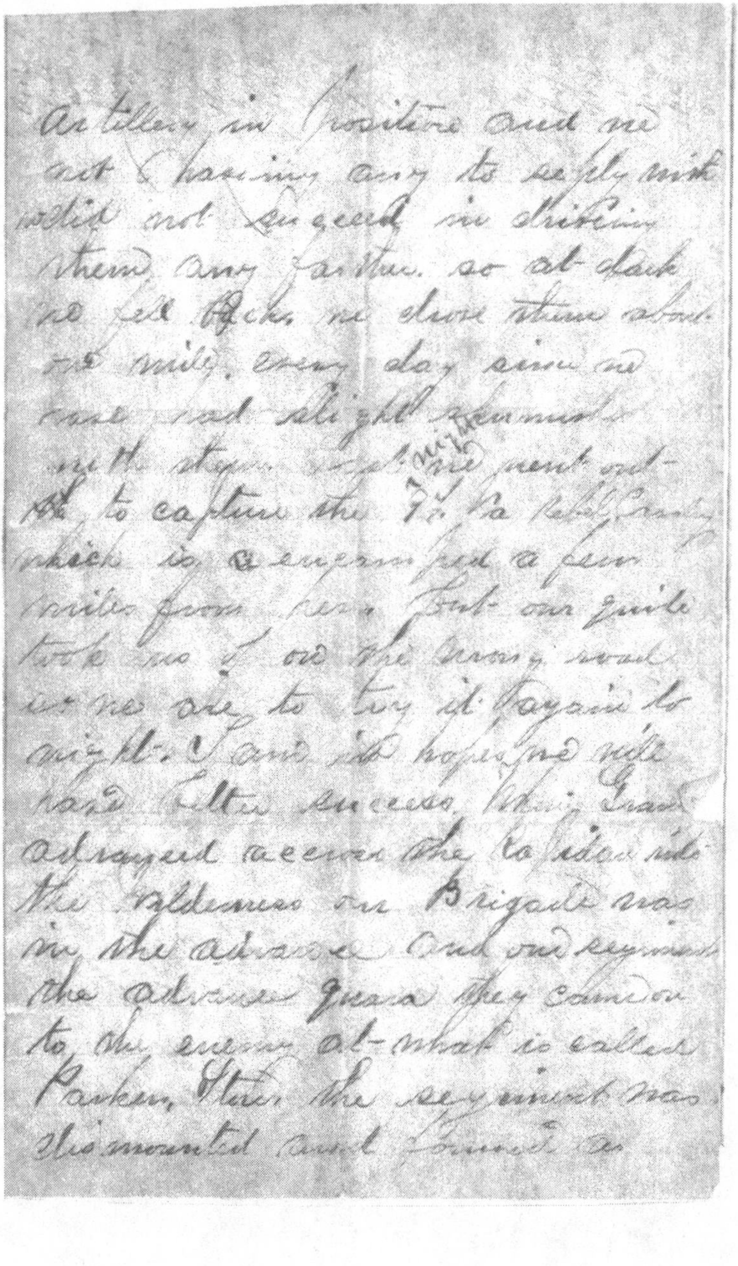

Artillery in position and we
not having any to reply with
which not succeed in driving
them any farther. so at dark
we fell back. we drove them about
one mile. every day since we
have had slight skirmishes
with them. night we went out
to capture the 7th Va Rebel Cavalry
which is encamped a few
miles from here but our guide
took us off on the wrong road
so we are to try it again to
night. I am in hopes we will
have better success. When Gen
advanced across the Rapidan into
the Wilderness our Brigade was
in the advance and our regiment
the advance guard they came on
to the enemy at what is called
Parker Store the regiment was
dismounted and formed a

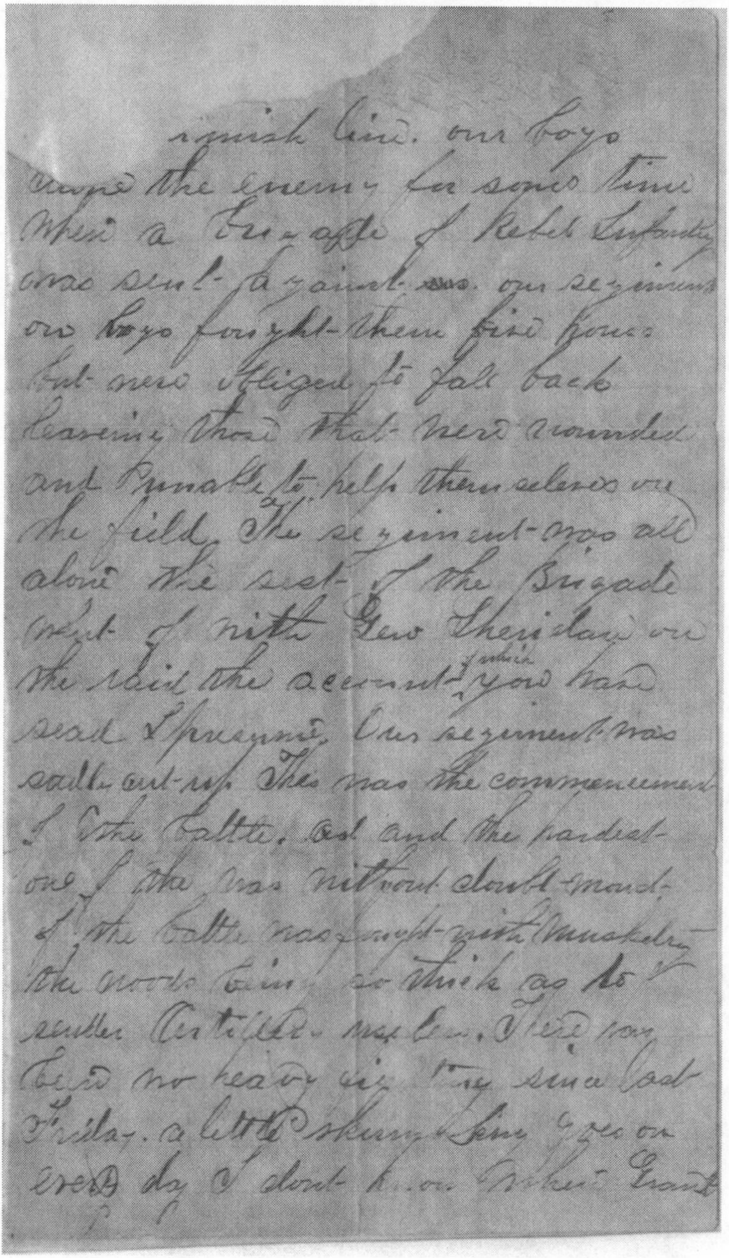
squish line. our boys
drove the enemy for some time
when a brigade of Rebel Infantry
was sent against us. our regiment
our boys fought them five hours
but were obliged to fall back
leaving those that were wounded
and unable to help themselves on
the field. The regiment was all
alone the rest of the Brigade
went of with Gen Sheridan on
the raid the account which you have
read I presume. Our regiment was
cut up. This was the commencement
of the battle. and the hardest
one of the war without doubt most
of the battle was fought with musketry
the woods being so thick as to
render artillery useless. There has
been no heavy fighting since last
Friday. a little skirmishing goes on
every day I don't know where Grant

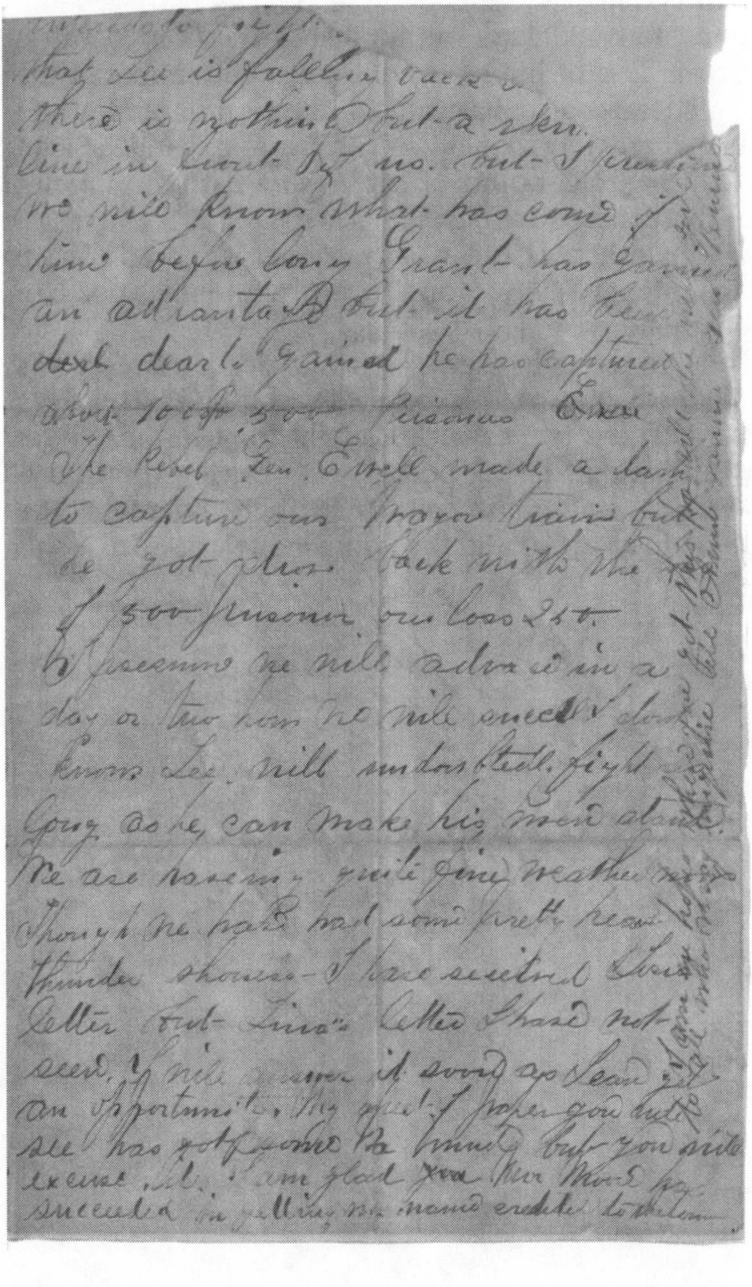
would do for it
that Lee is falling back &
there is nothing but a skir.
line in front of us. but I presume
we will know what has come of
him before long Grant has gained
an advantage but it has been
dearly gained he has captured
about 10 or 12,000 prisoners Even
the Rebel Gen. Ewell made a dash
to capture our wagon train but
we got him back with the loss
of 500 prisoners our loss 250.
I presume we will advance in a
day or two how we will succeed I don't
know Lee will undoubtedly fight
long as he can make his men stand.
We are having quite fine weather now
though we have had some pretty heavy
thunder showers — I have received Lina's
letter but Lina's letter I have not
seen, I will answer it soon as I can get
an opportunity. the sheet of paper you sent
me has got [illegible] but you will
excuse it. I am glad that Mr Moore has
succeeded in getting my name credited to the town

From the 4th of May through June, the countryside of Virginia became an open battleground. Union forces always outnumbered the Confederates, but the loss of life of Union forces outnumbered the Confederates also. Basically for the months of May and June, there were so many skirmishes and so much blood shed, the exact points of battle were hard to pinpoint for two consecutive days.

On June 11, the two cavalries experienced a sharp encounter at Yellow Stone Tavern, a few miles north of Richmond.

In the fight the rebel cavalry leader, Stuart was killed, which proved to be as devastating as Jackson's death. These two cavalries fought for two more days with Sheridan losing 5000 men. During the thirty-seven days after the conflict in the Wilderness, the Union lost 54,550 and the Confederates 32,000.

June 6, 1864 letter to Sister Cinty, my last before imprisonment..notice my "Stavered(Starved) to death":

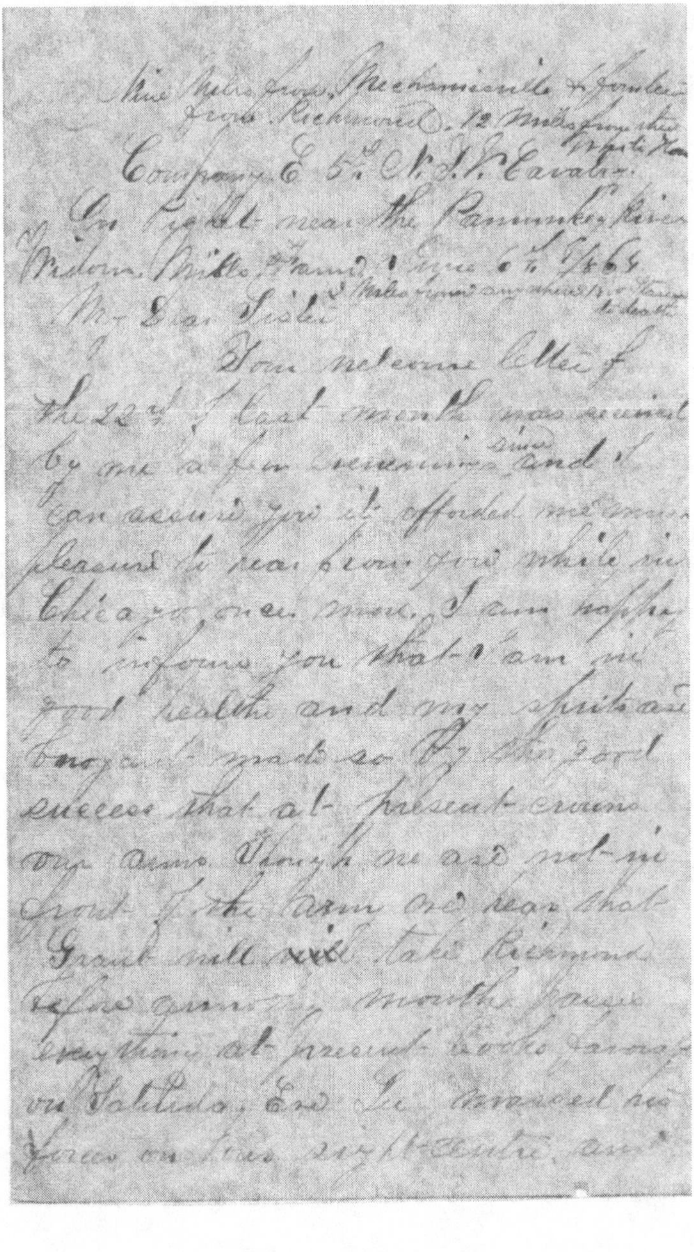

Nine Miles from Mechanicsville & fourteen from Richmond. 12 Miles from the White House
Company E 5th N.Y. Cavalry
On Picket near the Pamunkey River
Widow Mills Farm June 6th 1864
My Dear Sister 2 Miles from anywhere to Starved to death

Your welcome letter of the 22nd of last month was received by me a few evenings since and I can assure you it afforded me much pleasure to hear from you while in Chicago once more. I am happy to inform you that I am in good health and my spirits are buoyant made so by the good success that at present crowns our arms though we are not in front of the army we hear that Grant will take Richmond before many months pass everything at present looks favorable on [illegible]. Gen Lee has massed his forces on their right centre, and

and tried several times to break
through but did not succeed.
Grant has his forces all entrenched
and as fast as he advances he
entrenches himself there is a line
of earth works all the way from
the Rapidan that Grant has thrown
up. In the attack on Saturday night
(which lasted about five hours) the
Rebels left 2000 dead & wounded
on the field our loss was 300.
I never saw such determination among
the men of the army as at present
they all seem to feel as if they must
go forward and the men have a
world of confidence in Genl Grant
The army has never been better
manouvered then at the present
campaign. Our Co has lost its
usual number of Sergts this summer
our Orderly Sergt was killed a few
weeks since while we were

advancing on Milford Station
The first plattoon of our Company made
a charge over a bridge and the
planks were torn up on one end
and we did not see it untill we came
to the hole in the bridge so that we
crowded in together on the bridge
and it took a few minutes to get
of and the rebles were in the
woods a few yards ahead of us
and we were so exposed that
had there been many of them
they might have killed the whole
of us but no one was hurt but
the Lieut he was shot through the breast
just above the heart he got down
of his horse walked of the bridge and
died. We have had 2 Lieuts wounded
since. our Loss in Noncommisioned
officers has been larger than any other
Company in the Regt. We have had 3
Lieuts killed 2 wounded & one is now

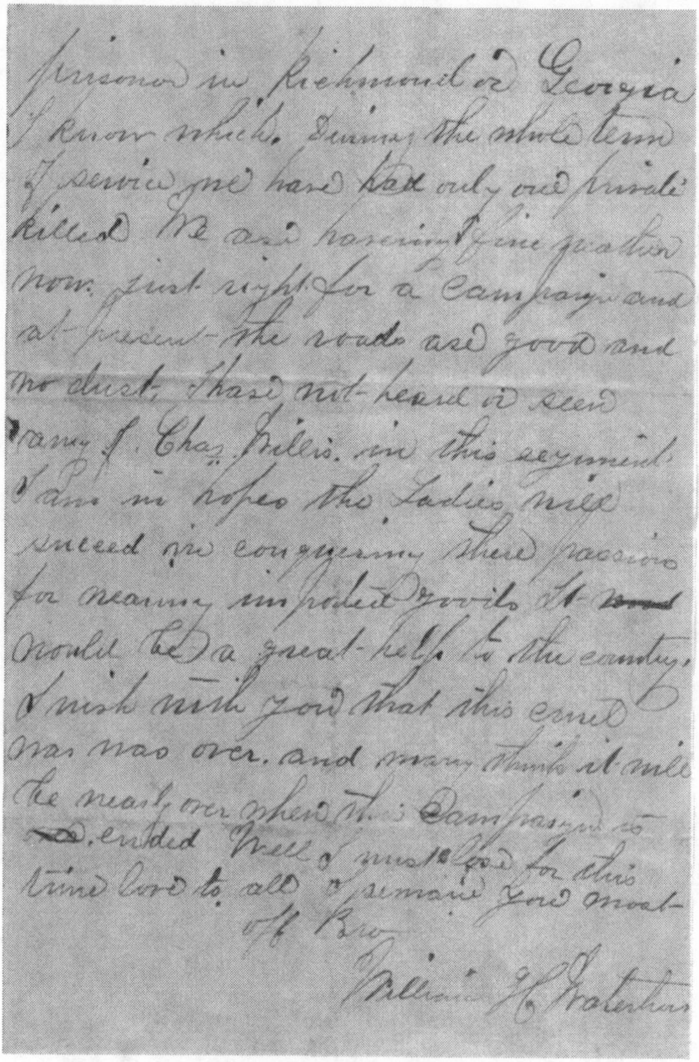
prisoner in Richmond or Georgia
I know which. During the whole term
of service we have had only one private
killed We are having fine weather
now just right for a Campaign and
at present the roads are good and
no dust. I have not heard or seen
any of Chas. Miller in this regiment
I am in hopes the Ladies will
succeed in conquering their passion
for wearing imported goods It
would be a great help to the country.
I wish with you that this cruel
war was over. and many think it will
be nearly over when this Campaign is
ended Well I must close for this
time love to all I remain your most
aff Bro
William H. Water[illegible]

There was the siege of Petersburg that the south held out with only a hand-full of men. It was after this siege, that the Union forces under Wilson and Kautz did heavy wreckage to the railroad lines from Petersburg to change the war. They started to return on June 24th, but at Stony Creek met a heavy Confederate cavalry and lost 1000 men in the next few days.

There was the siege of Petersburg that the south held out with only a hand-full of men. It was after this siege, that the Union forces under Wilson and Kautz did heavy wreckage to the railroad lines from Petersburg to change the war. They started to return on June 24th, but at Stony Creek met a heavy Confederate cavalry and lost 1000 men in the next few days.

14

CAPTURED ON JUNE 29, 1864

Between the 20th and 29th of June, 1864, my regiment took part in these raids. We were intercepted by the Rebel Cavalry at Reams Station near Stony Creek, on June 28th.

There were six hundred of us, the whole division, captured after being without rations for thirty-six hours. Finally when the rebs fed us on June 30th; it was a small piece of corn bread and bacon. We didn't realize that was a lot compared to what we would have in the months to come. One of the rebel soldiers even took my silver metal from me and my gun. That told me the honor the rebels practiced.

This ended my contribution to the 5th Cavalry brave fights, as I became a prisoner for the rest of the war. Believe me, I longed to be back with my regiment and would have exchanged gladly the gruesome acts of battles for what I endured in prison.

The following is a day by day journal of my horrendous, almost eleven-month imprisonment, starting in Salisbury, North Carolina, then four months in the hell hole of Andersonville, Georgia.

I probably lived through this eleven month period by being sent to Millen, close to Savannah for three months. Though it also was horrible, it wasn't as crowded and it had fresh water running through the camp. There were no tents, but we made burrows in the ground and covered them with any piece of cloth we could find. There were still thousands in this camp, but not as cramped as in the stockades of Andersonville, where up to a hundred persons would die daily.

Unfortunately when Sherman neared Millen on his march from Atlanta to Savannah, they moved us out to Thomasville and then back to Andersonville, arriving back on Christmas of 1864. During my eleven months in prisons, my weight went from 169 to 117 pounds. Reading back in my journal, it told me we only had a couple of days when the rations given would even start to be the minimum to live on. A small portion of rice with molasses would hardly be enough; neither would a piece of corn bread. We kept alive by believing that tomorrow we were going to be in the prisoner exchange group. There were many tomorrows, but thanks to God, it finally came on May 16, 1865 when we left for Camp Parole near Annapolis and truly when I arrived home on May 23.

To help understand the confinement in these prisons, I will borrow some historical descriptions: The most substantial prison holding former Andersonville captives was Camp Lawton in Millen, about forty miles south of Augusta. Camp Lawton was a stockade structure enclosing forty-two acres, the largest in terms of area. Set a mile from the Augusta Railroad, it was designed to hold up to

40,000 prisoners, although it never went beyond 10,000. By all accounts it was better than Andersonville, with its fresh water spring running through the property. Rations were more plentiful, yet disease and death abounded because many of the prisoners arrived terribly debilitated from their incarceration at Andersonville. In its few months of existence, nearly 1,000 died.

As Sherman approached, some prisoners were sent to South Carolina, the rest of us to Savannah. From Savannah, about 5,000 prisoners were transported down the Atlantic and Gulf Coast Railroad to Blackshear, a makeshift guard line with artillery pieces surrounding several thousand men in the piney woods of southeast Georgia. Blackshear lasted less than a month. Afterwards, the majority of us went southwest to Thomasville, Georgia, where the rail line ended. After two weeks of confinement there, we were sent back on a sixty-mile march to Albany where we re-embarked on the train arriving in Andersonville on Christmas Eve, 1864. You will notice that my journal ceases from leaving Millen until into March back at Andersonville because of this long way back, my pages were lost.

I do want to say that had it not been for my comrade and friend, Alexander Worthington, who kept my welfare at his highest priority while we were imprisoned, I would not have lived to tell my story. Shortly after our freedom, Alexander became ill with a disease contracted at Andersonville and died. I again give him my heartfelt thanks for his courage, support, help, and certainly, my life. Alexander's father, William G. D. Worthington, had been a judge in Baltimore.

Complete journal while imprisoned

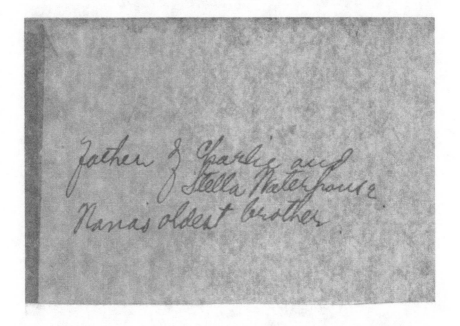

Note on the papers when found in the attic of the Waterhouse home in Maitland, Florida.

Wm H Waterhouse Journal 1865

Stony Creek Station June 29 Here we are prisoners. Our whole division was routed and I presume up captured.

June 30 We have lain here all day at Stony Creek Station. They say we will get some rations soon I am in hopes we shall for we have had nothing to eat for 36 hours

July 1st We laid and slept in a hog hole last night most of us rec'd a days rations last evening which was a small piece of C Bread & Bacon part of the squad went off for Georgia to day we expect to start to morrow July 3d We left Stony Creek S last evening at dark and arrived at Weldon N C this morning at 5 o clock we rec rations of meal and bacon which we cooked This evening we started for Raleigh N C

July 4th We arrived at Raleigh this morning about 8 o clock We rec'd rations of hard bread and no meat. To day is the Sabbath and the first we have spent while we have been prisoners we expect to start for Salisbury to day

To start you on your way with the Journal of Imprisonment: Page One:

Stoney Creek Station June 29 Here we are prisoners. Our whole division was routed and I presume captured. June 30 We have lain here all day at Stoney Creek Station. They say we will get some rations soon I am in hopes we shall for we have had nothing to eat for 36 hours July 1st We laid and slept in a big hole last night most of us rec a days ration last evening which was a small peice of C Bread & Bacon part of the squad went off for Georgia today we expect to start to-morrow July 3 We left Stoney Creek O last evening at dark and arrived at Walden this morning at 5 o'clock we rec rations of meal and bacon which we cooked This evening we started for Raliegh N C July 4 We arrived at Raliegh this morning about 8 o'clock We rec rations of hard bread and no meat. Today is the Sabbath and the first we have spent while we have been prisoners we expect to start for Salisbury today

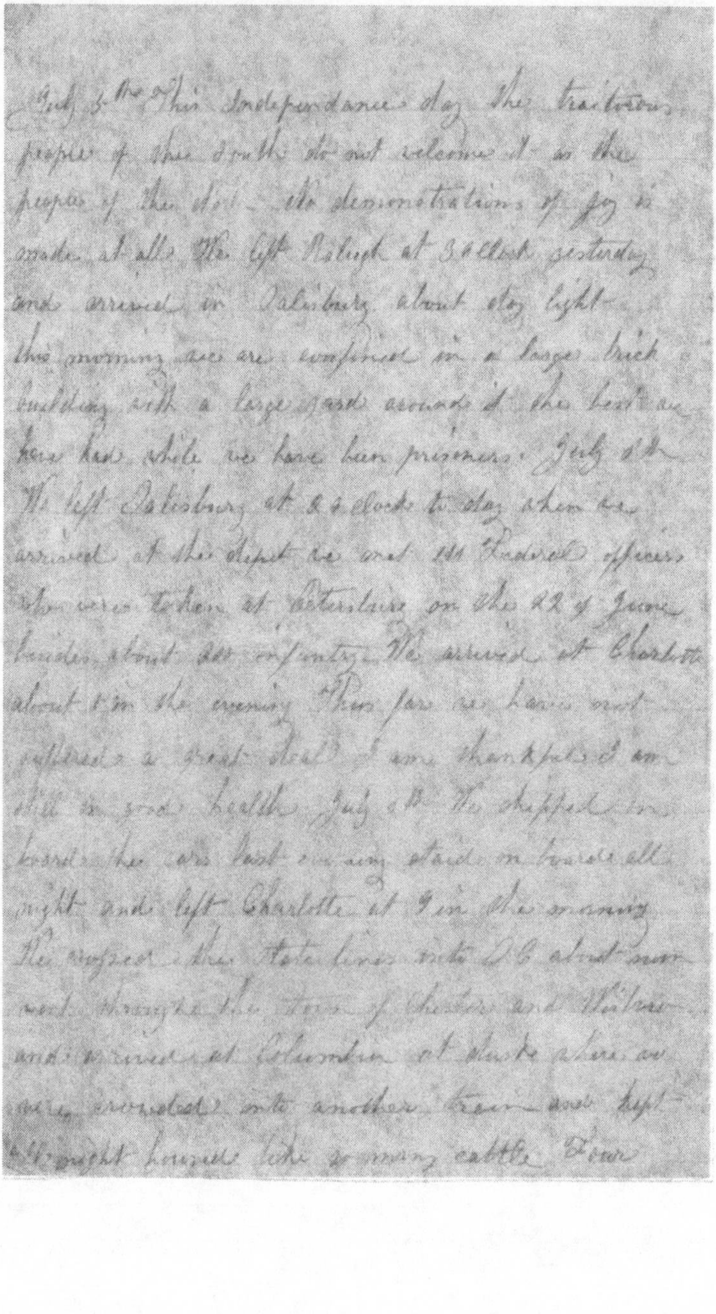

July 5th This Independance day the traitorous
people of the South do not welcome it as the
people of the North the demonstrations of joy is
made at all. We left Raleigh at 3 o'clock yesterday
and arrived in Salisbury about day light
this morning we are confined in a large brick
building with a large yard around it the best we
have had while we have been prisoners. July 6th
We left Salisbury at 2 o'clock to day when we
arrived at the depot we met 100 Federal officers
who were taken at Petersburg on the 22 of June
besides about 200 infantry. We arrived at Charlotte
about 8 in the evening Thus far we have not
suffered a great deal I am thankful I am
still in good health. July 7th We stopped on
board the cars last evening staid on board all
night and left Charlotte at 9 in the morning
We crossed the State lines into S.C. about noon
went through the town of Chester and Winsboro
and arrived at Columbia at dusk where we
were crowded into another train and kept
all night housed like so many cattle. Four

Yankee officers and one Sergt with a soldier of
Confederacy made their escape last night
July 8th We left Columbia last night passed through
several small towns crossed the Savannah river
at dark and arrived at Augusta about 10 at night
We have been living on three hard tack a day for
11 days July 9th We laid in Augusta all day
obtained 2 days rations of C Bread and bacon
took up the line of march or ride for our
destination at Andersonville we passed through
several stations We arrived at Andersonville
about noon and were put in the Stockade about
3 oclock the worst place we have been in yet
July 10th We have been 1 day and night in this old
Stockade over 6th new ones came in to day 5
were hung for murder and they were among the
prisoners The weather has been quite pleasant
God has been good so far in giving us health and
strength July 11th We have lain in prison all
day the weather has been extremely warm One
squad in Camp with another have dug up a pine
stump for wood and through the kindness of

Calion Austin and Jackson who gave us a blanket we were enabled to put up a tent. We rec rations of corn mush to day thus far our health has been preserved. July 12th Still we continue to abide in this old Stockade thus far we have enjoyed good health nothing new has taken place to day. There are from 40 to 80 a day die in this prison. July 13th We are still in this prison there has been considerable excitement in camp to day about parole and exchange of prisoners. I hope there will be an exchange before long. There was a man shot to day by the guard for being over the dead line. July 14th We have spent another day as prisoners of war. We still enjoy good health with the exception of Worthington who seems unwell to day. There was a great excitement among the guard. The commander of the post got information that some of the prisoners are going to make a break so he got the sergeants together and told them that he should open fire upon them if he saw any thing unusual soon after that he had his whole force turned out

July 16th We have spent another day in prison
and we have had quite pleasant weather;
Nothing new has transpired.
There are a number of petitions being drawn
up by men in camp to send to the Govrs
of the Northern States in regard to the
condition of the men in prison.
July 17 To day is the Sabbath how I would
like to be at home to attend worship.
There was a religious meeting meeting held
in prison and quite an interesting meeting.
July 18th We still continue in this prison
as prisoners of war and are likely to for
some time to come. We had our rations
stopped on account of some of the men
trying to dig out of the Stockade.
July 19th Still the weather continues pleasant
Thus far we have not suffered much from
heat God has spared me health and strength
and food enough to survive through all our
privations. Nothing new although there

are all kinds of reports
July 21th Still we are prisoners of war
The forces here are fortifying themselves
and reinforcements are constantly being
sent in they are gaurding against a
raid it is said July 21st Nothing new
has taken place to disturb the monotony
of this dread hole. Thus far we have
enjoyed good health and are in pretty
good spirits July 22 About 600 prisoners
came in to day most of them belonged to
Wilsons command while on the raid were
captured the 29th we still enjoy good health
and fine spirits July 25 The weather
continues quite pleasant nothing new has
transpired to day the enemy are still fortifying
around here July 29th To day is the Sabbath
There was service held in camp and quite
a large attendance There seems to be quite
an interest in religion in prison some are
seeking the salvation of their souls

July 25th Still prisoners of war There was a
report in the rebel papers that the
commission hade met and exchange had
been agreed upon to commence the 8th
of last month. July 26 Still the weather
continues pleasant for a few nights past
we have suffered from cold. There was
about 200 more prisoners came in to day
We have had a slight shower of rain
July 27th Still prisoners but hope the time
is not very far distant when we shall
again be free 200 more Yankees came
in to day July 28th Still the weather
continues pleasant nothing has occured
to day but the arrival of a few more
prisoners When the men went into prison
the rebels fired a shell over the Camp
I suppose they are afraid we shall break
out of prison July 29th Still prisoners
but as yet our health is good for which
we have reason to be thankful The number of
deaths from 8 last night to 8 this morning was 82.

July 30. Still the weather continues pleasant many seem to be confident that there will be an exchange the 6 of next month. I am in hopes there will. July 31st Sunday. Still we are prisoners of war we still enjoy good health while many in the stockade are dying. Nothing new has taken place to disturb the monotony of this prison. Aug 1st Cont. There is nothing new this morning a large number of the sick were taken out to day it is said to be paroled. The point of exchange is said to be Hilton Head S.C. Aug 2d. Still we are prisoners of war there is considerable excitement in camp to day in regard to Gen Stoneman's making a raid on this camp he is already reported to be at Macon. Aug 3. Still the weather continues pleasant. The report that Gen Stoneman was shelling Macon proved to be true for about 200 of his men were captured, they say Gen Stoneman was taken prisoner also. We had a severe thunder shower this evening. Aug 4th. Still we remain prisoners here and I presume are likely to for a month or more. 150 more prisoners came in to day.

July 30 Still the weather continues pleasant many seem to be confident that there will be an exchange the 6 of next month. I am in hopes there will. July 31st Sunday. Still we are prisoners of war. we still enjoy good health while many in this stockade are dying. Nothing new has taken place to disturb the monotony of this prison. Aug 1 (mistake) There is nothing new this morning. a large number of the sick were taken out today it is aid to be paroled. the point of exchange is said to be Hilton Head SC Aug 1st Still we are prisoners of war there is considerable excitement in camp today in regard to Gen Stonemans making a raid on the camp he is already reported to be at Macon. Aug 2 Still the weather continues pleasant. The report that Gen. Stoneman was shelling Macon proved to be true for about 200 of his men were captured, they say Gen S was taken prisoner also. We had a severe thunder shower this evening. Aug 4th Still we remain prisoners of war and I presume are likely to for a month or more 150 more prisoners came in to day.

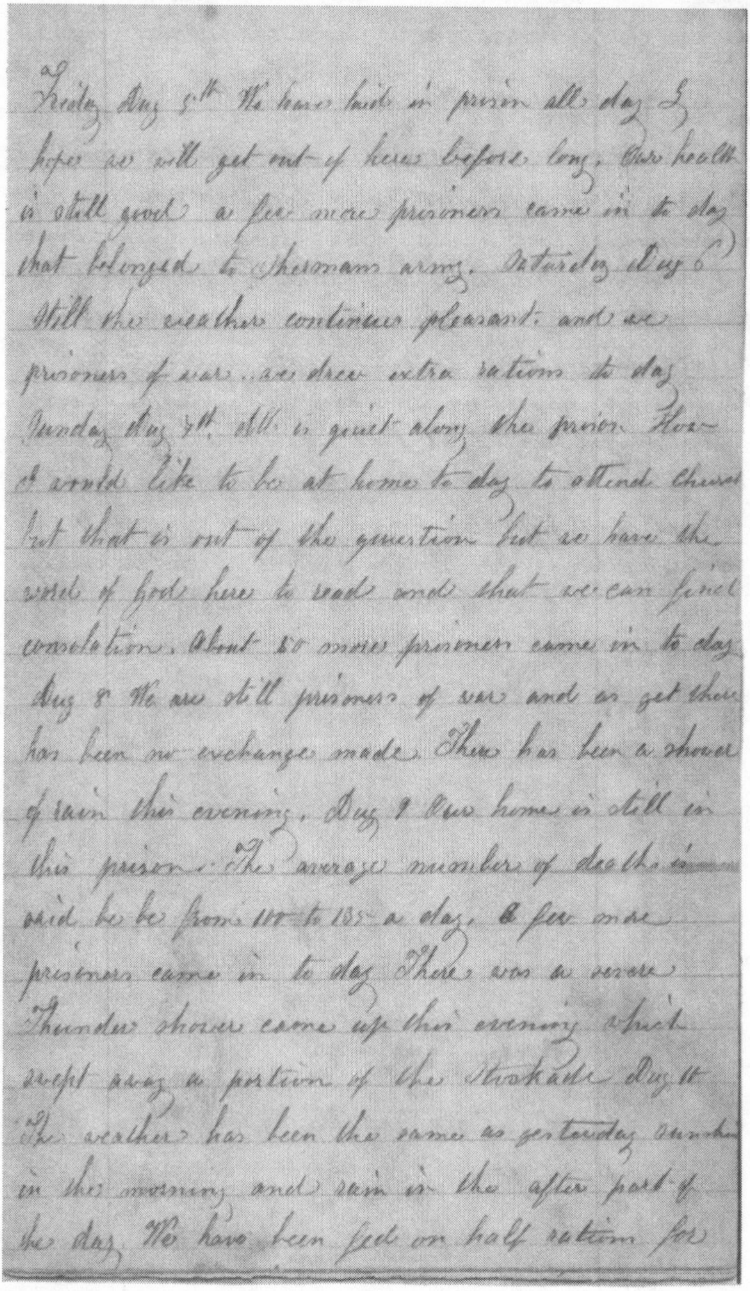
Friday Aug 5th We have laid in prison all day I
hope we will get out of here before long. Our health
is still good a few more prisoners came in to day
that belonged to Shermans army. Saturday Aug 6
Still the weather continues pleasant and we
prisoners of war. we drew extra rations to day
Sunday Aug 7th. All is quiet along the prison. How
I would like to be at home to day to attend Church
but that is out of the question but we have the
word of God here to read and that we can find
consolation. About 50 more prisoners came in to day.
Aug 8 We are still prisoners of war and as yet there
has been no exchange made. There has been a shower
of rain this evening. Aug 9 Our home is still in
this prison. The average number of deaths is
said to be from 110 to 135 a day. A few more
prisoners came in to day There was a severe
Thunder shower came up this evening which
swept away a portion of the Stockade Aug 10
The weather has been the same as yesterday sunshine
in the morning and rain in the after part of
the day. We have been fed on half ration for

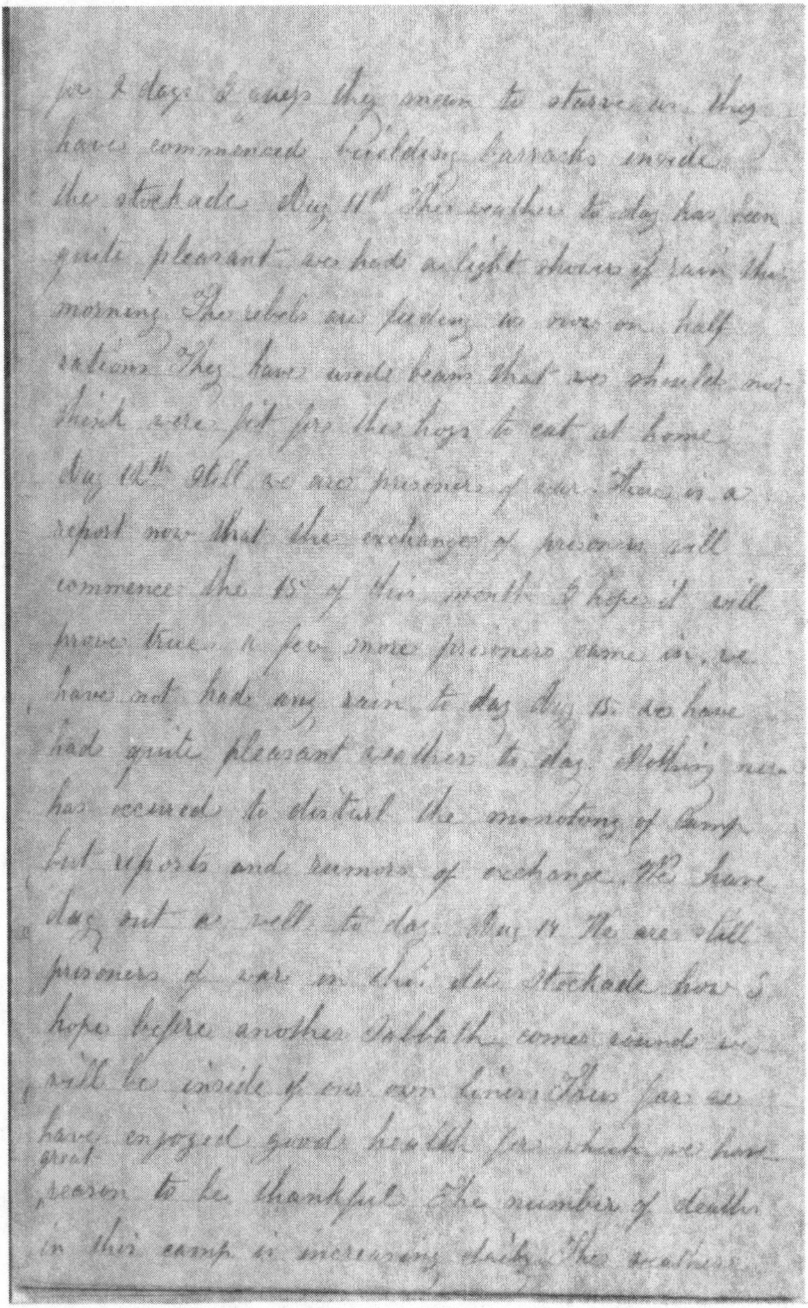
for 2 days & cups they mean to starve us they
have commenced building barracks inside
the stockade Aug 11th The weather to day has been
quite pleasant we had a light shower of rain this
morning The rebels are feeding us now on half
rations They have made beans that we should not
think were fit for the hogs to eat at home
Aug 12th Still we are prisoners of war There is a
report now that the exchange of prisoners will
commence the 15 of this month I hope it will
prove true a few more prisoners came in we
have not had any rain to day Aug 13 we have
had quite pleasant weather to day Nothing new
has occured to disturb the monotony of Camp
but reports and rumors of exchange We have
dug out a well to day Aug 14 We are still
prisoners of war in the old stockade here I
hope before another Sabbath comes round we
will be inside of our own lines Thus far we
have enjoyed good health for which we have
great reason to be thankful The number of deaths
in this camp is increasing daily The weather

is pleasant but warm. Some say the parole will
commence to-morrow. Aug 15 Still we remain
prisoners of war Nothing has transpired to break
the monotony of camp. The parole that was so
strongly rumored to commence to day has all proved
a failure Aug 16 We remain inside of of the
Stockade yet as prisoners of war a few more
came in to day from Sherman army Aug 17
Yet we are prisoners. I hope the time is not far
distant when we will be set free. One of our
number is quite unwell I hope he will get no
worse Aug 18 We are all pretty well to day but
awful hungry for the Confederacy are feeding us
on very small rations we dont get half enough
to eat Aug 19 Still the weather continues pleasant
but extremely warm Nothing new has transpired
to break the monotony of this dread hole
I am in hopes the time is not far distant
when we shall get exchanged or get more rations
Aug 20 The weather to day has been somewhat
variable at times the sun would shine out
extremely warm and then we would have a

slight shower nothing new has taken place to day
Aug 21st The weather to day has been most of the
time unpleasant Another Sabbath is past and
gone I hope we wont have many Sundays to
spend in this hole There is no news of note now
though some think the exchange is still going
on in some other part of the south Aug 22d
The weather to day has been quite pleasant a few
more prisoners came in to day Our health is
still good with the exception of Hayne Aug 23
We are having fine weather with the exception of
being somewhat warm It is now reported that all
the officers are taken out of this prison. Aug 24
Still the weather continues fine and we are
enjoying ourselves pretty well There is not
much excitement now in camp Aug 25 We are
still prisoners of war Thus far our health has
been preserved for which we have great reason
to be thankful We are now getting rations
uncooked if we can get wood we will fare better
Aug 26 The weather to day has been extremely
warm about 150 prisoners came in to day that

was captured in Florida there is no news of note
Aug 27 Still we continue prisoners of war there is
nothing new worthy of note. The usual number of
sick ~~[illegible]~~ continues to die here in this prison.
The rebels continue to fortify and build up
stockades Aug 28 Another Sabbath has come
we would like to be at home to attend
the worship of God, but that is out of the
question We still are in good health and pretty
good Spirits. Aug 29 Just two months ago we were
taken prisoners we had been in hopes by the time
two months were gone we would be inside of
the Union lines A few more prisoners came in
to day from Shermans Army Aug 30 Still we
are prisoners of war all is quiet within the
Stockade a few men made their escape by
cleaving off one of the Stockade logs. Aug 31st
Still we are having pretty fine weather though
rather warm Still in the enjoyment of good
health for which we have reason to be thankful
There has nothing new transpired to day

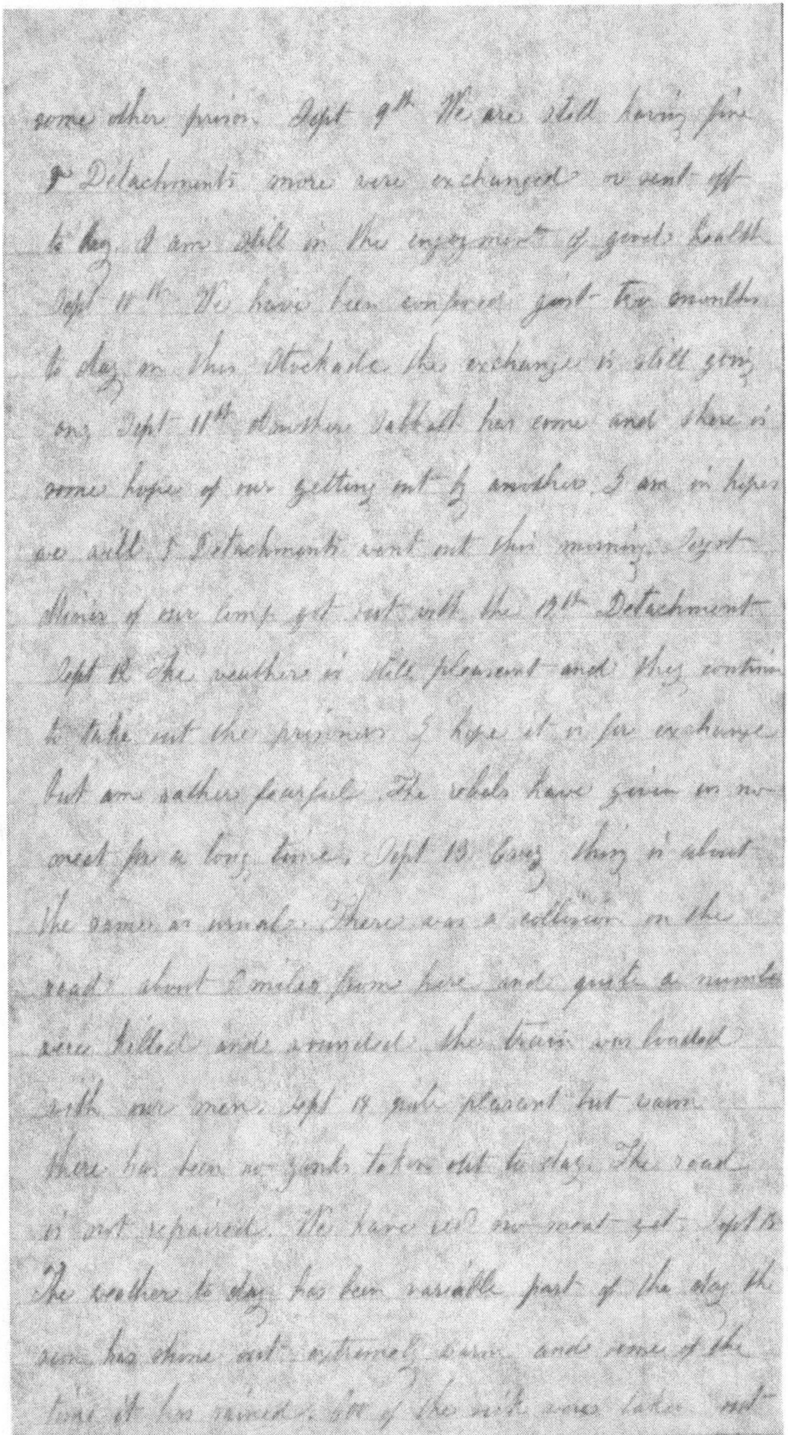

some other prison. Sept 9th We are still having fine
& Detachments more were exchanged or sent off
to day. I am still in the enjoyment of good health
Sept 11th We have been confined just two months
to day in this Stockade the exchange is still going
on. Sept 11th Another Sabbath has come and there is
some hopes of our getting out by another. I am in hopes
we will. 5 Detachments went out this morning. Sept
Three of our Camp got out with the 19th Detachment
Sept 12 The weather is still pleasant and they continue
to take out the prisoners I hope it is for exchange
but am rather fearful. The rebels have given us no
meat for a long time. Sept 13 Every thing is about
the same as usual. There was a collision on the
road about 2 miles from here and quite a number
were killed and wounded the train was loaded
with our men. Sept 14 quite pleasant but warm
there has been no yanks taken out to day. The road
is not repaired. We have had no meat yet. Sept 15
The weather to day has been variable part of the day the
sun has shone out extremely warm and some of the
time it has rained. 500 of the sick were taken out

to day The rebels were good enough to give us ~~some~~ a ration of beef this evening. Sept 16th The weather to day has been somewhat warm there has been no prisoners taken out to day Sept 17th There has been no more taken out to day it is said there is another prison somewhere I hope it is not so Sept 18th We still have fine weather 1500 of Sherman men were taken out this evening I am in hopes before another week comes around we will find ourselves in some other place than this Sept 19 We are having rather unpleasant weather now rather close and muggy I hope we will have a change before long, there has been a few more of Shermans army taken out Sept 20 The weather still continues the same it was said that 1800 more would go out last evening but they did not. Sept 21st The weather continues about the same There is no excitement in camp The remaining Detachments were reorganized counted off into squads of 90. 270 in a Detachments. Sept 22 Still we are prisoners of war without much prospect of getting exchanged or any thing else, There is no news of note Sept 23 All is quiet at the prisoners camp at Georgia

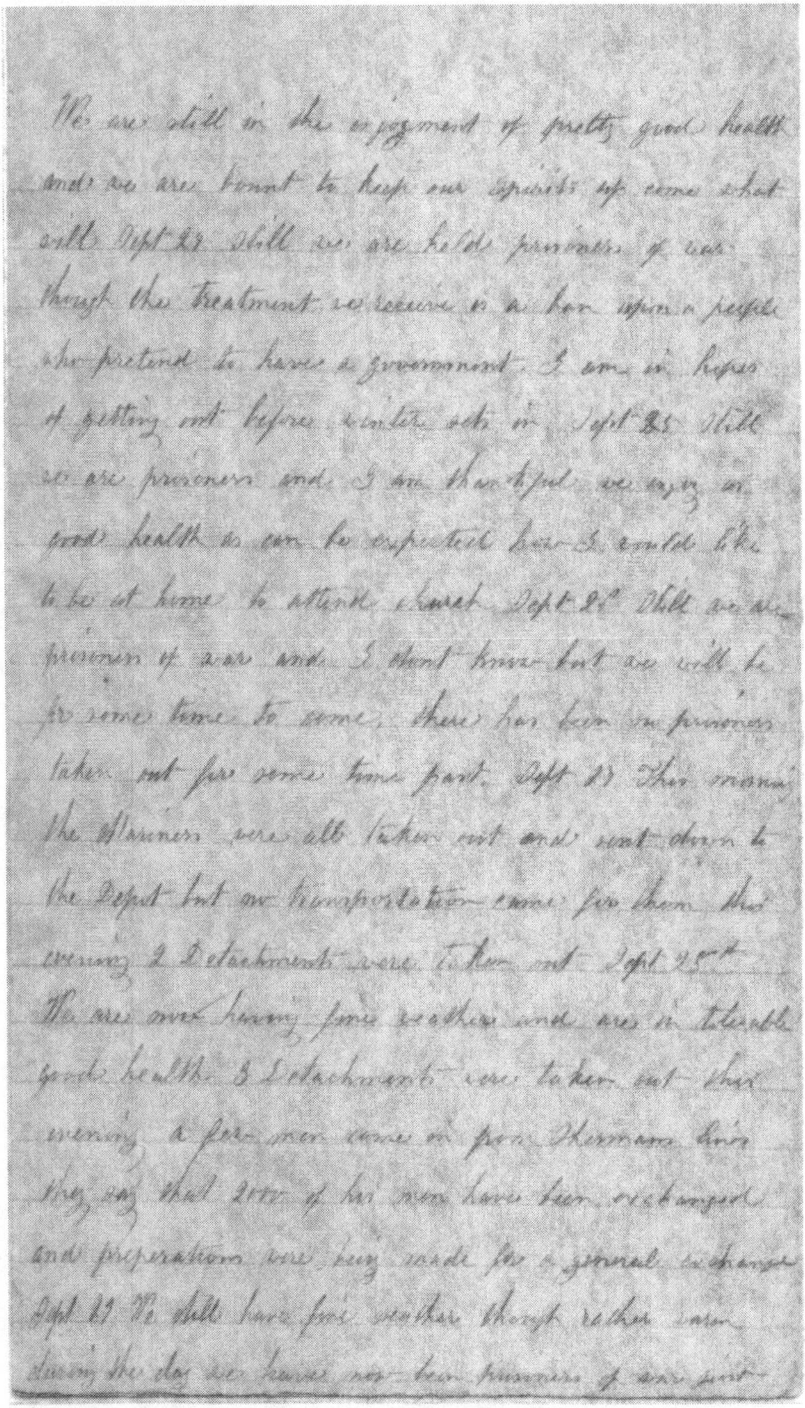
We are still in the enjoyment of pretty good health
and we are bound to keep our spirits up some what
still. Sept 22 Still we are held prisoners of war
though the treatment we receive is a [illegible] upon a people
who pretend to have a government. I am in hopes
of getting out before winter sets in. Sept 23 Still
we are prisoners and I am thankful we enjoy as
good health as can be expected here. I would like
to be at home to attend church. Sept 24 Still we are
prisoners of war and I dont know but we will be
for some time to come, there has been no prisoners
taken out for some time past. Sept 25 This morning
the Marines were all taken out and sent down to
the Depot but no transportation came for them this
evening 2 Detachments were taken out. Sept 26th
We are now having fine weather and are in tolerable
good health 3 Detachments were taken out this
evening a few men came in from Sherman's Army
they say that 2000 of his men have been exchanged
and preparations are being made for a general exchange
Sept 27 We still have fine weather though rather warm
during the day we have now been prisoners of war just

3 months I hope we will not be another month in Succession Sept 30th The weather continues pleasant there is no news some say the exchange will has left confined in the stockade about 4550 the weather in the middle of the day was extremely warm, Oct 1st 1864 The weather to day has been quite pleasant nothing new has taken place to break the monotony of camp. 4 Detachments were taken out this evening it is hoped for exchange. Sunday Oct 2d The weather to day has been extremely warm we still are prisoners of war and I dont know but we shall be for most of the winter Oct 3d Still we are prisoners of war there is nothing new of note we have had quite a severe storm of rain this afternoon there has been no prisoners taken out for two evenings. Oct 4th The weather to day has been quite pleasant this evening 4 Detachments went out Oct 5th The weather to day has been very pleasant all quiet at Camp Sumpter last night the rebels issued to us some soft soap a new thing in the line of soldiers rations Oct 6th The weather to day has been rather unpleasant This eve we pulled up stakes and went over to South gate but

we did not get out I presume we will get out
to-morrow night Oct 7th The weather to day has been
quite pleasant though the sun has not shone out
much We still are in the enjoyment of good health
We packed up thi we ready to go but did not get
out after all Oct 8th The weather to day has been
pleasant but the evening has been quite cool
there has been no more taken out. Oct 9 the
weather to day has been quite like the fall of the
year The rebels made us made us all move over
to the south side of the Stockade and formed us
into new Detachments To day is the Sabbath but
how little it appeared like Sunday at home
we still are in the enjoyment of good for which
we have great reason to be thankful Oct 10 Still
we are prisoners of war and are likely to be I guess
for the winter the weather is fine but the evenings
somewhat cool Oct 11th We still continue to have fine
weather Last evening we had quite a severe frost
The rebels issued to the sick Hard Bread and Bacon
This evening 37 men of Shermans army came in were
taken prisoners while guarding the R.R.

Oct 12th We are now having fine weather To day the
Police commenced laying out the streets we will
have to pull down our house and pitch over again
We recd rations of Molasses & Rice to day.
Oct 13th Still we are prisoners of war and I dont
know but we will be in Secession dominions during
the winter We moved our tents to day and are formed
in regular order we recd rations of S Bread Beef Bacon
and Beans Oct 14th The weather continues pleasant
There is no news of note to disturb the monotony
of the Camp. Our health is good as can be expected
though I think if we were in our lines we would be
on the sick list. Oct 15 We are having very fine weather
We recd rations of Rice Molasses & S Bread. Oct 16
The weather to day has been warm and muggy How
I would like to be home to attend church but that
is out of the question we still try to keep up hope
of getting out sometime. Oct 18 The weather to day
has been rather unpleasant All the rations we
recd this one was about 1/8 of pint of Molasses
& a pint of Beans. Oct 19th The weather has been about
the same as it has for a week 70 men out of

a Detachment was now sent out for the purpose
of fetching in meals we rations of C Bread Beef
Bacon and beans Oct 18th Still continue to have fine
weather I am suffering somewhat from a ~~some~~ cold
Oct 19th Still we are prisoners of war and I don't
see much prospect of getting out very soon I am
afraid we shall see the dawn of a New Year in this
prison if we should live Oct 20 The weather
is fine though the nights are cool we rec'd rations
of Rice Molasses and C Bread Oct 22 The weather
to day has been unpleasant and cold with a very
cold wind We have been at work building our
house to day Oct 23 The weather to day has been
rather pleasant I am not enjoying very good health
at present but trust I will soon recover Oct 24
We still are prisoners of war and I fear the time
is some ways off before we will be exchanged
I am feeling somewhat better to day Oct 25 There
is no news of note There is quite a large amount
of sickness in camp at present Oct 26 To day
the sky has been overcast with clouds and it
has the appearance of a storm gathering I fear

there will be a great amount of suffering should
a heavy storm take place report says that an
exchange will take place the 22d of next month
Oct 27 The weather to day has been rather unpleasant
there was a severe storm this afternoon we rec'd
rations of rice & Molasses Oct 28th The weather to
day has been quite pleasant I am now in the
enjoyment of pretty good health and if we could
get Uncle Sams rations we would soon be strong
we receive very small rations of C Bread Beans & Beef
Oct 29 It is now just 4 months ago to day since we
were taken prisoners I am in hopes we wont be
4 months more in the hands of the rebels rec'd rations
to day of Rice & Molasses Oct 30th The weather to day
has been quite pleasant We are still prisoners of war
although I am in hopes we wont be all winter the
rumor is now that 10,000 sick are to be exchanged
We rec'd orders this evening to be ready to move in
the morning at 2 o'clock. Oct 31st This morning at
2 we packed up and by 8 we were on the train
for for the prison at Millen the weather to day has
been quite pleasant but think it will storm soon

Nov 1st This morning we arrived at Millen at the
early hour of 2 o'clock. The ride was a tedious one
for we were in a box car the distance was about
150 miles from Andersonville and we are about 80
miles from Savannah. The weather was cold and it
rained some. Nov 2nd It has been stormy and cold
to-day we are in a better place than we were at
A[ndersonville] ... of Andersonville the prisoners are in here
who were sent from that place in Sept. since the
sun has shone out once more but it is quite cold
we are now in the 8th Div 1st Detach. we recd rations
for the first time in two days on account of Jeff
Davis appointing the 2nd day of this month as fast day.
Nov 3rd Still the weather continues cold there is no
news of note we recd rations of meal, rice, salt and
beef. Nov 5th The weather to day has been quite pleasant
We have dug a hole in the ground and put a
blanket over it so that we are quite comfortable
we recd 2 days ration of bread 1 days rice and beans
and 2 days salt beef Nov 6th The weather to day
has been quite pleasant. We are now pretty well situated
... of the rebels will give us plenty of rations as ...

we are now enjoying pretty good health for which we have great reason to be thankful Nov 7th We still continue to have fine weather there is quite an excitement in camp about exchange a Savannah paper states that 10,000 sick are to be exchanged next week. I hope it is so About 300 men have taken the oath of allegiance to the Confederacy. Nov 8th Still we continue to have fine weather The Presidential election takes place at the North were I at home I would vote for Abe Lincoln for the Chair Nov 9th The weather is pleasant There is considerable excitement about exchange. To days paper says it will commence next week I am in hopes it is so Nov 10th The weather to day has been cold and unpleasant. It is said that clothing has arrived from the U.S. Government for the prisoners I hope it is so for some are sadly in need of it Nov 11th The weather to day has been quite pleasant The rebels officers have been in getting the number of the sick and those destitute of clothing. Some were in also to get men to take the oath of allegiance to the Southern Confederacy about 100 were taken

in I think they are very foolish and are jumping
out of the frying pan into the fire. Nov 12 Still the
weather continues pleasant. The rumor to day is that
there is to be a general exchange to commence next
Tuesday there is more signs of exchange than I have
seen. Nov 13th The weather now is quite pleasant
though the nights are somewhat cool. 100 more men
came in from Andersonville these are the last
of all in that prison. We are now in the enjoyment
of good health for which we have reason to be thankful
Nov 14th To day the weather has been quite pleasant
We built a fire place and chimney to our tent to day
received rations of Sweet potatoes, beans, rice and Beef
it is said the sick leave to morrow. Nov 15th Still the
weather continues pleasant. This morning the worst
cases of the sick were taken out to be sent to our lines
for exchange. A few men from Shermans army came
in to day. The report is that a general exchange
is to take place hope it is so. Nov 16th Weather still
pleasant the sick that were taken out yesterday
came back to day they could not leave on account
of transportation It is said they will leave on Friday.

have gone out to day there is no news of note.
We rec'd rations of rice Beef salt & potatoes Nov 13th
100 men were taken for exchange There is nothing
of account transpired to day In the enjoyment of
good health weather fine Nov 14th 120 more prisoners
were taken out to day I wrote a letter to be taken
through to our lines by one of them The day was
cloudy a storm arising our rations this eve were better
than usual they have increased nearly one half.
Nov 15 The weather to day has been quite unpleasant
To day is the Sabbath I would like much to be at
home to attend the worship of God but such a
privilege is denied us about 400 were taken out
to day Nov 21st This morning we were routed out
about 1 o clock
of beds and camp and put on to the cars in all haste
We were started off for Savannah by & had arrived at
that city about 5 o clock in the evening It has rained
all day which made it very unpleasant and we rec'd
1 & ½ hard tack and a small piece of beef for 1

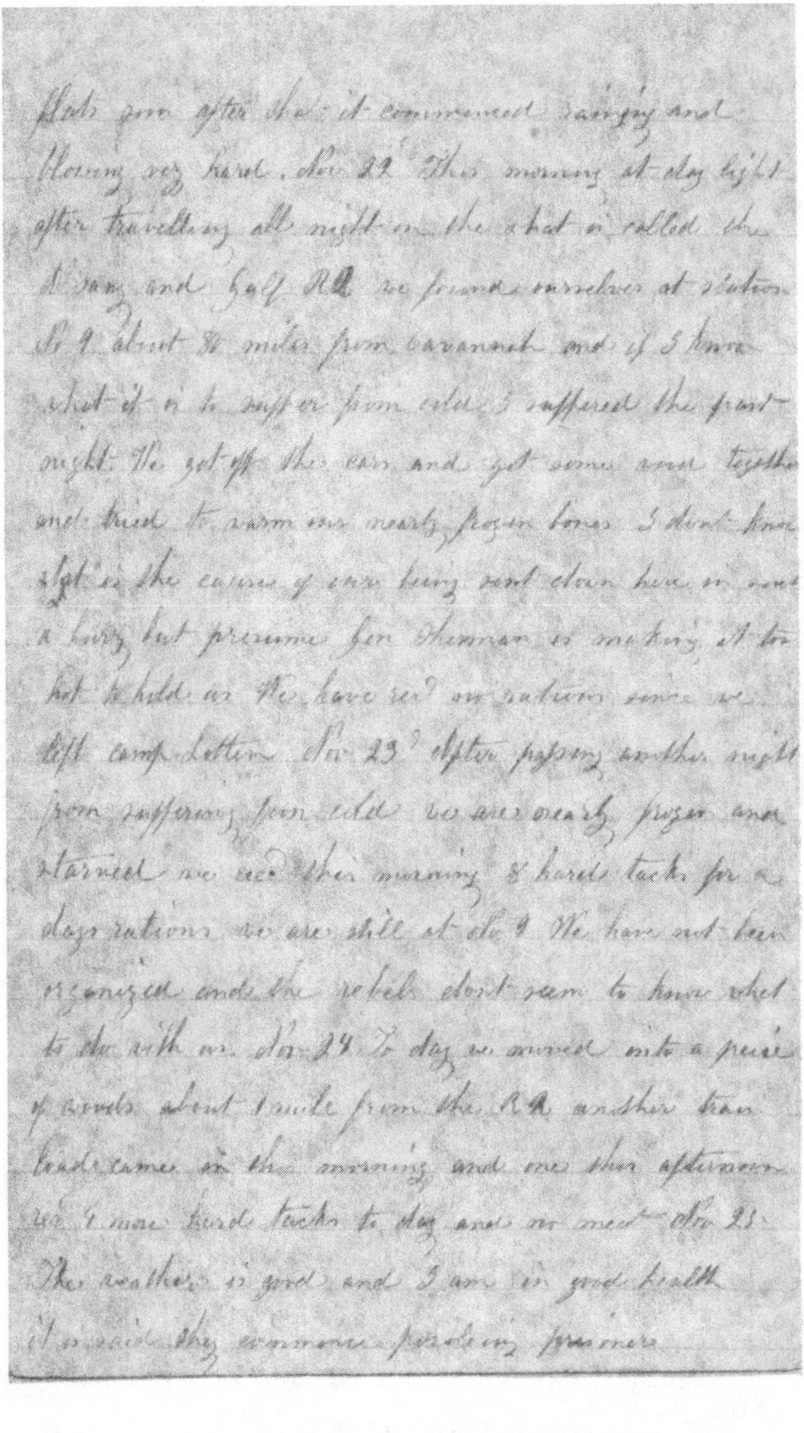
State soon after that it commenced raining and
blowing very hard. Nov 22 This morning at day light
after travelling all night on the what is called the
Savannah and Gulf RR we found ourselves at Station
No 9 about 80 miles from Savannah and if I know
what it is to suffer from cold I suffered the past
night. We got off the cars and got some wood together
and tried to warm our nearly frozen bones I don't know
what is the cause of our being sent down here in such
a hurry but presume for Sherman is making it too
hot to hold us. We have rec'd no rations since we
left camp Lawton Nov 23d After passing another night
from suffering from cold we are nearly frozen and
starved we rec'd this morning 8 hard tacks for 2
days rations we are still at No 9 We have not been
organized and the rebels don't seem to know what
to do with us Nov 24 To day we moved into a piece
of woods about 1 mile from the RR another train
load came in this morning and one this afternoon
we 4 more hard tacks to day and no meat Nov 25
The weather is good and I am in good health
It is said they commence paroling prisoners

to morrow We rec. Rations of hard bread, rice and
salt & Beef Nov 26 The weather to day has been
very pleasant and warm. 1000 men were paroled
to day & sent towards Savannah We have rec
rations of Corned Beef and Salt, Nov 27th The
weather to day has been quite pleasant. 1000 more
men were taken out to day but for some cause
or other we was not paroled or sent away. I wasnt
lucky enough to get out this time We rec two
days rations it is said we will go to-morrow we
are still in the enjoyment of good helth and in
hopes of getting home before long. Nov 28 We still
continue to have fine weather during the day it
is nearly as warm as June in York state We did
not succeed in getting away some say all the
transportation on the road is pressed for tran-
-porting troops between Florida and Savannah
We rec another days ration it is said in order to
be ready to move at a moments notice.
it is said that to-morrow the camp will be
reorganized Nov 29 The camp was reorganized
to day and it was found that the Yankees

Journal skips to March 17, 1865

Friday March 17 The weather to day has been very
warm and pleasant there is no news of note
It is reported through this camp that some
will leave to-morrow
Saturday March 18th We have had another
very fine pleasant day the exchange has
commenced at this camp at last three officers
and about 700 men were shipped The rebels
are taking none but Western men They say
the Eastern men will have to go to some other point
Sunday March 19th The weather still continues
pleasant There has no prisoners left here to day
It is said 1000 will go Tuesday next [illegible] is [illegible]
unwell I hope he will soon recover,
Monday March 20th Still we continue to have
pleasant weather there nothing taken place
to day worthy of note excepting the taking
of out Mechanics on parole of honor for
the purpose of building a bridge over the
Chatahooche river and making Bricks and
what I should call aiding and abetting
the enemy.

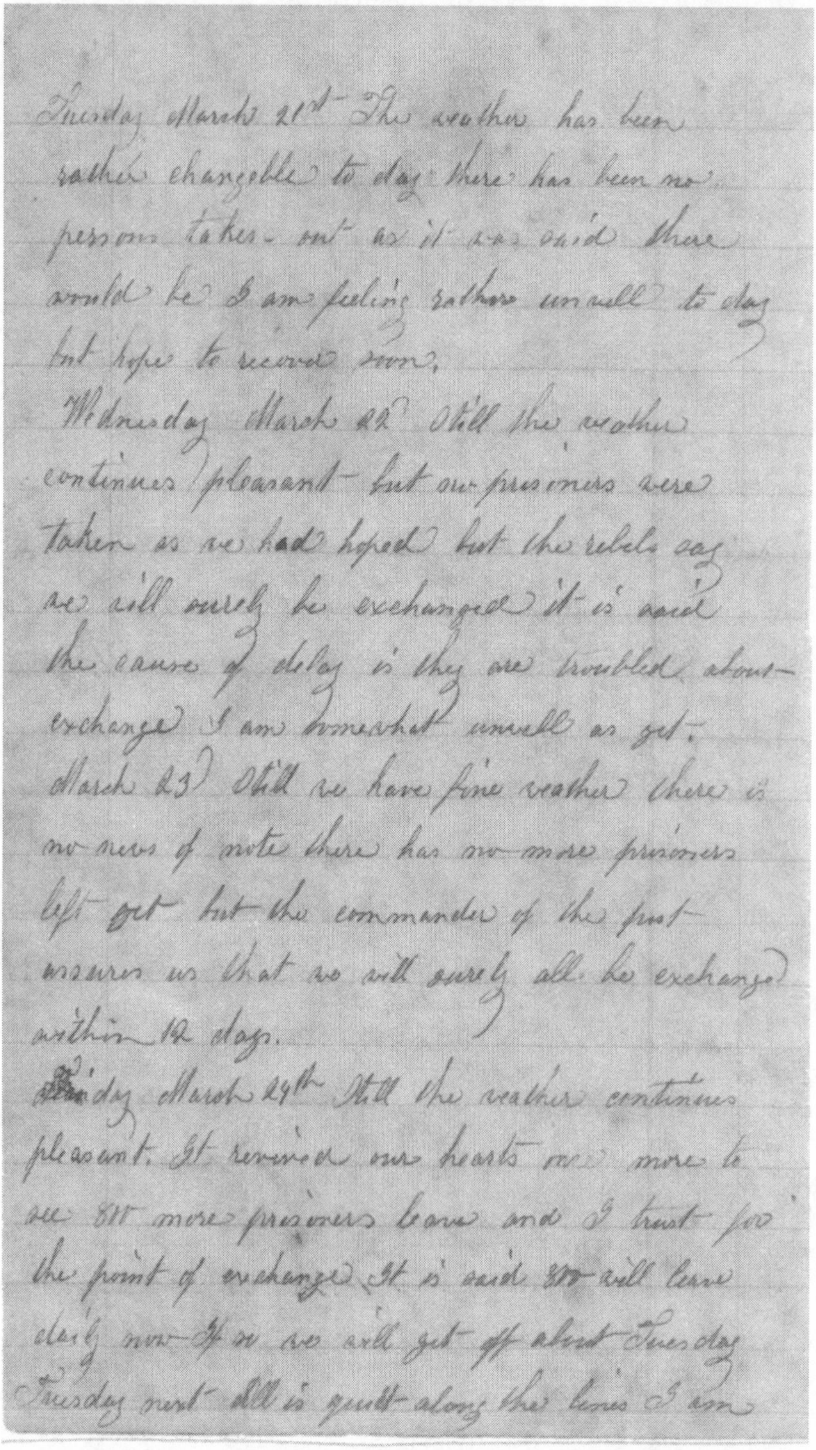
Tuesday March 21st The weather has been
rather changeble to day there has been no
persons taken out as it was said there
would be I am feeling rather unwell to day
but hope to recover soon.
Wednesday March 22d Still the weather
continues pleasant but our prisoners were
taken as we had hoped but the rebels say
we will surely be exchanged it is said
the cause of delay is they are troubled about
exchange I am somewhat unwell as yet.
March 23d Still we have fine weather there is
no news of note there has no more prisoners
left yet but the commander of the post
assures us that we will surely all be exchanged
within 12 days.
Friday March 24th Still the weather continues
pleasant. It revived our hearts once more to
see 800 more prisoners leave and I trust for
the point of exchange It is said 800 will leave
daily now If so we will get off about Tuesday
Tuesday next All is quiet along the lines I am

feeling quite well to day.

Saturday March 25th Still the weather continues pleasent 500 more left to day a large proportion being those who bought themselves out.

Sunday March 26th Another Sabbath has come around and we still are prisoners of war but the rebels assure us that before another week passes away we will be inside of Union lines I hope and trust it is so I am feeling quite well to day for which I have great reason to be thankful A is quite sick but I hope he will soon recover 600 more prisoners were sent off to day There was no service held in camp to day weather still is fine.

Monday March 27th Still we continue to have fine weather though it looks this evening as if it would storm before long 500 men were paroled to day but did not get away it is said that the train is broken down our men say they are paroled under the old Cartel of 1862.

Tuesday March 28th It has been rather unpleasant to day a greater portion of the day being rainy There has been no more prisoners taken out as yet I am quite well now
Wednesday March 29th The weather to day has been changeable but not very stormy It is now 7 months we have been prisoners of war as yet no more trains have come for the transportation of prisoners but the rebels tell us we need not worry for every thing will go off right again in a few days It is reported in the Rebel papers that our forces have made a raid on the R.R between Montgomery and Florida about 18 miles from the former place
Thursday March 30th The weather to day has been quite pleasant but somewhat gusty and blustering No more prisoners have been taken out as yet The Lt. commanding the post came in and told the boys that the point of exchange had changed from Vicksburg Miss to Jacksonville Fla and that we would all leave here as soon as transportation could be furnished [illegible]

Journal skips to May 16, 1865

May Tuesday 16th The weather still continues fine we arrived at Annapolis about 9 this morning We were taken off the steamer and marched up to Parole Barracks in the rear of St Johns College We will here get our Computation money and then be sent to Camp Parole about two miles from town The papers states that Jeff Davis is captured and I am in hopes it is so.
Wrote a letter home to day.

May 17th The weather has been quite pleasant but exceedingly warm we have been mustered for our Computation money to day wrote a letter to J H Ford of the 5th J C no news of note

May 18th Last evening we had a fine shower of rain and in consequence we have little cooler weather to day there has none of the prisoners been sent to Camp Parole nor none to Camp Chase Ohio We recd our Computation money to day mine amounted to $24.50 for [illegible] months at 25 cts a day

Friday May 19th The weather has been somewhat
variable to day We were all sent to Camp Parole
to day from which we will be sent to our
respective states and be mustered out of the
service of the United States.
Saturday May 21th The sky to day has been
beclouded most of the time but we have
had no rain at about 8 O Clock this morning
we were marched down to the wharf we then
took the steamer Conn for Baltimore we left
Annapolis about noon and arrived in Baltimore
about 2 O clock we there took the cars for Phil'a
arrived there about 1 O Clock the next morning
We there went to the Coopers Shop Refreshment Saloon
and got a lunch then all the N Y & Mass an R I
State troops were put on a steamer for N Y I was
unfortunate enough to be left behind but guess
I will be able to catch up with them before
they go to Albany if that is where they are going

Sunday May 21st It has been a wet stormy day
attended S School and service at the 3d
Baptist Church the S School was quite interesting
found Superintendent and teachers very kind
and Sociable the sermon was quite interesting
the text was taken from the 19 Chap of Leviticus
and 11th verse found a gentleman there of the
of Bodgy formerly from Southampton all the
members were very kind to me I expect now
to leave in the train from Kensington Depot
A gentleman came up to me and very kindly
asked me to go and take tea with him as
I had plenty of time I accepted this gentleman
names was Rushton after tea he took me down
to the Station the train left at 6 35 arrived
in N Y at 11,30 in the car paid my fare which
was $3.00

Monday May 22d 1865 In N Y city
and I end the journal
reached home on Tuesday.

On April 12, 1865, Lee surrendered. On April 15, Lincoln died. Johnston surrendered to Sherman. The Confederacy died. The fighting was finished, but not before taking a toll of 204,070 soldiers (94,000 Confederate, 110,070 Union) killed in battle and 414,152 (164,000 Confederate, 250,152 Union) dead from disease; a total of 618,222 soldiers in total. *Note: This is more than all of America's combined combats, without the Civil War, from Revolutionary War through the current combats in the Middle East.* The Confederates lost less in battle or from disease. The total loss, dead or disabled throughout the population caused by the rebellion had to have been over 800,000. Nearly three and a half million men met the call to arms. These estimated figures will never be fully certain as reports were lost or never made.

Now that Lee had surrendered, Grant could actively work on exchanging the prisoners back to their homes; something he would not do during the conflict because he felt the Confederate soldiers would return instantly to duty in the Army of North Virginia to appear against him and his Union prisoners would not return to their troop units, so exchange of prisoners became unnecessary to him. The South, when feeling they had to allow some prisoners leave due to the conditions at Andersonville, only paroled the ones from the West so they would have longer time to find their units.

15 *RELEASE, RETURN AND RECUPERATE*

MAY 16 -1865 May 16, 1865

Letter to Mother after my Release:

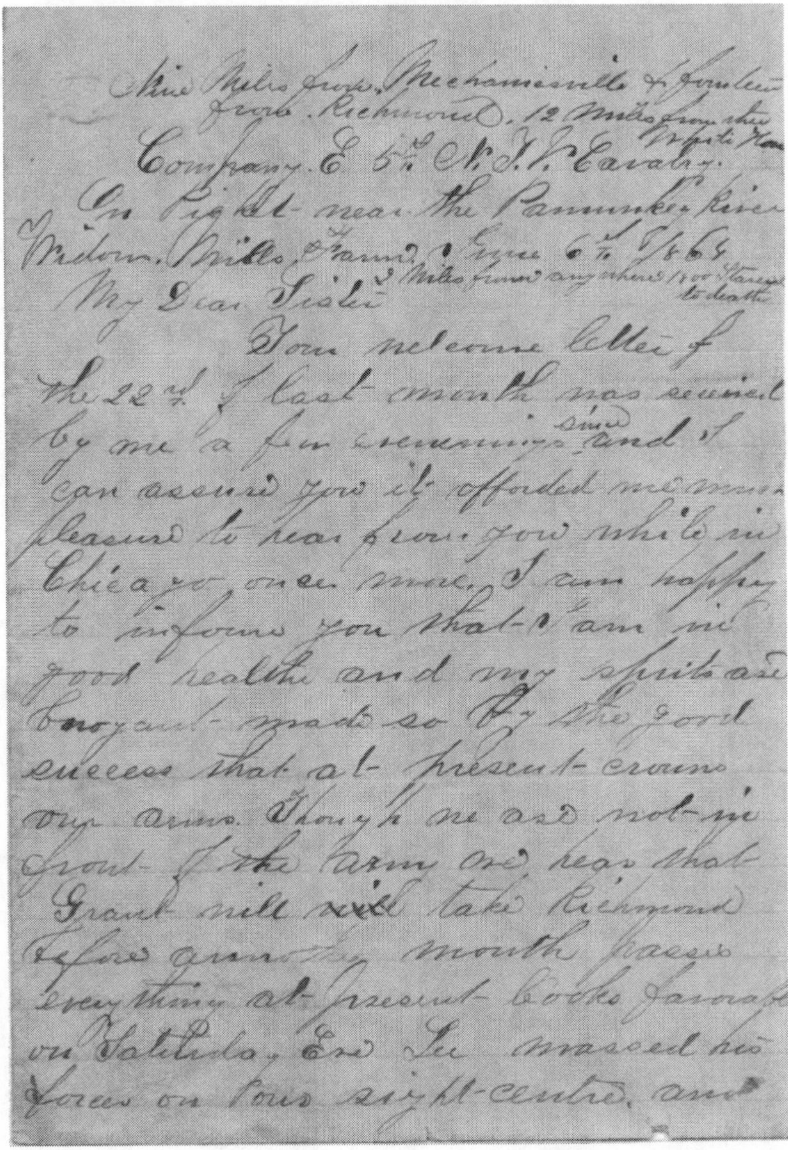

Nine Miles from Mechanicsville & fourteen from Richmond. 12 Miles from the White House

Company E 5th N. J. Cavalry.

On Picket near the Pamunkey River

Widow Mills Farm June 6th 1864

My Dear Sister 3 Miles from anywhere / 400 starved to death

Your welcome letter of the 22nd of last month was received by me a few evenings since and I can assure you it afforded me much pleasure to hear from you while in Chicago once more. I am happy to inform you that I am in good health and my spirits are buoyant made so by the good success that at present crowns our arms. Though we are not in front of the army we hear that Grant will ~~xxx~~ take Richmond before another month passes everything at present looks favorable on Saturday Gen Lee massed his forces on ours right centre and

and tried several times to break
through but did not succeed.
Grant has his forces all entrenched
and as fast as he advances he
entrenches himself there is a line
of earth works all the way from
the Rapidan that Grant has thrown
up. In the attack on Saturday night
(which lasted about five hours) the
rebels left 2000 ~~on~~ dead & wounded
on the field our loss was 300.
I never saw such determination among
~~as~~ the men of the army as at present
they all seem to feel as if they must
go forward and the men have a
world of confidence in Gen Grant
The army has never been better
maneuvered than at the present
campaign. Our Co has lost its
usual number of these this summer
our Orderly Serg't was killed a few
weeks since ~~[illegible]~~ while on duty

advancing on Milford Station
The first platoon of our Company made
a charge on foot over a bridge and the
planks were torn up on one end
and we did not see it until we came
to the hole in the bridge so that we
crowded in together on the bridge.
and it took a few minutes to get
up and the rebels were in the
woods a few yards ahead of us.
and we were so exposed that
had there been many of them
they might have killed the whole
of us but no one was hurt but
the Sergt. he was shot through the breast
just above the heart he got down
of his horse walked of the bridge and
died. We have had 2 Sergts wounded
since our loss in non commissioned
officers has been larger than any other
Company in the Regt. We have had 3
Sergts killed 2 wounded & one is now

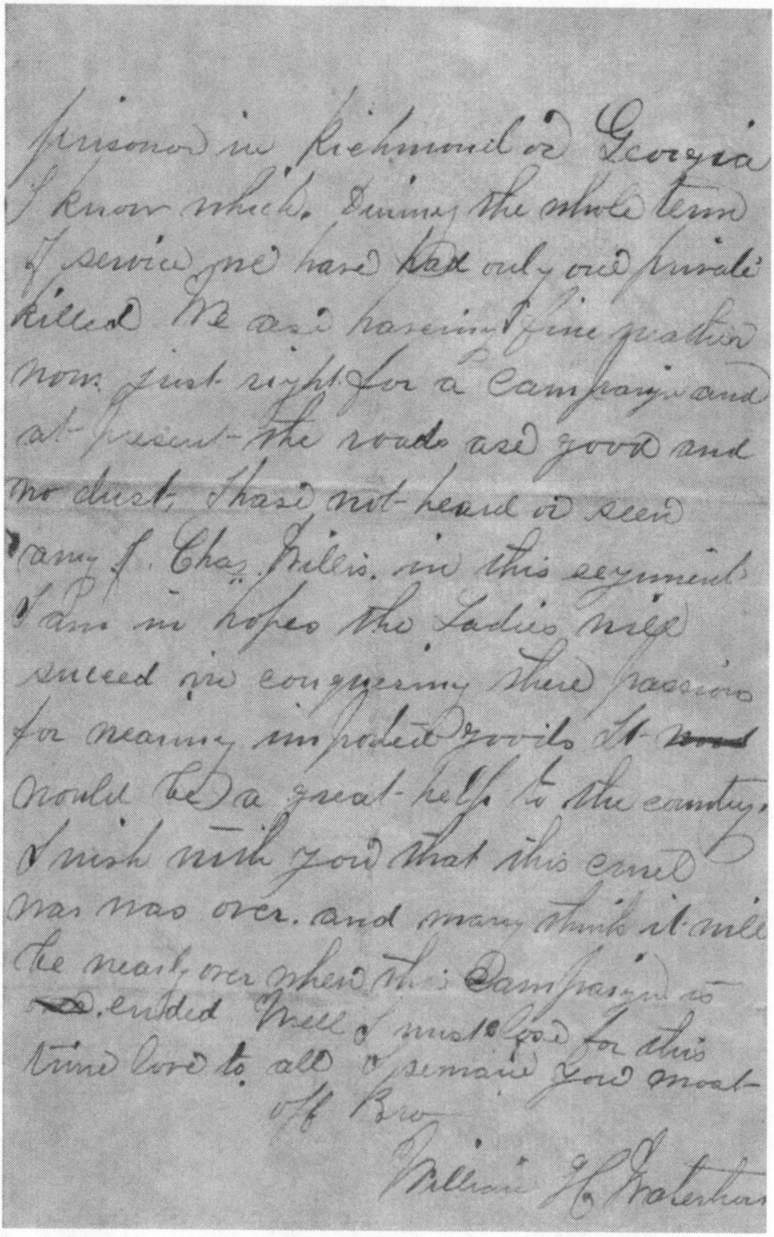
prisoner in Richmond or Georgia
I know which. During the whole term
of service we have had only one private
killed. We are haveing fine weather
now. just right for a Campaign and
at present the roads are good and
no dust, I have not heard or seen
any of Chas Millers in this regiment
I am in hopes the Ladies will
succeed in conquering there passion
for wearing imported goods It
would be a great help to the country.
I wish with you that this cruel
war was over. and many think it will
be nearly over when this Campaign is
ended Well I must go for this
time love to all I remain your most
aff Bro

William H. Waterhan

My journey home was long, complicated and tiring to be free but not really free. The month of April was spent day by day waiting to be transferred from Andersonville to Jacksonville and then waiting longer for the ship to be raised from the St. John's River. It had

May 24, 1865 Letter to Sister Cinty:

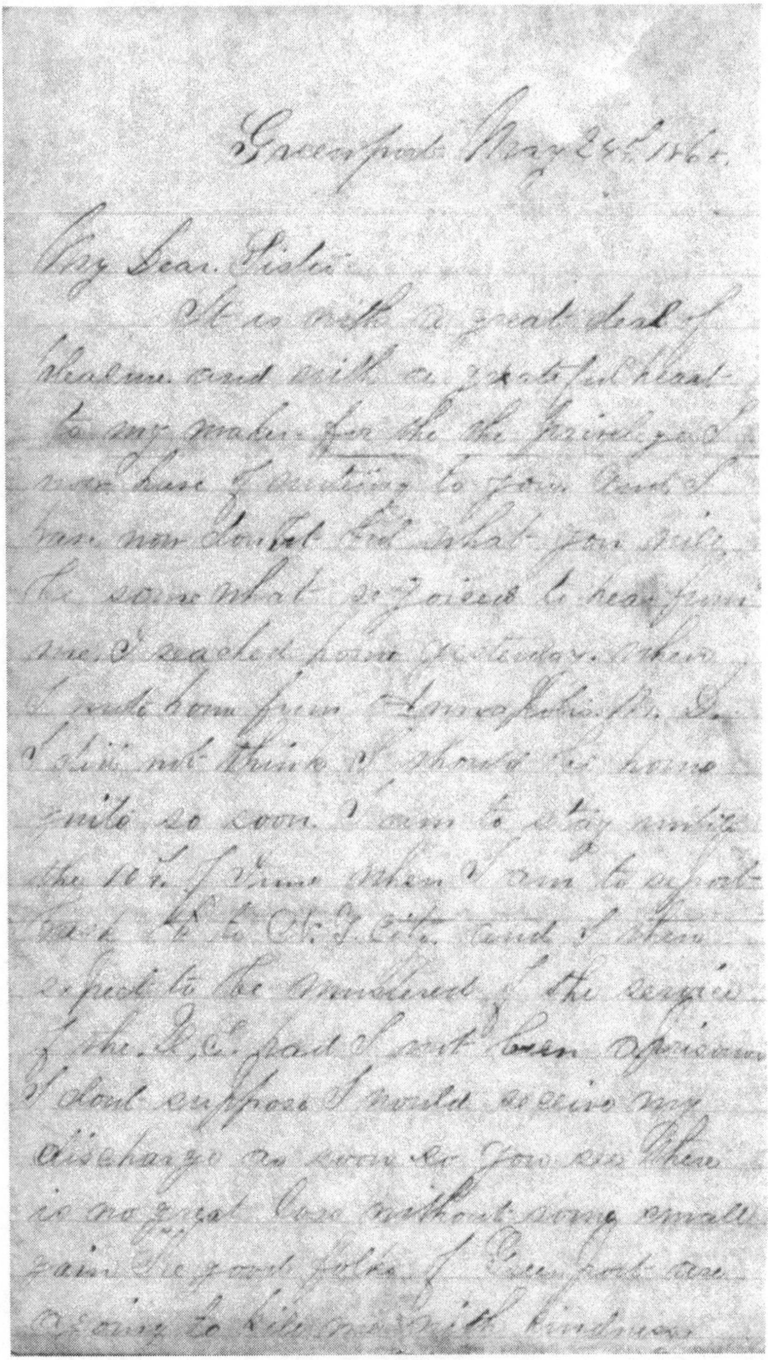

Greenport May 24th 1865.

My Dear Sister
It is with a great deal of pleasure and with a grateful heart to my maker for the the privilege of now here of writing to you and I have now doubt but what you will be some what rejoiced to hear from me. I reached home yesterday. When I wrote home from Annapolis Md. I did not think I should be home quite so soon. I am to stay until the 10th of June when I am to report back to N.Y. City and I then expect to be mustered out of the service of the U.S. had I not been a prisoner I dont suppose I would receive my discharge as soon as you see there is no great loss without some small gain. The good folks of Greenport are going to kill me with kindness

I guess for everybody is coming to
see me. And everyone wants to do
something. I am very thankful to
them. And I can appreciate there kindness
I think if anyone can. Mother tells
me you intend to come east. I am
in hopes you will as soon as possible
And I am hopes Willie will be able
to come on with you. And if he don't
have a good time fishing &c then
no one can. I fear I will have to be in
city most of next month after the 10th
But still I may not perhaps they will
muster me out inside of 36 hours
after I get there and they may be the
whole month about it. Mother says
you have been enlarging your family
by introducing a boy and it's name
is ~~Will~~ Wm. Now it must be either
its fathers or my namesake. I think I
will have to lay claim to it. And may
God grant that you may be permitted
to raise and that it may become a

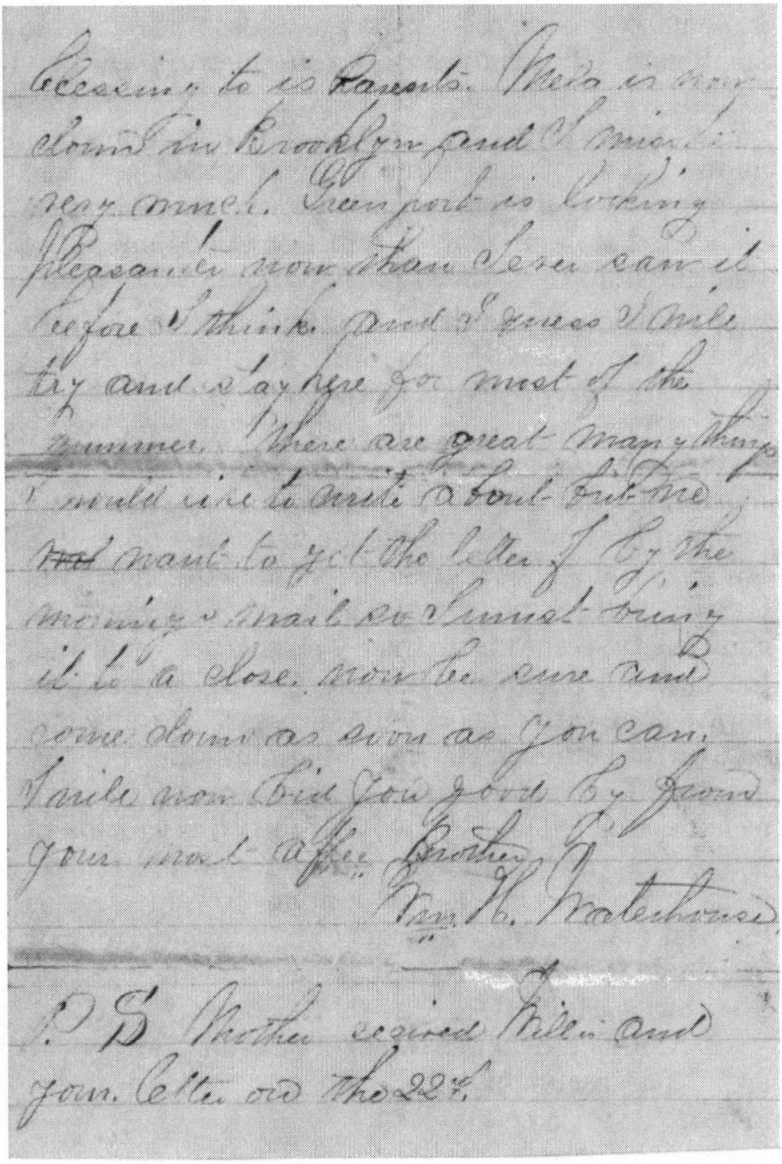
blessing to his Parents. Theo is now down in Brooklyn and I miss him very much. Greenport is looking pleasanter now than I ever saw it before I think and I guess I will try and stay here for most of the summer. There are great many things I would like to write about but we want to get the letter of by the morning mail so I must bring it to a close. now be sure and come down as soon as you can. I will now bid you good by from your most affec Brother
Wm. H. Waterhouse

P. S. Mother received Ellen and your letter on the 22d.

When I arrived home on May 23rd my strength gave out and I accepted the great love and care from my family and community. In this letter I expressed gladness and my philosophy "...had I not been a prisoner I dont suppose I would receive my discharge so soon so you see there is no great loss without some small gain." It took most of the summer to regain my health.

At one time I had thought about signing up for another tour of duty after the war ended and had mentioned it in my letters, but my loved ones seeing the emaciated state in which I returned talked me out of that decision; therefore, I mustered out of the service with my fellow 5th Cavalry of New York patriots at Hart's Island, New York Harbor, July 19, 1865, with the pension of thirty dollars a month.

Our commanding officer spoke: "After four years of hardship and honor, you return to your State to be mustered out of service, and to return once more to a peaceful life among your friends and loved ones. In a few days you will be scattered, and the Fifth New York Cavalry will be no more. The hardships you have endured, the comforts of which you have been deprived, the cheerful and proud manner in which you have always done your duty, and the successes you have met with on the battlefield, have won the admiration of every general officer under whom you have served. Surpassed by none, equaled [sic] by few, your record as a regiment is a glorious and honorable one. May your future lives be as prosperous and as full of honor to yourselves as the past four years have been to your country, to your State, and to the Fifth New York Cavalry.
(Signed,) A. H. WHITE,
Col. Comdg. Fifth New York Cavalry."

The regiment enrollment and losses were as follows:

Original number of men, 1,064; recruits added, 1,074; original, number of officers, 50; whole number of officers, 124; original officers remaining, 4; officers promoted from the ranks, 36; officers killed and mortally wounded, 8; officers wounded, 22; officers captured, 19; officers who died of disease, 4; officers dismissed by order of War Department, 5; officers resigned, 37; officers discharged at expiration of term of service, 13; enlisted men killed and mortally wounded, 95; enlisted men wounded, 236; enlisted men captured, 517; enlisted men killed accidentally, 18; enlisted men who died in Rebel prisons, 114; enlisted men who died of disease, 90; enlisted men discharged by reason of wounds, 25; enlisted men discharged by reason of disability, 295; enlisted men discharged at expiration of term, 302; enlisted men transferred to other commands, 103; enlisted men who re-enlisted in 1864, 212; number of battles fought, 52; number of skirmishes fought, 119; number of wounds received in action, 320; men lost in action and never heard from, 18; men remaining and mustered out with regiment, 694; original veterans remaining, 167; original horses remaining, 7.

During that summer of 1865, between Ma and Aunt Fan, the loss of most of my fifty-two pounds came back easily. The town folk amazed me with a hero's welcome. Some of my friends did not return as I mentioned in my letters and I remain in remorse for them. My sister and her husband Willis came for a visit. They again invited me to come to Chicago some day.

16

LIFE AFTER THE CAVALRY
1866 – 1882

At home, I became more settled. Once I had regained my strength and finished all the fishing and boating I had yearned to do, I started helping both Uncle Henry and Pa, but realized I was not content as I didn't have a profession. My sister, Cynthia, continually invited me to come to stay in Illinois. I looked for a profession and a wife.

Brother-in-law, William Willis, married to Cinty, had offered me an apprentice job in his and Uncle Levi's carpentry business in Aurora, Illinois, near Chicago. I had helped my other uncle and liked the work and always felt very close to Cinty and Willis. They had been staunch morale providers to me through their supportive letters during the war years. For me it proved to be a good move to Illinois in 1867. I learned the trade from Uncle Levi and his wife, Aunt Hattie, took very good care of me, but I lacked finding a mate. The young girls I met were much too frivolous for me.

On my trips home to Greenport and through my other brother-in-law, Horace Penny, married to sister Mela (Amelia), I met Sarah Conklin Penny, Horace's cousin. She was more mature, being born three years before me and raised in Southold's social circle. Her father, Henry Penny, had been Sheriff of Suffolk County, a highly elected office at the time, between 1844 and 1847.

Sarah and I were married in Riverhead, Long Island, on June 29, 1868 (a happier day than June 29, 1864!) and moved to Aurora to live, where our two children were born, a son Charles Booth on March 10, 1870, and a daughter, Stella Maud on August 28, 1871

After eight years, Sarah and I became homesick for Long Island and our families. My apprenticeship had made me ready to open my own business, but not in competition with my uncle and brother-in-law. We decided to return to Greenport in 1876. Both of my parents suffered from illnesses. Once back home I became established as a contractor and builder, constructing many houses and other structures in the eastern part of Long Island.

The following is a letter I wrote to the E 5th New York Cavalry in 1879, after receiving an invitation to their reunion, but not being able to attend due to my parents being ill. It sums up my feeling toward my military career and its members. I would have loved to have been there and gone through every battle one more time and seen all of my comrades, now without guns.

January 14, 1879 Letter to 5th New York Cavalry Reunion

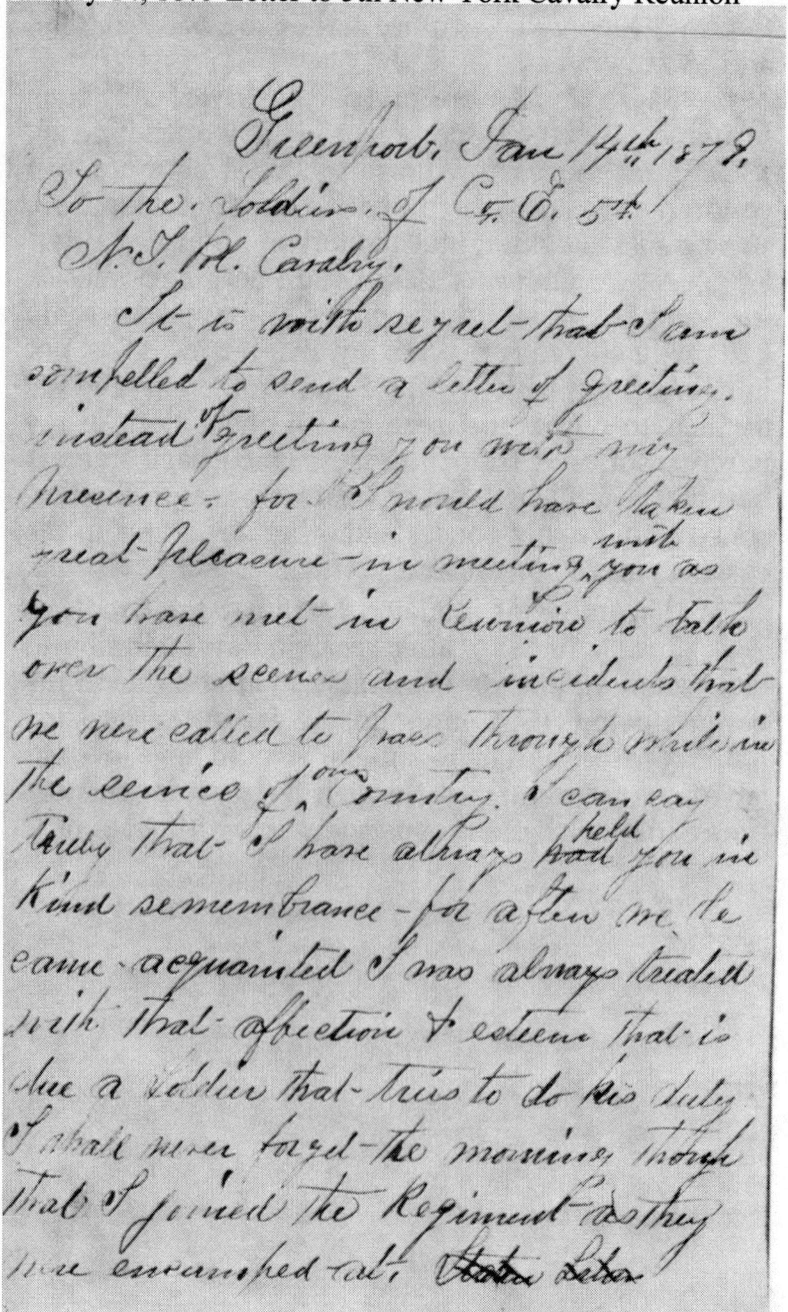

Greenport. Jan 14th 1879.
To the Soldiers of Co. E. 5th
N. Y. Vol. Cavalry.
It is with regret that I am
compelled to send a letter of greeting
instead of greeting you with my
presence - for I would have taken
great pleasure in meeting with you as
you have met in reunion to talk
over the scenes and incidents that
we were called to pass through while in
the service of our Country. I can say
truly that I have always held you in
kind remembrance - for after we be
came acquainted I was always treated
with that affection & esteem that is
due a soldier that tries to do his duty
I shall never forget the morning though
that I joined the Regiment as they
were encamped at ~~Staten~~ Staten

Stapleton, Staten Island - then (and it
was not to be wondered at) you received
me little coolly, for I came a stranger
among you and from another portion
of the State but I soon found warm
hearts & warm friends, and I have often
congratulated myself that my lot
was thrown in with such a noble
class of men. And it must afford
you much satisfaction as you are met
together to talk over Perils & Joys of
the dull monotony of camp life as
well as the exciting scenes of skirmishing
& Battle, Our first engagement is
as fresh in my memory as if it took
place but yesterday. our race up the
Shenandoah. after Ashby, and
the spot where the Gallant Spencer gave
up his life, and then after we got into
camp how we ground our Sabres. (not
according to regulations) but clean to the
hilt. Those were our Sanitary days we -

with our experience would convince to see, that repeated under the same Circumstances And then our retreat down the Valley across the Potomac into Maryland and soon we went back under Fremont; then scouted about Winchester where we done ample justice to the Cherries. Soon after Pope was in command then we was sent over into the Luray so on over to Culpeper, Orange, C.H. soon after the 2nd Bull Run; and then in the camp at Arlington, but space will not permit me to go through the whole of rouge, so I will hasten to the last engagement that I was permitted to participate in which was at Reams Station where I was taken prisoner also a number of others of our Co.; and it is very fortunate that so more were taken prisoners at the time for any one that was to pass or had to pass through the furnace of a Southern Prison will have its Harrowing memories.

indelibley stamped upon his mind. I
felt very sad when I learned of Alexander's
death he was a noble hearted man &
a true Soldier - I feel that I owe him
a great deal - for had it not been for the
Interest he took in my welfare I doubt
whether I would be as well off as I am
physically. for the all time of his imprisonment
his courage never failed and his Hope never
altered. and it makes me feel all the
more sad to think that he should have died
of disease contracted there. But by the
goodness of a Mercifull Lord. done but
my health was not injured in the least
while there.. but I must hasten hoping
that you will ever remember me kindly.
and that I may be permitted to see you
at your next Reunion. I remain your comrade
& fellow Soldier

Wm. H. Waterhouse

17

THE MOVE TO FLORIDA – 1882

My father died in 1880 and my mother in 1882. That same year, Sarah's sister, Clarissa and her husband, George Strong had moved to central Florida and told us how warm and beautiful it was there, plus the need for home builders presented a great opportunity. Long Island's cold, wet winters had proven that my imprisonment had left some inner scars becoming more apparent as years advanced. Florida's warmth certainly had a promising allure.

By moving and living in Illinois, we were more of a mind to adventure into unknown territory. I took Charles, a boy of twelve, and we went to Florida to investigate if all the things we had heard were true and that it would be fitting for Sarah and Stella to live there. Right after arriving, we found rooms in which to live at the home of Christopher Beasley, one of the first residents of the town and near the Strong's home.

We immediately saw the potential around us. One important fact was Lake Maitland stood as the last stop of the railroad line from Sanford and soon to be from Jacksonville, meaning many people were coming there looking for a place to live and a house to live in. We agreed such a move was worth the effort.

My letter to Sarah explaining this would be our home met with her approval. She had been trying to convince me for a long time, so my letter overjoyed her. Probably if she would have known some of the hardships coming up that first year, she may not have been as happy.

Our ladies followed us three months later, traveling first with a five day steamship ride from New York to Savannah. They then took a night boat via Sea Island to Fernandina, and then traveled in a combination freight and passenger coach to Jacksonville, spending that night in the St. James Hotel. The next day they boarded the old riverboat, DeBary, and spent the night coming up the St. Johns River to Sanford. From Sanford they boarded a train to Lake Maitland, the end of the line at that time.

When the train stopped at Mayo Station, a mile north of Lake Maitland, Charles got on and rode with them to Park Station near the Park House, a popular hotel. It was there I met them. We all stayed for a short time with the Beasleys until the household goods arrived and we could move into the rented Hungerford House and start our new life.

18

LAKE MAITLAND, FLORIDA – NEW HOME 1883 -1886

In 1883 I purchased a piece of land, one and a half acres on the south side of Lake Lily, from Edward C. Hungerford. The lake, named from the many water lilies that floated at its edge, wasn't in the center of town. Over the years many shacks had been built around it where some lived and fished. Mr. Hungerford changed that. Not only did he sell me land, but he gave a large parcel on the other side to Lake Maitland for a park.

Charles and I started plans to construct our house right away, but the first item we built was my carpentry shop so that I could start establishing myself in the community. Then we were chosen by Dr. Albigence Kingsley to build a wonderful house which was named *Under Oaks** on Oakleigh Drive. We proudly finished in record time. Learning the supplies available helped me next with our own home building and subsequent contracts.

**Note: This house has also been named 'Interlachen' and 'Oakleigh'.*

I wanted the best house I could build for my family, so spent a lot of time and precise detail work to make it happen. It took over a year to complete. The house's frame vernacular construction was one commonly built in the North during this time period, but the products we used were all local. I used heart of pine wood in the frame, the trim, the staircase and floor because once it dries and hardens, it becomes like stone. Cypress was used for the newel post on the stairs.

The two story floor plan allowed for a large parlor in the front western side with an archway into a nice dining room. Back of the dining room a door opened to the breezeway porch and a small pantry. On the northern side, the front of the house displayed the entrance vestibule. Inside, our lovely staircase flowed up some steps to a landing before turning and climbing the eastern inside wall of the house. Behind the vestibule was the living room complete with fireplace. This room also had a back door leading to the breezeway.

Upstairs were three bedrooms. Ours, facing the front on northeast side, was the biggest, complete with closets and a sitting area. The other two were for Stella and a guest room. From the back room was a corridor over the breezeway which led to another bedroom for Charles. This was over the workroom, where Sarah and the help washed, canned and sewed. For Sarah, I even installed a water pump inside this room, which was connected to an outside well. There were windows throughout both floors for cross ventilation. We completed the home in 1884.

It proved to be a comfortable and wonderful home for our family; one to satisfy all the family needs and one where Sarah could proudly entertain her friends in her parlor. Also it was only one hundred feet from her sister's house.

As soon as we finished our house, we built another exactly like ours and not very far removed from us. Two school teachers from Canada lived there. They were Emma and her sister Mary Dart.

NOTE: The Harris family owned it in mid 1900s. Then it stood empty, had a fire and was eventually torn down; it stood where current parking lot for the home is today.

Living in Florida took some getting used to with the heat, humidity, snakes and wild animals around us. The proudest moment for me was when I arrived home from one of my building sites, and Sarah showed me the remains of a snake, which she had clobbered to death. I knew we would make it from that time on; however, there were a few questionable times, such as when a skunk became cornered in the breezeway and let go all his gases on the newly washed clothes!

There were two stores in Lake Maitland in the 1870s, Vanderpool's Store and Turner's Store. George Stith built a new store in 1885 and Braxton Galloway built his about 1887. These carried a variety of basic goods, from canned food to sewing needles and kerosene, but when the stock ran out it took time to restock or when their limited items didn't cover our needs, then we had to hire a horse and buggy from the local livery stable to drive to Orlando for supplies. This happened weekly at first. We left after an early breakfast and it always ended up a struggle to arrive home before dark with no space empty in or on the buggy.

Sarah and Stella always knew when the Orlando stores had received a new order of hats or dresses and were ready with their lists urging me into another trip to Orlando. We even dined in a real restaurant in Orlando.

I loved our new location in Florida. Many wealthy people came to the Lake Maitland area to build their winter homes now that the train made the trip easier. I was fortunate to be in on the building of some of these homes, making my business flourish more than my expectations, and building houses for well known persons such as Charles H. Hall and Randall Bronson, as well as many others.

Life enriched me by being able to help a new little community become a town. From the very first, I tried to know everyone in Lake Maitland and help as many as I could. I loved having an active role in the development of the area. Four others, Edwin Turner, George Stith, Richard Packwood and T.W. Taylor, and I were elected the first aldermen in the election of 1885, serving under the first Mayor Josiah Eaton. During that year, I proudly delivered the Letters of Incorporation for Lake Maitland Township to the State Capitol in Tallahassee. This was a very proud moment. I continue to be an alderman and hope I always will have this honor.

For pleasure, I spent hours doing fine detailed work for special items. One of my proudest moments came in 1885 when I was asked to build the pews for the First Presbyterian Church of Maitland when it was built that year. I built them to last more than one hundred years. This became a special church for our family. Even Charles became the first superintendent of the Sunday School when he was only fifteen. *Note: Some of these pews still exist.*

Sarah, always being quite the lady, did suffer a bit at first, due to the lack of social events and the amount of nature and wild animals, crawling or walking, which appeared in abundance. In the winter season when the northerners returned, then Sarah found enjoyment playing Whist at the Park House Hotel with her genteel counterparts. She became involved with the church, giving a Pink Tea to raise money for the church bell. Being held during the busy winter season, everyone had to wear pink and they had enough funding to purchase the bell.

The next year, our family suffered some sadness, when my sister's husband, Horace Penny was killed. He was one of my wife's favorite cousins and we credited him as the one who introduced us. Horace was a Captain in the US Navy during the war, He had been wounded and spent time in the hospital, being released by May 20, 1864. After the war he reenlisted and enjoyed many years serving his country. In 1886, Horace was killed at sea in a storm, when a jib broke and washed him overboard. This saddened all of us knowing his wife Amelia, my sister, and their children would be alone and we were too far away to offer help.

Life in Lake Maitland continued to be good to us. I was well pleased to see an item in the March 11, 1892, Gate City Chronicle, Sanford, Florida, that named D. A. Morrison, W. H. Waterhouse and W. O. Ralls as first-class contractors and builders in the Maitland area.

Some of the happiest times in central Florida were my meetings with the GAR – Grand Army of the Republic – and I was the Commander of the Orlando Post for a few years.

One winter visitor, also a member of GAR with me and my neighbor, was Major Sidney Herbert Lancey. Writing under his pen name of Sidney Herbert, he was an editor of the *Southern Cultivator* and the *Journal* in Atlanta, a frequent contributor of articles to the *Savannah Morning News* and was considered a foremost authority on civil war history.

When he came to Lake Maitland as a season renter at the Park House, he could hardly get around due to his body being so full of Confederate bullets. The Major began serving in the Civil War as a chaplain in the US volunteers and then served in the First New York Cavalry until he was severely wounded in the first battle of Manassas. He suffered the rest of his life from these wounds, but the Florida climate brought him some relief and mobility.

One of the New York Times correspondents, William Drysdale, also a winter visitor to Lake Maitland wrote an account of meeting Sidney and seeing his famous tiny "literary den." Let me also explain it: After buying a house near ours, in a corner of his land, Sidney Herbert built a writing hut on it, which measured only eight feet by eight feet. His reasoning was no visitors could fit to bother him when writing. If more than one entered, the first would have to go in and move behind the door before the next could enter. Remarkably it had four rooms. The first was his library big enough for his writing desk and some shelves for his books, behind it was a kitchen with a stove holding a coffee pot, then a very small dining room and a storage area full of papers. Proudly he explained the reason it smelled like tar and paste was that he had sealed it tightly to keep out mice and bugs to protect his writing papers.

The Major introduced me to many of his writing friends who came every winter also. William Drysdale rented a little cottage from the hotel and would leave his papers in a closet each year until his return. Both of these men helped to find me some of the newspaper reports I included of the 5th New York's part of the war.

Sidney investigated and was able to find the Confederate soldier who had taken my metal pin (the one I had made in Stevensburg, Virginia in 1864) and my gun from me the day I was taken prisoner that same year. In 1907, forty-three years later, that metal giving my name and rank was returned to me along with an apology from Mr. William E. Gray. It was then carefully kept with the two metals that had been awarded me for my duty in the Civil War. Sidney wrote about this in the Savannah Morning News. My gun was never returned.

But I have to admit that some of my neighbors and best friends in Maitland had fought on the side of the South in the war. Most were members of the CVA: Confederate Veterans Association. There were many projects that the GAR and the CVA worked on together. One project together was to help fund the monument in Jacksonville to Confederate soldiers who lost their lives. So on June 17,1898, the Confederate monument was unveiled "In Honor of the Gallant Dead, We Boys in Blue Honor the Boys Who Wore Gray." In the speech at the ceremony, it was said the Gray believed in their cause enough to die for it and for this gallantry we honor those who fought, not their cause.

19

1887 ON

Charles was now attending Rollins Academy in Winter Park, Florida, where he studied for three years. Knowing his talents, he and I felt that he could accomplish more by studying architecture and working at it in New York City. During his seven years there, he secured positions in this line of work.

He met Lillian (Lilly) Huff, daughter of Peter and Amelia Huff of New York City. They married on January 21, 1896. In 1897, he opened his own architectural office in Passaic, New Jersey. Our first grandchild, Harold, was born January 9, 1898. His death in September, 1899, broke our hearts. A very sorrowful time for all of us. Happiness came again when twin daughters, Helen and Alice, were born August 3, 1900. They also gave us Doris, born October 25, 1904.

Charles was one of the leading architects in the development of Passaic for many years. Many times he brought his family to visit their grandparents in Florida.

Our daughter, Stella, also attended Rollins Academy in 1891 and 1892, then went on to study in the New York area. In 1901 she received her degree as a registered nurse at St. Barnabas Hospital, Newark, New Jersey and remained a nurse until 1916. We then asked her to come home to Maitland due to Sarah's illness.

I have continued my building and carpentry jobs throughout, along with enjoying my civic duties, and serving as an alderman throughout. It has been a full, good life. I now leave it, and my house remains as a legacy to future generations.

20

AFTER ALL

William H. Waterhouse died in Maitland on August 16, 1923, returning from a trip to Orlando. His funeral was held in the family parlor. Sarah Waterhouse's death followed in Maitland on March 29, 1924. Their graves are in the family plot at the Maitland Cemetery along with those of their children Charles and Stella and their three grandchildren.

Their daughter, Stella, remained in Maitland after her mother's death. Having been a nurse, she did help families in the town when needed, even delivering a few babies. Stella recalled the early days in Lake Maitland when attended school in a log house, different from Long Island's schoolhouse. She loved Miss Emma as teacher for elementary and Miss Mary later in a 'real' house, Packwood Hall where they put on plays for the town.

In 1924 Stella became the librarian for the Maitland Library (a building that Charles had designed on one of his many outings to Florida) and held this position until her retirement in 1954. She was known to pull some books off the shelves if she thought them "unfit" for children to read. Her name for the Waterhouse land was 'Three Pines' as she stated on her calling cards. In her later years, she was known as 'Miss Stella' by the town and could be seen walking into Maitland every day with a basket on her arm full of guava jelly she made from her guava bushes. On

Sundays she occupied her pew in the Presbyterian Church every Sunday until her death on February 6, 1966 at ninety-four years old. Another accolade, she was president for many years of the Needlecraft Guild and Garden Club. She was an honorary life member of the Maitland Woman's Club, and never retired from her civic work.

Stella ended the stalwart of the family with the homestead. She lived in it longer than any other family member and gave her whole life to the town of Maitland.

Because of this it is no wonder that perhaps her spirit lives on. William, in his will, left the house to Stella and Charles. She moved out of it and into the workshop on her own when Charles returned after his father's death making room for his family. Charles' wife was not fond of quiet Maitland and left the area right after her husband's unexpected early death the following year. The house now belonged to Stella.

Brother Charles was an outstanding member of the Passaic community, holding many directorships in successful businesses, offices in many civic organizations and receiver of many architectural awards. After he retired in 1926, he returned to Maitland to manage his citrus grove interests and lived in the family home. He died in 1927 after only a week's illness. Stella continued to live in the shop and rented out the big house to people from England.

Helen and Alice, the twin daughters of Charles and Lillie Waterhouse, attended Rollins Academy. Helen was a secretary for the New York City school system until she moved to Florida in 1946. She, too, donated her time to civic duties, working for the United Appeal Fund and as first president of the Maitland Historical Society. Friends remember her as always having a joke. She died in Deltona October 13, 1990.

Alice also became a secretary in New York. Alice loved to write poetry and was a member of poetic societies. She married Harry Peterson, whose first wife died in childbirth. Alice, Harry and his son

Robert(Bob),moved to Florida and rented a house in Winter Park until the English people left the Waterhouse home. When Alice's family lived in the main house in late 40's and 50's, Harry and Bob had to make some necessary repairs to the almost sixty year old home.

One interesting item they found when they repaired the plaster in the parlor walls was that they had been stuffed with horsehair between the outside wall and the brown coating, to which the plaster was then added. A unique insulation.

The family being very close, Stella visited the main house often and took a great interest in these repairs. One thing that distressed her was how they had painted the original varnished wainscoting in the dining room a light green along with the dining room table. After this, Stella restricted her many visits to the main house to only the family's big holiday dinners. Bob remembers Stella's actions and feelings on this change.

The Petersons lived in the family home in Maitland when Bob went to Winter Park High School. Bob is the one who found these great treasures in the attic of the Lake Lily home These priceless original letters of his great-grandfather, William Waterhouse, have been saved and will be available to view with the Historical Society of Maitland.

Bob graduated from Winter Park High School, spent four years in the US Air Force, mainly in Germany, then returned to graduate from the University of Florida's School of Engineering. He had a successful thirty year career with General Electric as an engineer in a Staff Management position. Most of his career was spent at a facility in Largo, Florida, owned by the Department of Energy (DOE) and operated by GE. They manufactured the highly classified devices called Neutron Generators, which were the triggers for some of our most sophisticated atomic weapons.

Two of his three sons graduated from the University of Florida with degrees in Building

Construction. After retiring from GE, Bob went into business with son Tom. They performed remedial work statewide on structures with settlement problems caused by unstable ground conditions (sinkholes). He now is semi retired living in Largo, Florida, with his wife, Sandra. He spends his time doing some contracting and fishing with his sons.

Alice died in 1983 and is buried with her husband (died in 1979), siblings Helen and Doris, parents and grandparents in the old Maitland cemetery.

Doris, the last girl of Charles and Lillie, graduated from Skidmore College in Saratoga Springs, New York. She married Eaton Rossell and had a daughter, Doris Ann Rossell. Doris died in 1972.

Doris Ann (Dodie) Rossell is an ordained minister in the Presbyterian Church USA. She has served a congregation in Abingdon, Virginia, been Campus Minister at East Tennessee State University in Johnson City, Tenn, designed and directed an institute on sex and values (VIACT), held the position of Director of Clinical Services at the Virginia Institute of Pastoral Care for 22 years and now is the owner and Director of the Dialogue Pastoral Counseling Center in Richmond, Virginia (www.dialoguecounseling.org). She is a Licensed Professional Counselor in Virginia and holds the title of Fellow in The American Association of Pastoral Counselors.

She has great passion for performing choral music, reading novels, cooking meals for friends and playing bridge.

Dodie has produced two videos: Living With Your Adolescent and Maybe Liking it and Caring for Aging Parents: Managing the Exchanging Roles. She is well known for giving presentations to church groups as well as civic associations. For titles of her presentation, go to her website:

www.dialoguecounseling.org.

In her involvement in the classical music scene in Richmond, she has been President and Concert Manager of CAFUR, a well respected choral group. In her tenure in CAFUR she brought to fruition three productions of J.S. Bach's choral works: St. Matthew Passion, St John Passion and the B Minor Mass. Presently, she is a member of the adult choir at Second Presbyterian Church, Richmond.

Dodie and Bob Peterson remain close and share mutual admiration for each other and their family.

Thanks to Marjorie Tope, an early member of the Maitland Historical Society, the Waterhouse Home is on the national Historic Preservation List and is a museum, open to the public at Lake Lily in Maitland, Florida, looked after by the Maitland Historical Society and Museums.

www.maitlandandhistory.org

William's Carpentry Shop, full of his original tools, sits next to the house and can be visited also. The original letters and tools, found in the attic by Bob Peterson, he has now donated to the museum home or the Maitland Historical Society's museum.

Harry and Bob also built a cottage next to the shop, connected by a breezeway. Helen and a friend moved into that cottage. This cottage is now the office for the Waterhouse Museum. Upon Stella's death, the main house went to Alice. The house passed on to Bob who eventually sold it to the city of Maitland.

In the 1960's and 70s, Harry, with occasional help from Bob, turned the parlor into a downstairs bedroom, added a bathroom downstairs, and added a small kitchen upstairs; thus. Alice and Harry could live downstairs and rent out the 'upstairs apartment.'

A year after Alice died her grandson, Tom Peterson, was staying in the house as he attended Valencia Community College. He rented the upstairs apartment to two other students to help with expenses. There was an instance one night after Tom had taken a final exam and feared that he had not passed it, meaning he would certainly have been out of college for good. He did what all college students do when worried, went out drinking to fortify himself. When he returned to his bedroom, which being to the back of the house on the side, was closest to the railroad tracks. He had become accustomed to its one middle-of-the-night clickity-clacking trip and usually waited for it to pass before trying to go to sleep. This night he wasn't quite asleep when his bed started shaking violently. He tried to sit up and found he could not. He kept trying, becoming upset that he could not sit up; it was as if someone was holding him in bed. He looked around and saw no one. Later the train suddenly went by so it had not been the train. He dismissed it as a bit too much to drink until something else happened.

One morning, one of the girls came down and asked Tom who 'Aunt Stella' was. Tom did not know. It seemed that 'Aunt Stella' had paid the girl a visit in the middle of the night and complained to her about the wainscoting problem.

When Tom, months later, asked his father about this, Bob responded, “No one knew about that except my father and me!”

So Miss Stella is still watching out after her parents' Three Pines home. Visit her, she would love to show you around.

EPILOGUE
From the author

A thought on the Civil War, which started out with a defiant step of many southern states to stand by what they thought was their right of personal property. Unfortunately their personal property was enslaving fellow human beings. But after almost three years, it then became a military campaign between two exceptional generals, each not brought into the campaign on beliefs, but locality of where they or their family lived.

General Grant started his offense against the Confederacy in March 2, 1864, with what was estimated as 1,000,000 soldiers in all areas versus, having 140,000 alone in the Army of the Potomac. The Confederate Army of North Virginia had less than 60,000. In all odds, this should have been an easy war to win now that all the six unqualified Union generals had been removed and the strong Ulysses Grant installed. But for the next thirteen months and ten days of continual fighting, the South held on. Only the amount of soldiers and supplies won the war finally. Neither General blinked in this fight. One did not outsmart or undo the other. History reminds us continually that even if the two had switched places, Lee in command of Grant's army would have won and Grant in command of Lee's would have failed. On the part of Lee, which with lack of men and supplies, the strategy resolved into a purely defensive scheme, and as such, will remain among the great defensive campaigns in history and continues to be studied as such.

CPSIA information can be obtained at www.ICGtesting.com
Printed in the USA
LVOW111223281011
252527LV00002B/1/P

9 781450 789431